ADVANCE PRAISE FOR *THE FUTURE IS DISABLED*

"Groundbreaking, hilarious, and brilliantly written, this book is a vital manual for navigating disabled grief, joy, and survival in pandemic times. If you need advice on how to crip mutual aid, how to make revolutionary disabled art, or how to make some really good chicken soup, this book has you covered. *The Future is Disabled* cements Piepzna-Samarasinha's status as one of the most important disability thinkers of our generation. They make the disabled future absolutely irresistible."

–JINA B. KIM, assistant professor of English and of the Study of Women and Gender, Smith College

"*The Future Is Disabled* is a timely and necessary collection of essays about what disability justice is, has been, and could be. It contains the disabled stories, secrets, knowledge, humor, and creativity that we need now and what we will need to create the just futures we deserve. The brown cripqueer femme love and hope and rage and grief contained in these pages is astounding and necessary— a gift to us all. It's the kind of book you dog-ear, write in, quote from memory, and pass along to every disabled-even-if-they-don't-use-that-word friend, lover, comrade, and fellow artist you hope to make a better world with. It's a community building tool and a personal balm for anyone invested in collective liberation, especially disabled people of color. Buy it. Read it. Pass it on."

–SAMI SCHALK, author of *Black Disability Politics*

"Leah Lakshmi Piepzna-Samarasinha has created a guidebook for Deaf, Mad and disabled activists and artists everywhere—a love letter to all of us in these times of change and speculative futures turned into lived realities. *The Future Is Disabled* dares to dream of a different   ꞏder how we will show up for each other in   es about our newly passed on kin and str   DJ groups from scratch. This book is everyt   nd

change, and at a time when the disabled and Mad futures described by Octavia Butler are settling in around us. Thank you, Leah, for helping us to dream, and helping us to consider what we need to do to survive into the future."

–SYRUS MARCUS WARE, co-editor of *Until We Are Free: Black Lives Matter in Canada*

"*The Future is Disabled* moves us past disability as an identity category, or awareness of disability justice as an anti-oppression check mark. By addressing her beloved community on her own terms, Leah Lakshmi Piepzna-Samarasinha teaches us that disability justice is a possible world that already exists, full of the love we deserve and the complexity we already embody."

–ALEXIS PAULINE GUMBS, author of *Undrowned: Black Feminist Lessons from Marine Mammals*

"*The Future is Disabled* is the kind of world making that has until now been reserved for science fiction. This book is committed to community, blazingly experimental, and embedded in the practical work of everyday disability justice.

"*The Future is Disabled* speaks in a multitude of voices, including words of wisdom, interludes, herbal remedies, recipes, 'autistic long form,' and access riders, to provide clear instructions on how disabled people can get free. Throughout this groundbreaking work, Piepzna-Samarasinha finds meaning in recent history, and leaves readers with no doubt that the disabled future is now.

"Piepzna-Samarasinha has provided us with a primer, a language, a lucid image, and a guide to disability justice, one of the most vital and rapidly expanding movements of our time.

"With reverence for the work of their contemporaries, elders, and the next generation of disability justice thinkers, Piepzna-Samarasinha sets out to honor, elegize, and create 'disabled and chronically ill citizen scientists.' *The Future is Disabled* will leave any crip saying, 'I could be disabled like that.'"

–Cyrée Jarelle Johnson, author of *Slingshot*

LEAH LAKSHMI
PIEPZNA-SAMARASINHA

THE FUTURE IS
DISABLED

Prophecies, Love Notes,
and Mourning Songs

ARSENAL PULP PRESS
VANCOUVER

ARSENAL PULP PRESS
Suite 202 – 211 East Georgia St.
Vancouver, BC V6A 1Z6
Canada
arsenalpulp.com

The publisher gratefully acknowledges the support of the Canada Council for the Arts and the British Columbia Arts Council for its publishing program, and the Government of Canada and the Government of British Columbia (through the Book Publishing Tax Credit Program) for its publishing activities.

Arsenal Pulp Press acknowledges the xʷməθkʷəy̓əm (Musqueam), Sḵwx̱wú7mesh (Squamish), and səl̓ilwətaʔɬ (Tsleil-Waututh) Nations, custodians of the traditional, ancestral, and unceded territories where our office is located. We pay respect to their histories, traditions, and continuous living cultures and commit to accountability, respectful relations, and friendship.

Lyrics from "THIS IS A PROTEST FOR YOUR HEART!!!" by Left at London are reprinted with permission.
"Pod Mapping for Mutual Aid" is reprinted with permission of Rebel Sidney Fayola Black Burnett.

Cover and text design by Jazmin Welch
Edited by Lisa Factora-Borchers
Copy edited by Jade Colbert
Proofread by Rachel Spence

Printed and bound in Canada

Library and Archives Canada Cataloguing in Publication:
Title: The future is disabled : prophecies, love notes and mourning songs / Leah Lakshmi
    Piepzna-Samarasinha.
Names: Piepzna-Samarasinha, Leah Lakshmi, 1975- author.
Identifiers: Canadiana (print) 20220228779 | Canadiana (ebook) 20220228957 |
    ISBN 9781551528915 (softcover) | ISBN 9781551528922 (HTML)
Subjects: LCSH: People with disabilities. | LCSH: People with disabilities—Social conditions—
    Forecasting. | LCSH: Social justice.
Classification: LCC HV1568 .P54 2022 | DDC 305.9/08—dc23

For Stacey, LL, Carrie Ann, Mel Baggs, Elandria,
Don, Eugenia, and Graeme, forever.

And for all of us—living, dead, and not yet born—
creating the disabled future.

Disability justice dreams got me this far,
and I'm going to keep betting on them.
—STACEY PARK MILBERN

I could cut my wrists up
I could put my fists up
Either way, I can't cheat death
I don't wanna live, that's fine
'Cause the years will still go by
I don't wanna miss them
I don't wanna miss them
I don't wanna miss them
Not this time.
—LEFT AT LONDON,
"THIS IS A PROTEST FOR YOUR HEART!!!"

Hard times are coming, when we'll be wanting the voices
of writers who can see alternatives to how we live now,
can see through our fear-stricken society and its obsessive
technologies to other ways of being, and even imagine real
grounds for hope. We'll need writers who can remember
freedom—poets, visionaries—realists of a larger reality.
—URSULA K. LE GUIN

I may be small, I may speak soft,
But you can see the change in the water.
—JAMILA WOODS, "ZORA"

TABLE OF CONTENTS

13 THANKS AND ACKNOWLEDGMENTS

17 INTRODUCTION
Writing a Disabled Future, in Progress

PART I
DISABILITY JUSTICE IN THE END TIMES

51 CHAPTER 1
"We Were Maybe Not Going to Save the World, but We Were Going to Save Each Other": How Disabled Mutual Aid Is Different than Abled Mutual Aid

71 TINY DISABLED MOMENT #1
Small Moments of Disabled Knowing

75 CHAPTER 2
Interdependence Is Not Some Giant Living in the Hillside Coming Down to Visit the Townspeople: The Church of Show the Fuck Up, in Real Life

106 TINY DISABLED MOMENT #2
"There Is No Disabled Community Here"

109 INTERLUDE
Pod Mapping for Mutual Aid, by Rebel Sidney Fayola Black Burnett

112 CHAPTER 3
Disabled Grief Technologies: Disability Justice Future-Building in a Time of Mass Grief

126 RECIPE
Rosewater for Crying Eyes

128 CHAPTER 4
Nobody Left Behind and Wanting to Run Like Hell: Disabled Survival in Climate Crisis

140   CHAPTER 5
Cripping the Resistance: No Revolution without Us

152   RECIPE
Stacey Soup

154   CHAPTER 6
Still Dreaming Wild Disability Justice Dreams at the End of the World

165   TINY DISABLED MOMENT #3
The Free Library of Beautiful Adaptive Things

168   CHAPTER 7
The Future Is Disabled (with Karine Myrgianie Jean-François,
Nelly Bassily, Sage Lovell, Sarah Jama, and Syrus Marus Ware)

PART II
THE STORIES THAT KEEP US ALIVE:
DISABILITY JUSTICE ARTS IN THE INTERREGNUM

177   CHAPTER 8
Twenty Questions for Disability Justice Art Dreaming:
A Winter Solstice Present

183   CHAPTER 9
I Wanna Be with You Everywhere (And I Am):
Disability Justice Art as Freedom Portal

197   CHAPTER 10
Disability Justice Writing, the Beauty and the Difficulty

212   CHAPTER 11
Autistic Long-Form, Short-Form, No-Form, Echotextia:
Autistic Poetic Forms

220   CHAPTER 12
Cripping the Book Tour

236   SAMPLE ACCESS RIDER

PART III

THE DISABLED FUTURE

243 TINY DISABLED MOMENT #4
ADA 30 / DJ 15

249 CHAPTER 13
Disabled Secrets

258 CHAPTER 14
What Really Happens in DJ Groups

263 CHAPTER 15
Home Is a Holy Place: The Sacred Organizing Spaces
of Disabled Homes

276 TINY DISABLED MOMENT #5
LL Comes to Me

280 CHAPTER 16
Loving Stacey: An Honor Song

301 TINY DISABLED MOMENT #6
Adaptive Trike

305 CHAPTER 17
Wild Disabled Joy: Disabled Pleasure Activism

325 CHAPTER 18
Wild Disabled Futures: The Future Is Now

THANKS AND ACKNOWLEDGMENTS

First of all, thanks to the Cheasty Greenspace, the urban forest in Beacon Hill, South Seattle, Duwamish territories, where I lived as an uninvited guest, tended and got taught by, and where I wrote this book. Thank you for being the land I listened to and built relationship with, for keeping me alive during the pandemic, and for being the container for so much writing and healing for the past seven years.

Thank you to this book, for showing me who you were and how you wanted to be written.

Stacey Park Milbern, thank you for being on my shoulder for every moment of writing this book, and for being one of the first eyes on some of these pieces as they came out. I miss you every fucking day and wish so bad we could write together, but in some ways, we still are. Your disabled Asian queer brilliance and care work built a movement, and your unconditional love changed my life and so many other crips' lives forever.

Thank you to Alice Wong for your endless game-changing disabled cultural labor and creation of a crip-writing empire with the Disability Visibility Project, for giving so many of these pieces their first homes, and being a comrade, writer-warrior, and sibling pie-lover. Thank you also for generously giving me permission to use "the future is disabled," a phrase you originated in your Crip Oracle work, as the title of this book.

Thank you to Shameless, GUTS, Disability Arts Online, PopCollab, Orion, Disability Visibility Project, Truthout, and the anthologies

Pleasure Activism, The Care We Dream Of, and *Disability Visibility* for publishing early versions of pieces in this book.

Thank you to DIS Summit, especially Sandy Ho for being another queer Asian Masshole disabled genius, creating the fully accessible DJ conference space of my dreams, and letting me help out. Thank you to CRIP FUND, Kripsignal, the Autistic Black, Brown, Indigenous, Asian, and Mixed-Race People of Color group, the DJ Money Group, GTFO, and Sick and Disabled Queers for all of our audacious disabled Mad ND imagining.

Thank you to all of my Patreon followers for supporting this work and allowing me to somehow afford to pay the whole-ass rent at my house where I lived without roommates for a big chunk of the pandemic. Thank you to everybody who hired me to do something for money.

Thank you to my disabled and ally writing coaching clients and my mentees in the Ki'tay D. Davidson Disability Justice Fellowship for the gift of getting to be your Disability Justice Brown Femme Writing Coach Taylor, and for the gift of being able to support and witness the disability justice literary canon we are making. WRITE YOUR BOOKS.

Thank you to Deana Haggag and everyone at US Artists for creating the Disability Futures Fellowship, the first big disabled arts fellowship ever and the first big fellowship I ever got in my life, for believing in my work and giving me the money that enabled me to survive the pandemic, support others in my community, and write this book. Thank you for believing in a disabled future.

Thanks to Brian Lam of Arsenal Pulp for taking a chance on me six years ago and championing my work and that of so many other disabled and/or 2QTBIPOC writers. I am so proud to be an Arsenal Pulper, to be published by an independent queer of color–led press, not a corporation, to work with a queer Asian publishing elder who made a press with the only Disability Literature section that I know of. Thank you for continuing to ask, "So, you got another book yet?" Thank you to TextaQueen for being the forever cover artist of my dreams and imagining a disabled brown portal to the future, and Jazmin Welch for patiently working with us, including when I got second-degree burns on my fingers on deadline day. Thank you to Cynara Geissler, Jazmin Welch, Jade Colbert, Jaiden Dembo, Catharine Chen, and the whole AP team for being stellar at your work bringing this book into the world.

To my dream editor Lisa Factora-Borchers. For everything, forever. More than an editor, you are a midwife, a portal, an alchemist. You listened hard, then touched on the right acupressure points to make this book so different from how she began, and exactly how they were meant to be. Your queer Asian femme spirituality, your word genius, your telling me that the first book was a mixtape and this was an accessible mansion. I am blessed to be able to work with you to bring these works into the world. Deep bows.

My big, wild disabled, ND, Deaf, and allied extended family in South Seattle, Oakland, T'karonto, Brooklyn, and beyond are the joyful heartbeat and bones of my life and our collective work. I think a lot about how different my disabled and neurodiverse parents' lives would be if they'd had access to this kind of community. I wish for everyone to have access to this kind of love and trouble. I am so blessed to get to coevolve, argue, play, explore, and create with you. Lisa Amin, William Maria Rain, Lucia Leandro Gimeno, Syrus Marcus Ware, Jonah Aline Daniel, Amirah Mizrahi, Ejeris Dixon,

Carolyn Lazard, Dori Midnight, Adrian Lowe, Tina Zavitsanos, Max Reynolds, Liz Latty, Kim Murray, Aruna Zehra Boodram and Surya Boodram, Chanelle Gallant, Zavisha Chromicz, Jen Deerinwater, Gabe Teodros, Annanda DeSilva, Reilly Joy, Chaya Klernet, Ryan Comet Alley, Neve Zique Mazique-Bianco, Kiyomi Fujikawa, Satchél Silvette, Vero Vengara, Dorian Taylor, Dre Avila, Kai Cheng Thom, Setareh Mohhamed, Gems Butler, Rebel Sidney Fayola Black Burnett, Elliott Fukui, Alice Sheppard, Meg Day, Dana Garza, Juba Kalamka, Patrice Strahan, Mere Guido, ChrisTiana ObeySumner, Andraéa LaVant, Sofia Webster, Jina Kim, Dr. Sami Schalk, Dr. Moya Bailey, Emi Kane, Ellen Samuels, Leroy Moore, Margaret Price, Eli Clare, M. Téllez, Ryan Li Dahlstrom, Teukie Martin, Dolores Tejada, Steph Lee, Tala Khanmalek, Mateo Medina, Teal Van Dyck, Sulan Mlynarek, Lenny Olin, everybody in the Sad Stacey Squad, the "It's Complicated" group, and many others for the conversations, mutual aid, disabled joy, and relationships this work is grounded in.

Thanks to Gabriel Teodros, whose Early show on KEXP was the soundtrack I wrote this book to, along with Dori Midnight's Spotify playlists.

Finally, thank you to my cat companion, Zuri a.k.a. Queen Zuri ZuZu of All the Land, for being perfect, and to the writers and actors of *Star Trek Discovery, Sort Of, We Are Lady Parts, Queen Sugar, Reservation Dogs, For All Mankind, Gossip Girl* (2021), *Good Trouble*, and more shows in my five TV subscriptions than I can remember, for keeping this crip going during the end of the world.

"Femme labor heals."
—BRUNEM WARSHAW

INTRODUCTION

Writing a Disabled Future, in Progress

THE DISABLED FUTURE

I believe in the disabled future.

This is a radical statement. Disabled people aren't supposed to be alive, take up space, exist—joyfully, complicatedly, thrivingly, ornery-ly—in the present. But the future? Nah. Double nah.

In the Bad Future of all kinds of dystopian imaginings, disabled people are either everywhere, with our pathetic, pain-filled, dysfunctional, broken bodyminds. We're the tragic autistic son in *Children of Men* who can't look up from his devices, the "disfigured" ugly babies produced by toxic waste and climate change. We're a cautionary tale told to children, warning them to fight climate change and fascism or just look what will happen. On the other hand, in so much utopian social justice–oriented science fiction, it's unquestioned that in the good utopian future, disabled people don't exist. Everyone eats organic, and disabled babies are eliminated before birth through genetic selection that no one ever calls eugenics.[1] In the happy future, we're all dead. And isn't it better that way?

Fuck that.

---

1 I love much of Marge Piercy's work, but for an in-depth, disabled critique of the ableism and eugenic elimination of physical disability depicted in the utopian future of her 1979 science fiction novel *Woman on the Edge of Time*, check out Allison Kafer's *Feminist, Queer, Crip*, an epic work of disabled feminist futurism in general, but specifically chapter 3, "Debating Feminist Futures: Slippery Slopes, Cultural Anxiety, and the Case of the Deaf Lesbians."

"Crip bodies were built for space travel. Crip minds already push the outer limits," Alice Wong, founder of the Disability Visibility Project, tweeted in 2016.[2] "We already master usage of breathing apparatuses and can handle challenging situations." A 2020 *Wired* article wrote about the buried history of disabled and Deaf people selected as some of the earliest astronaut trainees, because Deaf people were less likely get nauseous and used sign to communicate; because pooping is a major problem in space and it's easier when you already have a colostomy bag.[3] Disabled and Deaf gain[4]—the brilliance within our divergent bodyminds—help us take root amongst the stars, to paraphrase Octavia Butler. As white Jewish queer disabled writer Carrie Kaufman recently wrote, "Where do you (the abled) go when you leave us behind? Is it worth it?"[5]

At the core of my work and life is the belief that disabled wisdom is the key to our survival and expansion. Crip genius is what will keep us all alive and bring us home to the just and survivable future we all need. If we have a chance in hell of getting there.

Yet a major way ableism works is to erase us from ideas of the future. The science fiction future, sure, but also the everyday future of having any idea of what a disabled adulthood or elderhood could look like. Ableism isolates and keeps disabled, Deaf, and neurodivergent people from finding disabled, Deaf, and neurodivergent

2 Alice Wong (@Sfdirewolf), Twitter, August 13, 2016, https://twitter.com/SFdirewolf/status/764371929910218752.

3 Rose Eveleth, "It's Time to Rethink Who's Best Suited for Space Travel," *Wired*, January 7, 2019, https://www.wired.com/story/its-time-to-rethink-whos-best-suited-for-space-travel/.

4 Deaf gain is a phrase invented by Deaf people to describe the notion of Deafness as a linguistic and cultural advantage, not a loss or a state of being less than hearing people.

5 C.K. Kaufman (@rosesarespread), Instagram, January 24, 2022, https://www.instagram.com/p/CZHmO3xrDoP.

communities. It's common for parents or teachers to tell some disabled children they're "not like the others," for parents of autistic, Deaf, or disabled kids to deny our identities. Sometimes, especially for BIPOC people, this can be the best survival strategy we know, but being kept from each other also kills. Most people still draw a blank when you say the words "disabled community"—like, what is that? Autistic and disabled special-ed student Cole Sorensen writes, "Until I started college, I had never met an adult who was like me. I had other disabled friends, sure, but with no model of what my life could look like after graduation, I couldn't imagine much of a future for myself at all."[6]

This is why I believe some of disability justice's most important work lies in how we've created space for BIPOC people (and, secondarily, Others) to identify as disabled, chronically ill, Deaf, or neurodivergent, through our creation of Black- and brown-centered disabled, sick, Deaf, and neurodivergent communities and politics. Community building isn't always seen as "real activism" (whatever) but the work we do to create disabled Black and brown community spaces, online forums, hashtags, and artwork is lifesaving because it creates space for disabled BIPOC to *come out* as disabled. I mean big organized spaces, parties, and cultural events, and I also mean the disabled BIPOC version of "Hey, do you want some of my fries?": one disabled BIPOC person being friendly and Initiating Hangout Space with another, who might not be ready to be out yet.

6 Cole Sorenson, "No Place for Disability in Special Education," *Disabled Academic Collective*, August 28, 2020, https://disabledacademicco.wixsite.com/mysite/post/no-place-for-disability-in-special-education.

It's very difficult to organize for survival, power, and pleasure when people can't even admit they go to this school, you know?

Disability justice (DJ) spaces filled with disabled Black and brown people are crucial spaces for disabled, sick, Deaf, and neurodivergent BIPOC people to witness possible futures for ourselves, as we take in other Black and brown disabled people as possibility models and friends. *I could do it like that. I could have a life like that. I could expect my access needs be met like that. I could just say, "Hey, I need a chair or captions," easy like that. I could be disabled like that.*

Many Black and brown disabled people have been gatekept from claiming disabilities and excluded from mainstream disabled spaces for years by blatant and covert racism perpetuated by white disabled people and/or by the idea, *Yeah, I know about that group but they're all white people*, making it not safe or not worth the risk to go through the door. I've witnessed a fair bit of resentment and anger over the past decade from white disabled groups/people at the success of disability justice groups to attract masses of disabled BIPOC and ally BIPOC people. White-majority and -lead disabled groups' racism and lack of intersectional analysis and leadership, in tandem with the general ableism of the world, prevented that kind of community buy-in for decades. I didn't make the rules, though, and it's just a fact that racism is an impediment to movement-building and activist wins.

DJ community spaces lead by Black and brown disabled people are revolutionary spaces because they are often the only ones where disabled BIPOC feel safe to uncloset ourselves and speak our vulnerable and raw disabled BIPOC stories. I always insist on doing BIPOC-only disabled workshops because I know that when BIPOC who haven't had space to think about disability from a Black or brown perspective before finally get that space, our disabled BIPOC stories that come out—of pesticide and chemical poisoning from working in the fields and housecleaning, immigration denials and deportations, police murder, abuse in prisons and immigration camps, medical experimention and abuse on Black and brown bodies—are not ones we will ever feel comfortable sharing in front of white people. Doing DJ work in BIPOC communities means going into it knowing the stories of intergenerational trauma and pain from racist ableism are going to come out and there must be space to hold them with care.

As painful as they are, those stories and the spaces that hold them are places where we are birthing disability justice futures—our individual futures as disabled Black and brown people, and the big collective futures we are making together. They are spaces of "crip doulaing," a term created by disability justice organizer Stacey Park Milbern to describe the ways disabled people support/mentor newly disabled people in learning disabled skills (how to live on very low spoons, drive a wheelchair, have sex/redefine sexuality, etc.).[7] A doula supports someone doing the work of childbirth; a crip doula is a disabled person supporting another disabled person as they do the work of becoming disabled, or differently disabled, of dreaming a new disabled life/world into being. This is a very Black and brown disabled, collective way of doing the work.

It's radical to imagine that the future is disabled. Not just tentatively allowed to exist, not just *OK, I guess there's one white guy with a wheelchair, cool, diversity*. But a deeply disabled future: a future where

---

7 Stacey Park Milbern and Leah Lakshmi Piepzna-Samarasinha, "Crip Lineages, Crip Futures," *Care Work* (Vancouver: Arsenal Pulp, 2018), 242–43.

disabled, Deaf, Mad, neurodivergent bodyminds are both accepted without question as part of a vast spectrum of human and animal ways of existing, but where our cultures, knowledge, and communities shape the world.

What would a future look like where the vast majority of people were disabled, neurodivergent, Deaf, Mad? What would a world radically shaped by disabled knowledge, culture, love, and connection be like? Have we ever imagined this, not just as a cautionary tale or a scary story, but as a dream?

Some people have scoffed at me when I broached the idea of a majority disabled future—surely I don't mean this literally? But I kind of do. The climate crisis, pandemics, and the ongoing ecocide of settler colonialism and extractive capitalism are already creating the conditions for more people to get sick and disabled from viruses, heat waves, and wildfire smoke. I finished this book in winter/spring 2022, while the world was enduring the Omicron variants of the COVID-19 pandemic, going into its third calendar year. In early January 2022, Dr. Katelyn Jetelina,[8] the creator of the blog Your Local Epidemiologist, wrote, "Dr. Trevor Bedford, a brilliant computational epidemiologist and scientist, estimated that as of January 17, 4.5% of the US population recorded a confirmed case. After accounting for under-reporting, we should expect 36–46% of the US population[9] to have been infected by Omicron by mid-February."[10] By April, the

8 For more of Katelyn Jetelina, "Your Local Epidemiologist," see https://substack.com/profile/27227002-katelyn-jetelina.
9 Trevor Bedford (@trvrb), Twitter, January 19, 2022, https://twitter.com/trvrb/status/1483996723458445319.
10 Katelyn Jetelina, "State of Affairs: Jan 24," Your Local Epidemiologist (blog), January 24, 2022, https://yourlocalepidemiologist.substack.com/p/state-of-affairs-jan-24.

CDC's Dr. Kristie Clarke reported that almost 60% of everyone in the US caught Omicron in winter 2022, and in children eleven and younger, almost 75% had antibodies to the virus.[11] As of July 2022, we live in a world where government abandonment and ever-evolving viruses have made many people resigned to inevitably getting COVID.

We are in the third year of a global mass disabling event—the COVID-19 pandemic—where, as I and many other disabled activists and people have noticed and stated, *the world has been cripped*: The entire world has been immersed in a disabled reality for the past two years. Masking, handwashing, long-term isolation, awareness of viruses and immune vulnerability, the need for disabled skills of care, adaptivity, and virtual community-building are just a few of the dis-abled ways of being that everyone, disabled and not, have been forced to reckon with.

The COVID-19 virus and the failure to create a just global public health and economic response to support people undergoing it is also creating a disabled world in that mass numbers of people are becoming newly or differently disabled because of getting COVID, long COVID, and/or long-term CPTSD and other mental disabilities from the grief, loss, and stress of the pandemic. As Dr. Sami Schalk, author of *Black Disabled History* and a brilliant Black queer disabled scholar, tweeted in January 2022:

> It won't be long before basically a majority of adults in the US are disabled by long COVID and/or lack of access to healthcare because of COVID destroying our systems & the people who run

---

11 Joe Neel, "Most Americans have been infected with the COVID-19 virus, the CDC reports," NPR, April 26, 2022, https://www.npr.org/2022/04/26/1094817774/covid-19-infections-us-most-americans.

it. So start listening to disabled people about how to make more accessible worlds. And by long, I mean a generation or two. All these kids with long COVID, diabetes developed due to COVID, plus all the mental health effects of living among so much death & fear & callousness … they will all be disabled adults. And maybe our understanding of disability will change when the majority of people are dealing with PTSD and fatigue & such, but the fact remains that the bodyminds of this country are being disabled & debilitated at varying rates & only a disability justice approach will work.[12]

Some readers responded with outrage, calling Dr. Schalk's tweet "catastrophizing," to which she replied, "Disability is not a catastrophe to me. It's just a fact of life,"[13] which I witness as a very Black queer disabled femme way of understanding disability. And disability *is* a fact of life, now more than ever, in the midst of year three of a global disablement.

And that's just talking about the pandemic as a source of mass disability. There are also many other, non-pandemic ways the world is getting more disabled. More and more people are locked in prisons, both the regular kind and immigration detention, especially as the climate crisis pushes masses of people to flee land they can't live on anymore, because it's too hot or too flooded or too politically unstable because of the famine and stress caused by these things. Prisons are spaces where people get disabled, or more disabled.

12 Dr. Sami Schalk (@DrSamiSchalk), Twitter, January 10, 2022, https://twitter.com/DrSamiSchalk/status/1480612339472912394.
13 Dr. Sami Schalk (@DrSamiSchalk), Twitter, January 12, 2022, https://twitter.com/DrSamiSchalk/status/1481248719970394117.

Wars continue, as does settler colonial displacement in Palestine and global Indigenous communities, the wages of which are disabled conditions from amputation to PTSD.

We know the often-cited (by crips, anyway) statistic that 26 percent of United Statesians are disabled (according to the CDC), and that 1 billion people, or 15 percent of the world's population, are (according to the WHO). We also often say the actual figures are probably higher, but people are afraid to disclose or were like, *I don't know if what have counts* or *Oh, I'm not disabled, I just have a condition*. The real numbers of disabled people in the world are already probably a lot higher than the abled mainstream thinks, and those numbers are just going to keep getting higher.

Then there's the joyful parts of why the world is becoming more and more disabled. Fueled by the bold work of neurodivergent people, *especially* BIPOC neurodivergent people, more and more people are joyfully coming out as neurodivergent and/or autistic every day. Many of us are self-diagnosing, moving away from the gatekeeping of the medical establishment, with its insurance hoops, high up-front costs, and limited and outdated white cis-male MIC (medical-industrial complex) imaginings of what autism and other forms of neurodivergence are.

I often correct people when they ask me "when I was diagnosed with autism," to let them know that I use the phrase *when I came home / when I figured it out,* instead. I was doula'd and supported by autistic Black, Indigenous, and POC friends in recognizing that I have been autistic all my life, the child of two neurodivergent, probably autistic parents, and that the shame I carried from allistic abuse all my life was not because I was inherantly bad or wrong, but something I could set down. They, not a doctor, are the people who helped me figure out my neurodivergence. I'm not shaming anyone for going after diagnosis for any reason, including of course the need for accomodations, but I am sharing this story to name a way of knowing ourselves that breaks from the MIC. I now have a starter pack I send to welcome BIPOC people, especially femmes, who are questioning whether they might be autistic, filled with essays, memes, hashtags, and online assessment tools. Many people with all kinds of disabilities are doing the same thing, even when we also pursue an official diagnosis—the first hints we had POTS or EDS or fibro or Chiari formation or OCD often came from other disabled people with those body/mind conditions.

Because of the work of disability justce, more and more people are coming out as disabled earlier, saving us years of denial, isolation, and shame. All of this joyful, complicated claiming of names we call home as disabled people breaks with the MIC's chokehold on who gets to identify as disabled and who doesn't, on a strict medical diagnosis as equalling identity. I see masses of people claiming names and identities and communities on their own terms and without waiting for permission, because they feel like they have something to gain. This joyful, self-determined claiming of disabled cultures changes how many of us we think we are.

How does it change everything, to imagine and plan for a future where we are the majority—and not a terrible thing, but a source of possibility and power?

––––––

The second thesis of this book is: We won't be able to survive climate change, the rise of fascism and white supremacy, and unending pandemics, we won't be able to create the just future we all still hope will show up, without disability justice and disabled skills.

In the words of my friend and comrade, Black disabled trans artist and organizer Syrus Marcus Ware, "There is no revolution if disabled people aren't in it."[14]

I am a pragmatist; I want us to win. And we are not going to win freedom and liberation from all forms of oppression if we do not systemically confront and destroy both internalized and externalized ableism. Talila Lewis, Black disability justice writer and organizer and co-founder of HEARD, says, "I laugh when people talk about racism and ableism separately—it's literally impossible to take them apart." The working definition of ableism that Lewis has revised for years, as of January 2022, reads, "A system of assigning value to people's bodies and minds based on societally constructed ideas of normalcy, productivity, desirability, intelligence, excellence, and fitness. These constructed ideas are deeply rooted in eugenics, anti-Blackness, misogyny, colonialism, imperialism, and capitalism. This systemic oppression that leads to people and society determining people's value based on their culture, age, language, appearance, religion, birth or living place, 'health/wellness,' and/or their ability to satisfactorily re/produce, 'excel' and 'behave.' You do not have to be disabled to experience ableism."[15]

What happens when we, the disabled margins (to paraphrase the late, great bell hooks) are the center? The multiple norms? What

14 Leah Lakshmi Piepzna-Samarasinha, "Cripping the Resistance: No Revolution without Us," *Disability Visibility Project*, August 24, 2020, https://disabilityvisibilityproject.com/2020/08/24/cripping-the-resistance-no-revolution-without-us/.
15 Talila Lewis, "Working Definition of Ableism – January 2022 Update," *Talila A. Lewis* (blog), January 1, 2022, https://www.talilalewis.com/blog/working-definition-of-ableism-january-2022-update.

would this world be like if we succeeded in flipping the world so that no one was exposed to eugenics, abled expectations of normality, intelligence, productivity, desirability, and the negative ways the MIC currently uses diagnosis, and everyone benefited? Because, as Lewis says, "you don't have to be disabled to experience ableism": ableism warps and lessens everyone's experience of the world, from shame about asking for help to ideas of intelligence, worth, and who has the right to have a family. I think of Toni Morrison's line, "I stood at the border, stood at the edge and claimed it as central. I claimed it as central, and let the rest of the world move over to where I was."

What is the world we could make then?

What are the worlds we are already making?

I AM A DISABLED FUTURIST. AND I AM NOT THE FIRST.

Far from it. Though it might surprise the abled (what doesn't), disabled people think about, make art about, and create the future *all the time.* A decade ago, disability justice performance collective Sins Invalid made a TIME MACHINE that was in the foyer of our 2011 show (it looked like a giant Japanese paper lantern people could walk or roll inside of), where audience members could record messages to the disabled future and listen to ones Sins artists had prerecorded. Mia Mingus wrote one of my favorite pieces about crip futures in Octavia's Brood, where disabled people escape eugenicist genocide on earth to create a loving, traumatized disabled planet of collective disabled farms that receive crip infants. Alice Wong has been using the term "crip futurism" with her Disabled Oracle Society project. White queer disabled science fiction writer Nicola Griffith has been using the term "crip futurism" since 2017. We have to fight to have a future, always, in a world trying to kill us, which means daily struggles to survive, create joy and organize, and reckon with technologies like CRISPR and VOXZOGO—the former, a gene-editing technology trumpeted as delivering a future where many disabilities will be "edited out" of disabled fetuses (for those who can afford it); the latter, an injectable drug approved in 2021 to end dwarfism in dwarf young people, potentially eliminating all future generations of little people.

As a lifelong brown queer crip science fiction reader, I would argue that science fiction has engaged critically with disability and neurodivergence for fucking ever, including when mainstream literature ignored disability. Science fiction is full of disabled writers and writers writing disability, both those who claim the D-word publicly and those who don't—or aren't—but who consistently write worlds that go beyond disability as tragedy or nonexistent, where disabled main characters live within and transform apocalypse out of their disabled genius and guts. I find this to be especially true of science fiction writers who aren't white. Look at how hard disability shows up in the worlds created by Octavia Butler, Larissa Lai, Nalo Hopkinson, Nnedi Okorafor, Rivers Solomon, Thirza Cuthand, the Metropolarity collective (Ras Mashramani, Alex Smith, Rasheedah Phillips, and M. Téllez), and Cherie Dimaline, to name just a few. Pandemics and the ways people altered by infection learn survival from that alteration?[16] Indigenous children stolen into new residential schools for medical experimentation/abuse for a cure, after white people lose the ability to dream?[17] Lauren Olamina as a hypersensitive neurodivergent

16 Larissa Lai, *The Tiger Flu* (Vancouver: Arsenal Pulp, 2018).
17 Cherie Dimaline, *The Marrow Thieves* (Toronto: Dancing Cat, 2017).

fibromyalgic leader, her leadership both stressed and lifted by her disabilities?[18] Okorafor's Onyesonwu in *Who Fears Death*, whose existence and heroism emerges out of the survivor PTSD they've had from their birth as a child of mass rape, and who uses uses her survivor/PTSD magic to regrow her and others' clitorises after undergoing FGM? Burnt-out trans sex-working engineered lifeforms pissed off at the ways they can never get access to good health care and getting off through a motel hookup anyway, and autistic-coded bioengineered, humanoid'ified space plants who have mixed feelings about others fighting for them without asking what they want?[19] Autistic Black wounded healers on a generation starship divided by race and class?[20]

It is not an accident disabled, and non-disabled, BIPOC write science fiction where disability isn't a sidenote to the future. It's also not an accident sci-fi fandoms are full of disabled and neurodivergent nerds. Obviously not all science fiction is disabled/anti-ableist like the examples I gave above. There's plenty of science fiction that ignores disability or parrots unquestioned ableist tropes: *Battlestar Galactica* sending the only character who needs adaptive tech into the sun; Marge Piercy's good future in *Woman on the Edge of Time*, where Mad people are respected but physical disability is eliminated without a second thought, an *of course* prenatal genetic editing; or *Star Trek's* Captain Pike ending up in the Beep-Beep Machine, a terribly designed wheelchair where his scarred and nonspeaking body is displayed as a monstrosity for the rest of the crew (in the twenty-third century they can design a bad wheelchair but not an AAC device,

18 Octavia Butler, *Parable of the Sower* (New York: Four Walls Eight Windows, 1993).
19 M. Téllez, "Heavy Prosthetic" and "Heat Death of Western Human Arrogance," *Venus Squared Saturn* zine, 2020, and *Cyborg Memoirs*, https://cyborgmemoirs.com/.
20 Rivers Solomon, *An Unkindness of Ghosts* (Brooklyn, NY: Akashic, 2017).

I guess). I don't think it's a coincidence that those three examples were written by white people, or that BIPOC science fiction writers have a more abundant track record of writing realities full of disability, whether they are utopic or dystopic or complicated. Even non-crip/sick/ND BIPOC science fiction writers are more likely to write crip futures, I believe, because we live within our own disabled histories of medical experimentation, genocide as the end of the world that's already happened, your uncle's leg amputation after Israel shoots a rocket into his house, or working three jobs while sick.

Black abolitionist organizer and science fiction writer Walidah Imarisha wrote something I and many people have come back to in recent years, a holding on to the possibility found in science fiction to imagine futures in times of chaos: "For those of us from communities with historic collective trauma, we must understand that each of us is already science fiction walking around on two legs. Our ancestors dreamed us up and then bent reality to create us."[21] Imarisha has spoken about being a descendent of enslaved Black ancestors, a descendent whose existence is a wild dream her ancestors invoked. "I am my ancestors' wildest dreams" is a phrase on T-shirts and graffitied walls in the past decade, speaking to the ways we draw from our ancestors' called-insane imaginings to inhabit the improbable present we've inherited and created. Disabled people are constantly creating an improbable crip future in the face of all that wants to eliminate us. (Disabled creativity is one of the core crip superpowers.) Crips thriving and not dying, as we are, and making vibrant-ass disabled presents and futures is a dream made flesh that comes out

---

21 Walidah Imarisha, introduction to *Octavia's Brood: Science Fiction Stories from Social Movements* (New York: AK Press, 2015).

of our unending crip majestic tradition of bending reality. We bend time to create crip lives that are beyond what anyone has told us was possible, all the time. We do shit we're not supposed to do, when people are staring and when ableism makes us so invisible we could rob a bank and they'd miss it.

SOMETIMES THAT HOPE IS YOU: MAKING UP STORIES TO SURVIVE

It's not a secret, my *Star Trek Discovery* superfandom. I have a LOT of feelings about this show. If you haven't had the chance to watch it or think *Star Trek* is full of weird Kirk dudes, you are not wrong but let me explain: Rick Berman, who controlled content on *Star Trek* for decades and is widely critiqued for his homophobia and sexism (making all the women characters wear corsets, banning any depictions of cannonical queerness or transness from the show), finally stepped down, *Star Trek Discovery*'s showrunners are Nigerian producer Olatunde Osunsanmi and queer white producer Michelle Paradise, and *Star Trek Discovery* is, well, Black, African, Latinx, Asian, gay, nonbinary, trans, disabled, millennial, and weird as hell. Anthony Rapp and Wilson Cruz are married and bitch about Cardassian opera while wearing space pajamas. It's gay like that.

For those who aren't familliar, *Disco* tells the story of Michael Burnham, Black feminist weirdo Starfleet officer, transculturally adopted by Spock's parents after her parents are presumed dead after a Klingon raid on their research facility. A lot of shit happens over four seasons, but basically, as my frantic recruitment to the fandom often describes it, this is the "Bridge of Gay Haircuts" where Michael saves the galaxy and (eventually) Starfleet through what I would argue is a deployment of an organizing politic rooted in Black feminist Bernice Johnson Reagon's "Coalition Politics: Turning the Century"[22]—just in the twenty-third century. There is a LOT of disability in *Disco* (all the spoiler alerts, but among other juicy bits, Young Spock breaks out of a future psych ward by kicking his shrinks in the face and stealing a starship, Keyla Detmer is a disabled femme navigator who flies the ship with her prosthetic eye and adaptive headset worn over her undercut, while she makes eyes at her platonic life partner, Joann Owosekun, who also has an undercut). I am not alone in my intense crip-of-color *Disco* fandom, as Alice Wong has multiple posts about *Star Trek Discovery* on the Disability Visibility Project. We may have also made a shirt on Teespring listing a bunch of women and nonbinary characters from season 1.

Star Trek Discovery was a big part of what kept me alive during Trump's presidency. Everything was horrible. I had chosen to move to Seattle in 2015, which meant living in an open-carry state with an enormous armed white-supremacist history and present-day militia reality. Trumpism meant that Black queer and trans disabled people I loved were beaten up or doxxed by Proud Boys and fascists, sometimes to the point of leaving the state. I stopped going to Olympia, the state's capital and longtime punk weirdo haven, because it had become normal for white militia jackasses with AR-15s to run screaming through the streets every weekend. All of this, along with wildfires, Brett Kavanaugh, attempts to kill Medicaid and the Affordable Care Act and doom all of us to a more certain death—oh yeah, and Trump's attempts

---

22 Bernice Johnson Reagon, "Coalition Politics: Turning the Century," in *Home Girls: A Black Feminist Anthology*, ed. Barbara Smith (Kitchen Table: Women of Color Press, 1983).

to just be a dictator forever—made for a lot of being frozen with anxiety. It was hard to imagine something beyond just survival, let alone a wild good future.

Disco helped. Seeing a future where things were really fucked up but a bunch of neurodivergent multiracial nerds with Black feminist leadership saved the galaxy and revived the Federation through queer chosen family helped. Seeing a future where queer characters came back from death to their lovers helped. There were some really dire Trumpian days that I got through by pretending I was on the uss *Discovery*, in my head.

White trans science fiction writer Charlie Jane Anders writes in her book *Never Say You Can't Survive* about being bullied as a trans learning-disabled kid and how the story-creation she did to survive lead to her career as a science fiction writer. "I think there's a thing we naturally do when we're in the middle of hardship and political torment, which is that we retreat into our imaginations," she writes. "It's no accident that a lot of social justice nerds are into *Star Trek*. You can also survive when times are hard by making up stories of how they could be different."[23]

A lot of the writing I did during the Trump era that is in this book was doing that: surviving by making up stories about how shit could be different, i.e., how disabled people could survive and make something less gross than what we were in. I, in my own halting, cripping way, was groping toward both imagining something audaciously better than the disaster we had, and documenting what I was noticing, in

---

23 Charlie Jane Anders, inteviewed by June Thomas, "'You Can Form a Little Bubble of Imagination Around Yourself': Author Charlie Jane Anders Explains How Fiction Can Be a Balm during Hard Times," *Slate*, August 17, 2021, https://slate.com/culture/2021/08/never-say-you-cant-survive.html.

DJ movement and community, about how we were trying to make it happen. Like Michael Burnham, we were working in less-than-ideal conditions, often in utter peril, with crewmates suffering from CPTSD who got into huge fights with each other. Yet, with a ragtag bunch of imperfect people in a bad mood, we were still able to do things to Fight Evil and Survive that kept ourselves alive.

Because look at what happened in the midst of all the destruction of Trump and the triple pandemic. Mask giveaways in the tens of thousands. DJ books, sections of bookstores and libraries, performances, collectives, Instagram feeds, hashtags, online groups, Zoom sex parties and dance parties and stim parties and hangouts. *We*—disabled people—saved Medicaid and the ADA (Americans with Disabilities Act). We taught all of North America how to make air purifiers out of box fans and a twenty-dollar furnace filter from Lowe's[24] and how to use masks for smoke and then viruses and what the different kinds were. We got the use of electroshock on autistic youth banned at the Judge Rotenberg Center (even though the law banning it has since been blocked again). We organized massive campaigns like #PowerToLive,[25] spreading information about how to make dry ice and use generators to power life-supporting access and medical equipment, like ventilators and wheelchairs, after Pacific Gas and Electric (PG&E) with no warning cut off power to most of Northern California in an attempt to stop wildfires; and #HighRiskCA to reverse statewide legislation barring crips from the

---

24 Mike Senese, "Build an Affordable Air Purifier with a Box Fan and Hepa Filter, *Make*, November 16, 2018, https://makezine.com/2018/11/16/build-an-affordable-air-purifier-with-a-box-fan-and-hepa-filter/.
25 For more information about the #PowerToLive coalition and their life-saving information-gathering, see https://www.powertolivecoalition.org/.

front of the line for vaccines. We stopped medical rationing in triage from being a reality—so far. We had care circles, even when we were beyond exhausted and overwhelmed with rage and despair. Us, a whole lot of traumatized, pissed-off disabled people who were supposed to be the first people to die, who absolutely refused to be sidelined or forgotten about.

Some people may read this book and be confused: where's the futurism? Where's the shiny robot arms, the aspie supremacy fueling the space race, the cure? This is another one of those few ways disabled futures get talked about: shiny cool supercrip ones. But I am writing a *disability justice* futurism. Where the disability in the future is not about the 40K cybernetic arm that doesn't work and nobody who isn't a one-percenter can afford anyway—but all the disabled survival strategies, communities, and tech we create by and for ourselves as disabled BIPOC people.

If this life often feels like the apocalyptic science fiction novels I read as a teen and twentysomething come true, what is also true is that we—disabled people—are the heroes, surviving it and helping everyone else know how to survive it. We are the ones who know, more than anyone, the technology of how to actually care. We taught the world how to mask, wash your hands, boost your immune system with herbs in the kitchen rack, organize for vax equity and against care rationing. We were making a future in the present in grief and terror and uncertainty and loss, as we got good at doing this work in utter bullshit that made my little early 2010 apocalypse fears look like cupcakes. In our big projects, tiny invisible moments, "stupid" ideas, art, projects, lawsuits, private moments, adaptive device libraries, hustling money out of brick walls. Our Crazy leaps of faith, archiving, caremongering, troubleshooting, crip doula'ing a new world into birth.

CARE WORK IS GRIEF WORK

I also wrote this book out of my disabled grief (its subtitle could be "Grief Work"). I needed to write a disabled future because of my giant disabled grief. Two of my closest queer, BIPOC, fat disabled femme beloved friends who I made DJ with, Stacey Park Milbern and Lucia Leandro Gimeno, died in 2020 and 2021. Two of my oldest psych survivor comrades, Don Weitz and Graeme Bacque, died in the span of two weeks during September 2021—Graeme hit me up on Instagram to tell me Don had died, then he passed weeks later. My birth father died of cancer, my birth mother, already disabled via polio, cancer, and abuse, got COVID in her long-term care facility. Countless friends and family members of friends and loved ones got sick and died, to the point where I can't even remember all of their names without some serious scanning of my phone. We were scared there would be disabled killing camps during COVID, and that didn't quite happen, but I think we are seeing a holocaust of disabled people dying both from COVID and "related" causes—heartbreak, multiple access denials that pile up and make you sicker, COVID mixed with other ongoing conditions—that results in mass death anyways.

For a lot of the past two years of the pandemic, deep in those multiple layers of grief, I lurched from emergency to emergency, worked really hard at keeping my head above water, and pretty much could focus only on the victory of every day being one more day I didn't get COVID. I wrote this book from my grief couch, my

I'm-a-hard-femme-but-I-cry-every-day couch. I needed to make something out of my and everyone's unending chronic grief that broke me open. I needed to alchemize it to survive. I needed to record what we've been doing, and how we are surviving all we have lost. And to write some of what has been lost. To write that disabled history in the making.

Making a future in nonideal conditions, in the middle of utter disaster, grieving, panicking, mourning, PTSD'd out, deeply depressed, fumbling, fucking up, and trying again, is a crip way of making a future.

CARE WORK 2: THE RECKONING

Care Work is a tough act to follow. It's comforting to remember that I didn't know what the hell I was doing when I wrote it. I thought it would just be an ... essay book. Yeah, a bunch of essays! I'd written a bunch of shit, I could just slap it together and make a book. I didn't think it would be a disability book, no way—I mean, did I even have the expertise to write that? But then the more I pounded out the first draft on my back porch in the summer of 2017, the more I realized that all of these essays, they just happened to have a lot to do with disability and care webs. Books are anarchists. They're like kids: they tell you who they are, they do not stay what you imagined they would be.

In writing this book, even after *Care Work*'s unexpected success, I wanted to stay in that disabled space of not knowing what the hell I'm doing, but just ... doing it. I wanted to stay in a disabled writing space of messiness, uncertainty, and not being an expert. Who the hell am I anyway? Not the one voice, not an academic, not an expert.

Just a nobody who is a somebody, like every disabled person. This is an important stance to hold on to, more than ever, now that DJ turned seventeen years old and some of us have been able to access grants and some kinds of recognition, while some of us remain in the middle of nowhere, trying to eat, wondering if we've been forgotten. (I would be remiss in not stating that there are plenty of us who are both.) We didn't make disability justice to make a star system of cool disabled celebrity activists lording it over everyone else. We made DJ out of a knowledge of the ways disabled BIPOC and queer/trans people have been shut out from our disabled gifts being witnessed and respected, including especially those of us seen as "stupid" ugly or whose access needs are too troublesome. I believe in a movement without a star system, where we all get to shine.

In the spirit of not becoming assimilated or co-opted, in writing this particular wordhouse, I wanted to keep the crip snark, the sense of no bullshit, and as my friend Cyrée Jarelle Johnson calls it, my "peculiar kind of autistic charm." (Thanks, Cyrée.) I had a Post-it note reading I AM TRYING NOT TO BE BULLSHIT above my desk for most of the final year I was working on this book. So much of our disabled lives gets the voice boiled out of it to be as bland as a homecare instructions pamphlet. I wanted to keep the crackass-yet-compassionate sense of humor that I love about us. I still don't want to translate to abled people. Maybe I need to do so a little less, because of the work we have collectively done.

This is also a book written and edited with a sense of urgency. *Care Work* took almost a decade to write: published in 2018, some of the essays in it were first written in 2009–2010. I had what felt like plenty of time to polish it. I pushed myself to get this collection out quickly because I felt like the world might need it as the pandemic went into year three. I feel a lot of nerves about this decision, but it is a disabled choice I have made. The more time goes by, the more I feel the urgency of documenting our movements, our movement moments, our small disabled moments. Time goes by fast, and our leaders and beloveds die, especially during the pandemic. If 2015–2018 were "the femme suicide years," when many beloved queer femme artists and activists killed themselves, 2019–2021 were the "name a disabled fat BIPOC who wasn't murdered by the MIC during a pandemic" years. As Corbett O'Toole says, "Every disabled leader who dies takes a library of knowledge with them that they often didn't have the time to write down."[26]

This is in some ways a book of disabled secrets, of movement moments and conversations we have on voice memes and texts, in the moments where someone is dropping off some soup, of the real-deal complexities of putting disability justice into practice. I wanted to write down and share some of those small, real moments of trying to figure out how the fuck to make the 10 Principles of Disability Justice work in practice, or the shit that happens in every single DJ collective I've ever known, or tiny moments of disabled love, solidarity, figuring it out, and frustration. I wanted to continue to build on where *Care Work* left off. It's been truly wild to see DJ and also things not-quite DJ explode in the last three years, and for people to name *Care Work* as being a part of that work. I'm very honored and glad. I also feel like a lot of what I wrote—particularly about interdependence—just barely started to scratch the surface, and was at risk of causing harm

26 Corbett O'Toole, personal conversation with the author, August 2020.

if it was not advanced with more nuance. As the triple pandemic[27] hit and all of a sudden "mutual aid" was on everyone's lips and people were eager to bring me soup when I couldn't leave the house because of Viruses in the Air, as the requests for workshops grew, and as my own experiments with giving and receiving care got bigger, I wanted to write it down—more of the specific, true-fact moments of what happens when we try to care for each other and keep each other alive.

The back of my 2007 Honda Fit is covered with many obnoxious bumper stickers, because I am that kind of person: the biggest just says BOOKS CHANGE LIVES, all caps. I've based my whole writing career on that belief. It was true when I was an abused disabled autistic weird brown ten-year-old whose books were her friends, and as an angsty survivor autistic loner twenty-year-old with no money or social capital, for whom library books were a portal, a solace, a community in a backpack, a world(s). This way of being with books is a disabled writing and reading story. Crips are isolated everywhere, even in places where we have friends and community, but we have books in our beds. Books are a community organizing tool, a friend, a home. You listen to the audiobook over and over to hear a crip voice when you're stuck in the house; you read disabled books when you can barely say the words out loud, or you are the only disabled queer Black person you know, or no one can visit you in the hospital because of COVID regs. I am one of many late-realized autistic people for whom my autistic community was the #ActuallyAutistic hashtag and autistic Instagram, years before I had autistic friends.

---

27 The triple pandemic is a term created to refer to the interrelated trifecta of the COVID-19 pandemic, white supremacy/fascism, and economic depression.

Books are a particular kind of disability justice organizing tool. Eli Clare told me that when he wrote *Exile and Pride* he was kind of faking it: he wrote about having a radical disabled queer community that he didn't have yet, but his writing called it into being. Over and over, I see disabled writers writing our communities into being through this kind of crip writing alchemy. I think of queer disabled poet Laura Hershey's self-published zines and chapbooks like *Spark Before Dark*, or the vast influence of different Old Autistic generations of writing, from Mel Baggs' Ballastexistenz blog to many other older autistic websites you can only find on archive.org. Or the influence of Aurora Levins Morales's blog and books, Leroy Moore's decades of Black disabled hip-hop labor and archiving, Alice Wong's Disability Visibility Project—just three of the disabled BIPOC writers whose cultural work has been foundational to building disability justice. (Being a disabled writer also means writing knowing that someone has probably written what you've said before—it's just lost in a zine from twenty years ago, a crip first-gen website that didn't get renewed, an out of print book.)

This is, like everything I do, a love letter to other disabled QTBIPOC. Others can listen in, but you are not my primary audience—disabled BIPOC are. And like the best love letters, one of the ways this book femifests love is by honesty and real talk. Being real about disability justice, about what it means to try and love and care for each other, how it's messy and not simple. We are never, ever served by prettying shit up and making it simple or "nice." We are not a nice people, but we are extraordinary and wonderful. And, as Alexis Pauline Gumbs once wrote, "the future deserves a present where our truths were spoken."

This is especially true in these extremely perilous times, that are both full of all my hugest dreams for a disability justice revolutionary future and all my deepest fears that we will be eliminated, despite all our brilliance. I completed this book in January 2022, when the more-contagious-than-measles Omicron variant of COVID-19 has ripped across the world, pile-driving hospitals, pushing exhausted people—parents, workers, caregivers, teachers—to the breaking point, especially with a now total lack of the skimpy social programs (expanded unemployment and aid payments, eviction moratoriums) that had helped people in the first two years of the pandemic; and forcing many disabled people back into isolation in our homes in an attempt to dodge the variant.

On January 10, 2022, CDC director Rochelle Walensky, speaking on *Good Morning America*, said it was "really encouraging news" that most people who'd died of the Omicron variant were living with comorbidities, a.k.a. being disabled. "These were already people who were very sick," she said, implying that our deaths didn't matter. Her words hit so many disabled people in a place that was already black and blue. I thought I was OK, until I started sobbing in the middle of explaining where to get a pulse oximeter to a friend whose seventy-two-year-old mother had just had a direct exposure. Early January 2022 was a really low moment for a lot of disabled people. We were into the third calendar year of the pandemic, we had busted so much ass keeping each other alive, and yet, it felt like we were screaming into the void in the face of this matter-of-fact embracing of eugenics. I had no illusions that Biden would be some magic fairy godfather, but I thought there might be some improvement when Trump was out of office. But here we were, a year into the Biden administration, hearing the head of the CDC blandly state that our disabled deaths were encouraging news, and that they didn't matter at all.

The collective response of the disabilitysphere was swift. Black disabled activist and writer Imani Barbarin issued a call to arms in her viral January 8 TikTok video when she said:

> I'm livid—and you should be too ... Don't let the scientic jargon fool you. The CDC director is encouraged that 75% of the people who died of COVID, of the omicron variant, were disabled. What she doesn't tell you is the the majorty of these deaths are Indigenous and Latinx people. Also what she's failing to tell you is that 30 million Americans have four or more comorbities. When we live in a racist ableist society who do you think those people are? Those of you who think your safe, how many variants will it take before you're disabled and therefore disposable? Every single one of you should be livid, because we are all being left to die.[28]

Barbarin began the #MyDisabledLifeIsWorthy hashtag which quickly gained ground with thousands of disabled people, fearing for our lives, posting our rage, grief, and fear online, and insisting on our right to survive. Disability Visibility Project founder Alice Wong added, "I'm so sick of having to argue that our lives are valuable. And yet—here we are."

And yet here we are. It's disorienting. On the one hand, disabled people are making more beautiful books, survival hacks, organizing, and communities than ever before. There's a disability section of the *New York Times*, my publisher has a disability literature section

---

28 Imani Barbarin, "I'm Livid," January 9, 2022, Facebook Live video, 0:59, https://www.facebook .com/watch/?v=346681473949731.

filled with disabled BIPOC writers. Many people, either newly disabled or affected by COVID, are getting hip to disabled organizing and perspective and skills. More people than ever are talking about and practicing access and care and centering disability justice in their organizing and everyday life.

And simultaneously, we are in a time of a huge backlash. Eugenics is taken for granted, spoken about offhandedly as pundits and officials say that we must "learn to live with the virus" and "go back to normal." Many of us can't live with the virus, and a "return to normal" means a "return to the ableist bullshit that partially receded over the last few years of immune awareness, masking, CART and ASL on Zoom, mutual aid, and remote work." As I copyedit this book, the mask mandate in my home state of Washington expired a few days ago, a move echoed across North America, even as a new Omicron variant begins to peak again in Europe, and there's an eerie feeling that the powers that be are encouraging a mass forgetting of the last two years of disabled reality.

Walensky weakly apologized and tried to walk back her statement, but nothing really changed in terms of the CDC's failures to center and protect disabled and immunicompromised people. As Mia Mingus wrote in her essay "You Are Not Entitled to Our Deaths": "We know the state has failed us. We are currently witnessing the pandemic state-sanctioned violence of murder, eugenics, abuse and bone-chilling neglect in the face of mass suffering, illness, and death.[29] In my and many others' nightmares, this is a final solution for disabled people: all COVID mitigation strategies are thrown out

---

29 Mia Mingus, "You Are Not Entitled to Our Deaths: COVID, Abled Supremacy & Interdependence," *Leaving Evidence* (blog), January 16, 2022, https://leavingevidence.wordpress.com/2022/01/16/you-are-not-entitled-to-our-deaths-covid-abled-supremacy-interdependence.

the window so abled people can shop, work, and watch football, and disabled people either die or stay within our immune-safer bubbles for the rest of our lives. I believe in disabled resilience, but my suicidal ideation popped up again when I thought about that. I don't want a future where I never get to have in-person communion with people I love again, where I get harassed for wearing my N95 in the supermarket, and/or where most of the people I love are living with even more disability from long COVID with no government support, or are dead.

When my fear and disabled despair gets big, I remember: there're still more of us than them. There are more of us all the time, and especially more of us because of COVID. And disabled people are (some of) the best goddamn people in the world. Our disabled love and all our brilliant collective care and crip ingenuity, that we've done before and through the endemic, is love work that's not going anywhere. We're not going to stop dreaming.

As it turns out, a lot of oppressed communities have a lot of practice dreaming in the middle of complete despair. One of my favorite comic artists, Gaytor Al, has a beautiful six-panel comic she drew for Nakba Day 2021. The Nakba, or catastophe, is the day the Israeli government expelled Palestinians from their lands in 1948, and is marked by Palestinians and allies globally as a day of mourning and memory. The way Gaytor Al writes about the hard work of continuing to dream justice in the face of decades of brutality speaks to my own experiences of the difficult necessity of dreaming a disabled future in times of fascism and eugenics:

It is a hard day to have hope—every year, but especially this year. Somehow, though, it's still there, the single bulb improbably illuminated on a dead string of Christmas lights ... This date never passes without dredging up the (maybe apocryphal) words of David Ben Gurion, the first Israeli PM, in response to the Nakba: "the old will die, and the young will forget." Like hell we will. It's more than stubborn torch-carrying, though. It's muscle memory, what my body does when I drink too-sweet Lipton on a particularly clear morning or read about kids flying kites in Gaza. It will be there until I die or until Palestinians walk through Jerusalem without identity cards, two things I have no choice but to believe are equally inevitable.

Her comic shows her iconic alligator main character dreaming, her head on a pillow as an outline of East Jerusalem is slowly filled in with rich color above her, and the words, "We have dreamed, every night, for 73 years, of a free Palestine / And we will dream the same dream / Every night / Until we meet her."[30]

Dreams are some crazy, feminine, irrational Mad shit. Not serious, right?

But we, disabled people, we dream a lot. In psych wards, of dead friends, of getting out of our parents' basement apartment, on day 645 of pandemic not-leaving-the-house, of lovers who will be sweet to us in autistic, Deaf, disabled ways. We haven't stopped dreaming all through Trump and the pandemic. We go to bed every night dreaming of the disability justice future. And we will keep dreaming these wild disability justice dreams, every night and day, until we meet her.

We are meeting her right now.

30 Gaytor Al (@gaytor_al), Instagram, May 15, 2021, https://www.instagram.com/p/CO5zNlLDlLB/.

PART I

DISABILITY JUSTICE IN THE END TIMES

I believe that our ancestors laugh,
cry, rage, love, celebrate us.
We grow knowledge and movements with them.
—STACEY PARK MILBERN

We are our own best strategy to win.
—STACEY PARK MILBERN

"We Were Maybe Not Going to Save the World, but We Were Going to Save Each Other"[31]: How Disabled Mutual Aid Is Different than Abled Mutual Aid

I want you to know this: Disabled people kept each other alive during COVID-19.

We kept each other alive when we were alone. We kept the two or 2,000 other disabled people we were connected with alive. And we shared our knowledge with everybody else.

This is not new. Like every kind of oppressed people, disabled people are geniuses at staying alive despite everything. And we are often the only ones who remember each other and get in the trenches and kick ass to save each other when everyone else "forgets" about disabled people.

We were keeping each other alive before COVID, and we will keep on keeping each other alive. We also care for each other when we die, and through all that happens after. Even when we or the people we love die, the love we made through the care we created is not useless or wasted. But the ways we kept each other alive during COVID

---

31 Sandra Alland, Facebook, August 18, 2021, https://www.facebook.com/sandra.alland/posts/1734987846689065.

is nothing short of a heroic, epic miracle battle. Something there should be an giant saga-type movie about, but probably won't be.

However, the ways we kept each other alive are often completely incomprehensible to abled people and neurotypical people. Period. And when abled and neurotypical people think and talk and write books about mutual aid, that term, often ascribed to white anarchists, is what non-white, working class/poor, trans, sex-work, and disabled communities have practiced for forever. "Mutual aid": that term that has gotten so popularized on the front page of the NYT in the past eighteen months, in ways that would shock the shit out of my zine-reading nineteen-year-old self. The kind of non-disabled "mutual aid" that has been popularized during COVID didn't always talk about disabled-specific ways of surviving. So I'm going to write it down.

If you're reading this, maybe you don't need me to tell you. You're already disabled, and you figured out ways to keep yourself and other disabled people alive every day since February 2020, and you still are. You know what you're doing.

But maybe you do need to hear it anyway. Because you need to know that what you do counts. That what you do is real.

And maybe if you're new to disabled anything, maybe all of this will be mind-blowing information.

So buckle up and settle in for the ride. Let me tell you some shit.

SOME WAYS WE KEPT EACH OTHER ALIVE

When I think about disabled mutual aid, I think of a million examples of subtle, diverse forms of disabled survival work. Work that is mostly not seen as "real work."

I remember the first few months of the pandemic. We were all so fucking scared. There was no good information out there about the virus. Even my doctor, who I usually trust, told me, "Don't worry, most people will probably get a mild cold. It's going to blow over in a few months."

From a lifetime of knowing that the medical industrial complex lies, especially about pandemics that are going to affect oppressed communities more intensely, me and all the crip people I know didn't trust the information that was out there. The voices on the radio and TV kept saying, "Don't worry, only the elderly and immunocompromised will die." We were the elderly and immunocompromised.

Many disabled, elderly, fat, immunocompromised, and vulnerable people went to heroic measures to defend our communities and our selves. When I look at the strategies we created, they can fall into roughly six categories: public campaigns and information sharing, crip research, crip resources share, crip checking in and collective care, creating disabled community spaces, and getting people money.

We created organizing that was public, like work by Disability Justice Culture Club,[32] the East Oakland–based disability justice community center DJ activist Stacey Park Milbern founded in her house, which early in the pandemic created crucial infographics that spoke to the fears sick and disabled people were feeling when we were really scared and isolated, acknowledging that we were in the unknown, but emphasizing that we could take care of our existing disabilities, protect each other, and share information. The NoBody Is Disposable Coalition, a Bay Area–based coalition of disability, fat, and healing-justice groups who feared care rationing and the "ICUgenics" policies

32 Disibility Justice Culture Club on Facebook: www.facebook.com/disabilityjusticecultureclub.

being discussed that would deny care to people deemed low on the "quality of life" triage list—disabled, fat, and old people—created know-your-rights, COVID-safety, and patient advocacy guides advising folks on how to prepare advance directives and medically advocate for ourselves, including having a one-pager telling their story hung around their necks to try and get medical staff to see our lives as worth saving. The coalition also created organizing campaigns pushing back against care-rationing policies being debated—on social media and in meetings with health care policy directors and public health departments on the county and state level—which lead to many of those policies being withdrawn. Fat Rose, an organization of radical anti-fascist fat people, many of whom are disabled, created and shared crowdsourced safety strategies focused on fat and disabled people's bodies.[33]

I share these stories both to record stories of disability justice organizing that are often erased or forgotten, and because I think it's important to articulate that disability justice campaigns to share information and fight back against policies that would kill us overtly ARE mutual aid.

And: it's also true that the vast majority of COVID safety organizing created by disabled people was more private. It lies in all the everyday, word-of-mouth, not-so-public efforts to spread information, tools, scripts, and safety strategies, spread crip-to-crip, in texts, phone calls, voice memos, and online messages.

In writing this, I need to remember the everyday flavor of our days in the pre-vaccine COVID times in disabled communities I am a part

---

33 "Know Your Rights Guide to Surviving COVID-19 Triage Protocols," *NoBody Is Disposable*, https://nobodyisdisposable.org/know-your-rights/.

of. The disabled survival work we did, the strategies we invented. We stayed up late researching what scientists were saying, reading every article and sharing them. So many of us reduced our contacts to the bare minimum, or zero. So many of us didn't see or touch another human person for a year or more. Some still aren't.

In the first few months of COVID, I went on night walks so no one would be around to breathe on me, even with a mask on, because we just didn't know. When someone did walk toward me, I ran off the road and turned my head so I wouldn't breathe in their outbreath. I wiped down every door knob, light switch, and car handle with bleach or alcohol twice a day. (My car still has a bleach stain down the side.) We shared recipes for homemade hand sanitizer and where to buy the fragrance-free kind, and made contact-free distro boxes for it on our blocks.

We figured out ways to use our crip skills—already highly polished from years of navigating crip isolation—to navigate kind of living in an airlock for months. We innovated. All those Zoom crip dance parties and craft nights and hangouts and going deep into fandoms and leaving contact-free baskets of extra veggies on the stoop, those were and are lifesaving crip mutual-aid survival.

The ad hoc "crip mask brigades"—disabled people sharing info about masks to people who were new to them—were huge. We spread the word about when Vogmask and other N95 equivalents went on sale, bought them for each other in the ten minutes before they sold out, and mailed them to each other. Crips found medical fabric, sewed and mailed out masks to crips in other cities. I had three N95 masks, ones I'd already used a bunch, saved from wildfire season the year before. I used them sparingly on the rare occasions I left the house. There were no N95s for sale anywhere in North America, and people were being scolded about masking at all, let alone using N95s. But months before the CDC would say JUST KIDDING, PLEASE MASK, me and every crip I knew were wearing masks whenever we had to go into a grocery store or any other crucial inside place. People edged away from us. They thought we were sick, they thought we were crazy. They were right, but not in the way they thought. We were sick, crazy people who were determined to stay alive.

Some days it felt like half of what I did in a day was engage in convos with folks on social media sharing research (like "The Risks: Know Them, Avoid Them,"[34] a crucial piece of early popular research by epidemiologist Erin Bronage about aerosol transmission) about how masking was a good, lifesaving choice for everybody, but ESPECIALLY for other disabled people. We shared data dashboards and talked about community rates and different levels of exposure, from harm reduction onward. I witnessed so many disabled people deep in science Twitter and medical research, sharing early data, sharing knowledge we were already versed in from our lives as immunocompromised people about sanitation and immune support—all the ways we keep germs away from us. It was disabled people who first understood that viral load—the amount of virus one is exposed to—is a factor in whether one might get COVID. I feel like one of my almost-daily acts of support was sharing microcovid.org, a tool made by immunology and data nerds in San Francisco that helps you calculate the actual risk of daily activities based on your city and its current rates, type of mask worn and vax status, and how many people are

---

34 Erin Bronage, "The Risks: Know Them, Avoid Them," *Erin Bromage: COVID-19 Musings* (blog), May 6, 2020, www.erinbromage.com/post/the-risks-know-them-avoid-them.

around. We need to give ourselves credit, and get credit, for being the disabled and chronically ill citizen scientists and information sharers we are.

Before the pandemic, disabled people with multiple chemical sensitivities/injury, asthma, and other immunocompromised conditions have been masking to stay safe—from chemicals and fragrances but also viruses—for a long time. Disabled mask users did crucial work when we shared our existing knowledge of the different kinds of masks that exist (cloth, medical, N95, P95, respirators), brands, where to get them, and how to stop glasses from fogging and preserve lipstick. Many of us did a kind of community PSA creation on social media, talking about our historic and current-day masking practices, as immunocompromised and vulnerable folks. We possibility-modeled for mask using when we talked about our hacks to make masks cute and breathable and what our favorite kinds were, making mask using familiar and relatable. I didn't see any cute ads extolling masking put out by my city, state, or federal government, but I sure as hell saw disabled queer people flagging #Mask4Mask. I posted photos on Instagram of me wearing my mask, and some friends later thanked me for being an early crip proponent of masking, that me talking about why I masked was probably why they had worn masks and were alive.

For most of spring and summer 2020, none of my crip friends in New York could find any N95s and, unlike me, they lived in small apartments in buildings with shared ventilation. The small dyke-owned garden and pet-supply store in my neighborhood was selling

KN95 masks,[35] the only place that had any, and they only had ten or twenty on hand at any time. We were going there to get seeds, manure, and cat food because they'd moved all of their operation outside; you could pay for stuff online and go pick it up from a shelving unit by the sidewalk. I would buy as many KN95s as I could afford and mail them to folks in NYC with nettles I'd picked in the park and cedar and rosemary for lung steams from my garden and the woods next to my house.

Then there was the collective care and the creating of disabled community spaces. Friends who were disabled but less immunocompromised than me texted saying they were going to the grocery store and did I need anything? They went through all the picked-over grocery stores and found cheese, flour, and yes, toilet paper. I remember them setting the bags down on a rock twenty feet away from my front door, and us waving, with masks on, from a distance. I remember my friend making medicine and dropping off jars of tea on the doorsteps of all the Elders she knew. The Disability Justice Culture Club was organizing drop-offs of food, masks, and hand sanitizer to disabled people in Oakland. Friends and I co-organized a group disabled watch-party when *Crip Camp*[36] went live on Netflix, the first social event any of us had attended in weeks and with a truly epic thread of over 150 texts. My friend Lucia Leandro Gimeno[37] tuned in from the hospital, one of the first times I'd heard directly from him since a

35 Tim Chan, "N95 Masks vs. KN95 Masks: Which Work Best to Protect against Covid When Traveling?" *Rolling Stone*, April 9, 2022, https:// www.rollingstone.com/product-recommendations/ lifestyle/n95-vs-kn95-masks-1044184/.

36 Netflix film *Crip Camp*: https://cripcamp.com.

37 More on Lucia Leandro Gimeno at the Disibility Art and Culture Project: http://dacp.art/2021/ 07/27/lucia-leandro-gimeno.

medical crisis that spring had brought him to the ICU. He texted how much it meant to him to be in disabled space.

We also came together and got each other that form of mutual aid called money. Crip Fund,[38] an ad hoc group of disabled friends, mostly queer and mostly BIPOC, came together and raised money to give to disabled BIPOC in dire situations, via Venmo, no questions asked. When COVID hit and lockdowns happened, disabled people with precarious income lost a lot of that work, because clients stopped seeing sex workers, because small businesses shut down, because nobody was spending money on stuff we sold or services we offered, because everyone was broke, or we stopped doing the work we were doing because the exposure risks were so high. A little-discussed thing that happened in early COVID was that when government offices shut down—that included Social Security. Anyone who's ever been on SSI or SSDI or other benefits knows that they're always writing you telling you there's a problem with your account and you need to come to the office to fix it. This was still happening, except all the offices were closed. We heard about many disabled people who had lost their check and were in dire straits because there was no one at the office they could see to fix it.

The Crip Fund collective summed up this disabled, pandemic economic moment when we wrote:

> They say COVID-19 doesn't discriminate, but we know sick and disabled people are disproportionately affected by pandemics and public health crises long before and well after corona. Officials say people will die, but we say we aren't dead yet. When anyone (and

38 "About Crip Fund," *Crip Fund*, updated June 20, 2020, https://cripfund.wordpress.com.

what right now can feel like everyone) says it's only the old and unhealthy who are dying, we say stop racist-eugenics now. Much love to all life!

Some of us are losing work due to the closings and coming up short on rent, food, meds, pay for care work, etc. Some of us never had a job in the first place and live off of disability income—which always comes up short. Some of us are stuck at home well before lockdown and some are still looking for housing. We know that ableism, American individualism, and racial global capital want us dead and will try to kill every single one of us. But we also know they can't kill us all! The time is now. It was actually weeks ago but we were in bed. Still are. What we want is free but groceries, rent, and healthcare still aren't. Please give if you are able, or share where you can, or just vibe something good.[39]

All of these are crucial ways we kept each other here. We put in so much disabled work.

But, somewhere in that mess of early-middle days of collective disabled terror and life struggle, I reached out to a large local mutual aid group because I wanted to know if there was anything I could do to help out—if I could be a part of this big "mutual aid" thing that I kept seeing buzz about online. They said sure, they were going and buying groceries for disabled people who were immunocompromised and couldn't go into stores and would I like to help with that? I told them that I was one of those disabled, immunocompromised people for whom a grocery store was unsafe and asked if there were any accessible things I could do. I never got an email back.

---

39 "About Crip Fund," *Crip Fund*, updated June 20, 2020, https://cripfund.wordpress.com.

None of the things I listed above, the disabled mutual aid we were already doing, was on their list of tasks to sign up for. What we were doing didn't fit into their ideas of what mutual aid is, because they were thinking of it from an abled perspective of abled people are the ones who do the work, disabled people are the recipients. But every single thing listed above—and many more that I haven't listed, don't know about, but are happening right now by disabled people—are forms of disabled mutual aid. They are all innovative and life giving. They all count.

DISABLED PEOPLE DON'T DO MUTUAL AID LIKE ABLED PEOPLE DO. THE WAYS WE DO IT DIFFERENTLY ARE A BIG REASON WHY ABLED MUTUAL AID FUCKS UP.

A brief history of the mutual aid revolution/resurgence of 2020. The term "mutual aid" was popularized by the anarchist philosopher Peter Kropotkin in his essay collection *Mutual Aid: A Factor of Evolution*, which argued that cooperation, not competition, was the driving mechanism behind evolution. I first heard it used in anarchist and antiauthoritarian activist circles I was in in my early twenties to mean a radical model where care was not one-way or transactional: people came together to help each other. However, while the word may have been created by anarchists, the practice of communities caring for each other has been practiced for millennia as a basic form of survival. As my friend and collaborator Ejeris Dixon points out in their essay "Fascists Are Using COVID-19 to Advance Their Agenda. It's Up to Us to Stop Them" the woman down the hall from me may never have used the term "mutual aid," but when she says, *I know you* *have asthma, I'm going wipe down the elevator with bleach twice a day,* she's practicing it.[40]

In 2020, in response to the COVID-19 pandemic, the economic depression and care crisis that emerged from it, and the Trump administration's wholesale, genocidal abandonment of the US population, large mutual aid collectives sprang up all over North America and beyond to meet the needs that were not being met by federal and state governments. These collectives were incredibly creative in their strategies to address people's needs on a massive scale, ranging from networks of people cooking and dropping off meals and masks to people they didn't know, to innovative new strategies, like the networks of free community fridges that sprung up on the sidewalks of Seattle and other cities.

Some of these mutual aid networks understood how mutual aid could easily turn into charity—with all the gatekeeping and barriers to accessing care and support, and "prove you're worthy and not scamming us, we'll tell you what you need and you better be grateful and accept it" ableist, racist, and classist ideologies that can infest many nonprofits—and they worked hard against that. CareMongering Toronto was one of them and was incredible. A mutual aid Facebook group started by Indigenous and Sikh queer women and Two Spirit people organized around Indigenous and Sikhi principles of caring for communities, Caremongering had 25,000 members at its height and moved mountains to get isolated, often desperate people the food, meds, money, rides, and diapers they needed. Because of the

---

40 Ejeris Dixon, "Fascists Are Using COVID-19 to Advance Their Agenda. It's Up to Us to Stop Them," *Truthout*, April 11, 2020, https://truthout.org/articles/fascists-are-using-COVID-19-to-advance-their-agenda-its-up-to-us-to-stop-them/.

Indigenous and Sikh principles they were based in, which forbade denying people care, the administrations continually shut down anyone who guilt-tripped people about asking for help too often, accused people of scamming, or tried to tell people what they should really be asking for. Its size and popularity show that those principles worked and were enormously successful in getting help to people.

But there were many other mutual aid groups I witnessed that didn't do so well, where people's whiteness, racism, and ableism crept in and suspiciousness and gatekeeping of resources did occur. I also saw many mutual aid groups who seemed to not be thinking about disabled people or ableism at all when they talked about their goals for organizing. They didn't seem to understand that disabled people were organizing, that we were people other than faceless recipients of care. These groups seemed to be ignorant of the specifically ableist and racist histories of charities and how those dynamics easily creep into mutual aid. I wasn't ever sure if they were thinking about disabled people when they talked about mutual aid, and it seemed strange that disabled people were never mentioned when they eagerly defined what mutual aid was. Not only were they not thinking about ableism, they seemed to talk about "mutual aid" without ever referencing that sick and disabled people had been practicing it for years, that there might be something (or like, a lot) to learn from us, and that *a pandemic is a disabled event*.

If I had a dollar for every time I saw people using the term "collective care" without ever mentioning that it was invented by radical disabled women and nonbinary people of color who were and are part of the disability justice movement, I would be able to pay off my student loan debt.

The erasure of the intellectual and activist labor of disability justice activists—particularly disabled BIPOC women and nonbinary people and/or femmes—makes me want to scream. But it also has giant implications for whether the shit works or not. If you don't do mutual aid / collective care knowing that we invented the term "collective care," because we wanted something radically different than the charity model that was excluding and killing us—something where disabled people could lead and provide and cocreate care, where what care looks like is *fundamentally different*—you are not only being ableist; you will lose.

Our disabled strategies are fundamentally different, and they work better.

THE QUALITIES OF OUR SURVIVAL: HOW DISABLED PEOPLE DO IT DIFFERENTLY

I've thought about the qualities that make disabled mutual aid different then abled mutual aid a lot. One day I started writing about it on Twitter. Here's what I've come up with, a list of some distinct disabled qualities I witness showing up in crip mutual aid work:

Crip mutual aid isn't always a big public thing. In fact, it usually isn't, because it's often not safe for us to be public about our needs. There's the gawking and the gross-out, the suspicion that we're scamming or faking, the fear of losing eligibility to safety-net programs like SSI and SSDI and others, the social capital we're pretty sure we'll lose if people know about some of our "stuff."

There's also the fact that some of our needs are literally illegal: if we need criminalized medication, or if we are making money off the books or in "creative" ways that SSDI/SSI can't know about. We need to have control over who we allow to let try and help us because we know the likelihood of anything from getting abused to having an extremely annoying interaction is high. We need to have a little trust, or a lot, to do some of the things crip mutual aid actually involves.

Crip mutual aid is often low-key. Often small scale, offline, quiet, and invisible (to some). It doesn't have to be a big (public) deal. It doesn't have to be huge, with thousands of people in a spreadsheet. And it usually isn't—because a thousand-person spreadsheet is inaccessible to our brains, or because we can't find the fucking spreadsheet. ;)

The ways our care and kindness flourish in small crip moments is a characteristic of the way we do mutual aid. Crip space is (often) small space. Smallness can be more agile and effective, and that's great, because crip webs of trust are small. Most people don't have a gigantic disabled community, they have maybe one friend, or two to six people they can kind of trust.

Often the kind of stuff we do is like three people checking on each other. A couple years ago, me and some friends in South Seattle started a Signal thread called Kripsignal. We use it to check on each other during climate events like heat, smoke, or snow and figure out how we can help each other get what we need. We also send bad jokes, memes, tacos, and Venmo. *Bad jokes, memes, tacos, and Venmo count as mutual aid.*

With disabled mutual aid, the stuff we do to help each other doesn't look like a big deal or fall into "dramatic rescue of the cripples" tropes. They're preventative. They're casual and loving. They're about disabled noticing and caring. Kripsignal is a lot of us just checking in on each other and seeing how things are going. It stops things from getting bad before they do. And it calms our "we're going to be the crip dying alone in an overheated/flooded apartment" terror. It comes from a place of simultaneous disabled consciously remembering each other, and our crip realities, and keeping it low-key, not in that frenetic I'M HERE TO RESCUE YOU! Captain Save-a-Crip way that is both stressful and eyeball rolling.

"Low-key" is sometimes code for "low sensory overload," and so it's accessible in a particular kind of tonal neurodivergent way. YMMV (your mileage may vary), and I'm not saying this is the One Way, but it's a quality I keep seeing in disabled spaces and relationships. When you've been told all your life that your bodymind is a big stressful emergency panic and then nothing helpful can actually happen to make things easier, "Hey, no big deal, but you got enough ice and a fan? Wanna watch some internet TV?" said in a chill way, is a gift.

Crip mutual aid is crip creativity. Like the hangouts I had with the same friend all through the first pandemic year, where I would pull up in the disabled parking spot in front of their low-income building and they would roll out in their powerchair and we would have a one to three-hour-long shouted conversation with masks on through my rolled-down window. We could both sit, and we could be in each other's non-virtual company. We'd pass things—apples they'd gotten from the fruit guy, weed gummies, baked goods, an extra KN95—through the window. I am not joking when I say those hangouts kept me alive. A lot of weeks, or months, they were the only in-person contact with friends I had. So did the ways my crip friends agreed to hug, wearing masks and holding our breath, outside, when we hadn't been touched for months.

Crip mutual aid is not a romanticized, sanitized version of care, it is fucking real. I've seen a lot of abled new converts to mutual aid sigh romantically at all the "community care!" memes out there. When I look at the swoony graphics and memes about the joys of care, I remember my friend, a disabled, fat, mixed-race queer and trans elder, texting because their PCA had come to work sick, not wanting to put them in a bad spot, and worked without a mask on for a few hours before telling them they were ill. My friend, worried they'd been exposed to COVID, texted a bunch of people they knew and said, "OK, we're going to set up a system, everybody sign up on this Google doc. I need someone to text me in the morning and at night, to make sure I'm responsive. Let's do it for the next four days, I'll get tested too but I want you to check in on me. If you don't hear back from me, I give you permission to call 911, let them know that I'm fat and they need to bring an accessible stretcher, and this is where my apartment is."

That's the kind of shit I'm talking about. It's love, and it's the real fucking life-and-death deal. And it's not something that my friend would've trusted some random abled on a mainstream mutual aid Instagram with. What they did worked because of crip-on-crip relationships and trust that had been building for years.

Crip mutual aid knows that caring for other crips is not always fun. It means caring for people who will piss you off, irritate, and trigger you. It means having to figure out what your limits are, what you have the spoons to do, and where you draw the line. It means knowing that people who have needs that need to be met are often in a bad mood and will ask you to do some ridiculous shit. It means having to figure out time and again the line between support and saving, between interdependence and codependence. I'm still figuring it out.

Related to this, **crip mutual aid has a lot less of what I think of as ABLED PANIC** and that's why it works.

What do I mean by this? Well, you've probably seen a certain kind of Zoom thrown by abled/hearing people who've never done it before, right? They are so stiff. They are terrified that SOMETHING WILL GO WRONG. When it takes the CART transcriber a minute to get assigned or if someone says hey, the ASL interpreters are cut off, they go silently into a frozen panic. They keep apologizing. They totally freak out whenever there is any kind of glitch, and when there it is, they say, "We have to keep going!" Going, going, going!

In contrast, a lot of what epitomizes crip mutual aid is how matter-of-fact and down-to-earth it is. When CART stops working, we all just stop and go to the bathroom or whatever while it gets fixed. If there's a glitch, we just stop and fix it and we don't look surprised because we aren't, and we don't panic because this happens all the time. If we need to reschedule, it's not a big deal.

As an important footnote to this: It's not about having no sense of time and no one showing up for anything ever. Often when I see abled people encounter disabled people talking about "flexibility" and "sustainability," I see their faces close up. I believe they imagine that if we have a more relaxed approach to time, nothing will get done and all productivity will go out the window. It's as if there's either rigid abled schedules on the one hand or a complete hippie lying in a meadow orgy on the other. But in fact, disabled spaces I have been in do care about schedules. We need shit to stop when it stops so we can pee or go home or catch our ride or relieve our care attendant or do the next thing. We need structure and a sense of what is happening if we're more neurodivergent, anxious, or any number of other body-mind realities. I think it is a crucial point to note that one can be both easy about time and have a clarity around time boundaries, and I see this in disabled organizing and being.

Crip mutual aid doesn't think the pandemic is going to be a short-term thing, that the worst is over and we're on our way back to "normal." I've seen so many mainstream mutual aids scale back or close up shop because of a sense that the pandemic is over, right? I haven't seen any of the underground or overground, informal crip networks and projects stop. We were sick and disabled before the pandemic and we know all about how things don't go according to plan, how timelines stretch out, how people stop calling after two weeks, which is the longest they can conceive of a body/mind emergency happening. We know about not ever being able to go back to "normal." We know crip needs stretch out long like the horizon, like forever.

My friend San Alland, in a remembrance of their friend Callie Gardner, wrote about how the two of them checked in on and supported each other during the pandemic: "We were maybe not going to save the world, but we were going to save each other." That hit me in the heart. There's been so many times in my life where my goal has been we need to save THE WORLD, anything less is nothing, inadequate.

But we, in our small crip cyphers, are the world.

And the small, low-key things we do, in the crip genius ways we do them—with ease and without abled panic—are the opposite of nothing. They are everything.

SMALL MOMENTS OF DISABLED KNOWING

There's so many tiny moments of disabled intimacy and knowing that the abled world doesn't have words for. So we, the disabled, don't always have words for them either. But they still exist. We're still making them happen, all the time.

"*This* is the 'most accessible route'? That's what the Airbnb lady said?" I say.

"Yeah," says my friend Jonah. We look at each other and just start cracking up.

We're the only two queerdos with canes in this weird bougie neighborhood that is deliberately very hard to find, like down fourteen one-way side streets, where the fragrance-free-ish Airbnb is. We very much want to go to the amazing park with the ocean view and the railroad tracks and salmon-spawning creek we have been told about. The "most accessible trail" to said park is a muddy dirt trail that plunges below us. It's almost total slope. Like, we could maybe use some ropes to get down it.

We look at the map: the actually more accessible trail is almost a mile's walk away, and then it's even farther to get to the beach. We probably don't have spoons to walk it and also get through the park and also get back.

"Welp."

"You wanna try it?" they say.

"Yeah. OK. We can always stop. We can go as slow as we need," I say, those kind of crip chants we say to each other. Jonah nods. We start slowly, slowly easing our way down the hill.

We are in constant contact as we descend. I don't mean that we talk all the time—that kind of chatter wouldn't be accessible to either of us—but we are always crip-noticing and looking out for each other. Jonah says "Nice foot placement" on the way I place my feet at an angle as we descend a step at a time; I tell them it's a balance hack against sliding that an old friend who's an amputee showed me one day when our adventurous clambering down to a promised-on-All-Trails clothing optional beach turned into two hours of descent.

"I like your branch grabbing!" they holler as I grab small branches to brace myself as I go lower. We walk. We marvel as the muddy deer trail turns into a paved, accessible path. We stop when we need to catch our breath. My paper NIOSH N95 is working OK—I keep the bill of my rain jacket, zipped over a parka, pulled forward to keep the water off. I occasionally ask permission to pull it off. There's no one on the trail but us and it helps me to gasp some deep breaths of unfiltered air.

As we stumble on and the trail opens up to a clearing, we see that there's a parking lot! "Shit, *this* would've been the most accessible path! Why don't they ever consider cars as access?" one of us snorts.

We find a circle of stumps under uncut cedar and fir to watch the water, the crows, to talk and catch up with each other. Then we look together for the gate a purple-haired queerdo getting out of hir car told us about. We walk through, and north, to a bridge to the beach that is accessible on the way in, stairs on the way down. We note that the metal stairs are scary because you can see right through them to the ground plunging away below, encourage each other to walk down as quickly as we need for anxiety, as slowly as we need holding on to the rail with both hands, taking each stair with two feet then moving forward—for autism and balance and pain.

Finally we get to our prize: a winter beach that's totally deserted except for two public works workers who keep their distance from us. We flop on the ground. We get plastered with rain and water. We talk, and are silent, and watch the ocean. We're happy.

On the way back, when we get to the first big hill—because all that descent on the way down means ascent on the way up of course—my friend says, "I'm starting to get a little overwhelmed at all the uphill." I just hear them. I don't tell them *don't worry it'll be fine* or try and panic-fix it. We just witness each other. We walk even slower. We groan. We stop more. My breath is coming faster. One of the last times, we hear, before we see, a great barred owl. We stop and listen to her hooting.

When we get to the top, they say, "Without you here, I would've given up. I wouldn't have even tried that trail. I would've taken one look at it and been like, hell no, I'm going back to bed."

I laugh in recognition. "Oh, me the fuck too."

So much of the time when I get an anxious, "How do we make our group accessible?" question from some well-meaning abled person, I don't know how to answer the question. I mean, I do—there are so many access suggestions and audits and resources and essays, and I will send them all to them.

But what it's harder for me to convey is how real access, crip-made access, is the rich and flexible and subtle dynamics of noticing each other, working shit out, trying things, moaning and groaning, laughing and stopping, and negotiating we find as disabled people in disabled-on-disabled friendships, like mine with Jonah.

I love so many of the access tips and tools out there. But some well-meaning ableds using one for the first time might say, *Look at that hike, oh, there's no way that's accessible for the "differently abled."* And they wouldn't have been wrong to not hold their team-building hike on that trail or whatever.

But crip access is also a knowing, a dynamic, built out of a disabled-disabled friendship that has been building knowledge of each other's bodies and minds for years. Something more fluid and complicated and sarcastic and knowing. The ways we spot and witness and notice and praise and support each other. The ways we let ourselves laugh crip-ruefully "what the fuck?" at this totally inaccessible "most accessible path," stay with each other, fall on our ass, know that stopping or turning back at any time is possible, and slowly make whatever way we want, together. These small moments of disabled knowing, the ways I know Jonah knows me and that their knowledge is not static.

That disabled knowing, the sweetest crip kiss, one of the things that makes a fucking amazing disabled life.

CHAPTER 2

Interdependence Is Not Some Giant Living in the Hillside Coming Down to Visit the Townspeople[41]: The Church of Show the Fuck Up, in Real Life

WE'RE ALL GOING TO FUCKING DIE IF WE MAKE CARE OUT TO BE MORE SIMPLE THAN IT IS

I was at the 2017 Allied Media Conference, the one everyone went to after Trump was elected, hoping to get some answers that would save us. There was a very beautiful closing ceremony during which someone handed me a packet of five fava beans seeds and a small pamphlet that said things like "Transformative justice: don't throw anyone away!" and "Disability justice is collective care!" It was super sweet, but I thought, *If all we have is this pamphlet and five fava bean seeds, we're all gonna die.*

The first essay in *Care Work*, "Care Webs: Experiments in Creating Collective Access," is a fifty-page banger that kicks off the whole book. It was a risky choice, starting a book with an essay the size of a short

---

41 This title is a riff off of / reference to Yaslin Bey's song "Fear Not of Man" on his 1999 album *Black on Both Sides*. In it, Bey talks about how people ask him all the time about the future of hip-hop, as if hip-hop is something separate from them—some giant mythical creature coming down from the mountains to save or destroy everyone—rather than understanding that all of them *are* hip-hop, that they will make what hip-hop turns out to be out of their choices and actions. (This is a dry-ass paraphrasing of the song, but getting permissions to quote the whole thing from Sony felt too hard for me.)

novel, but I did it on purpose. I knew the stuff we were doing as dis-ability justice people experimenting with care webs—care created and performed by disabled people for each other, mostly outside of state systems—was at the heart of every other form of DJ activism we were doing. The collective access and care we were creating was necessary for us to be able to do anything else, and the community and love created in those spaces was a form of activism in and of itself. The concept of interdependence—that all people have needs, that none of us can get through the world solely on our own, and that having needs was not weak or bad or shameful—was an excit-ing and revolutionary part of the work, a break from and add-on to the disability rights movement's ideas of independence. I wanted to document those crucial experiments in outside-the-system care we were creating as disabled people, and provide some models and best practices for how care webs could be organized.

As the world got wilder under Trump and the pandemic, I got asked to do a lot of panels and workshops and talks on How to Care Web. The complete failure of the US government to advance any kind of organized and effective public health response to COVID fueled massive interest in care collectives and care-centered mutual aid in 2020. The concepts of care and care work received mainstream atten-tion in a way that completely blew my mind. I'd never expected to hear a US president utter the words "care work" on national TV, nor did I expect the term "the care crisis" to be coined and used, a lot, in mainstream media.

But there was a care crisis, and it was hard to ignore. Schools and daycares were closed, or would open but then close for three days to three weeks any time a kid had COVID symptoms, sending everyone home to their parents. Parents, particularly not-cis-men parents, went completely batshit trying to work and care for kids at home, driving many to the breaking point by the time of the Omicron surge of 2022. It became very difficult for many disabled people to hire a personal care attendant, because they were quitting in droves as they got sick, or because the work is so badly paid and risky. In turn, many, many people turned to mutual aid and care collectives for their disability or mental health care needs and crises. PCAs were scarce and medical centers and hospitals weren't an option—people were scared of getting COVID if they went, because hospital beds were full of COVID patients and people in crisis. A lot of people had and still are having severe mental health crises, but a lot of psych wards were closed in order to free up beds for COVID patients, and if you got in, a lot of the time being in the psych ward meant being stuck in a windowless room in the ER for days, or talking to a psychiatrist on an iPad. As both mass abolitionist resistance in the streets and fascist organizing against it ramped up in the summer and fall of 2020, healers and street medics stepped up their work. People had a sense that the revolution might be here as systems failed and city councils voted to take money from the police and put it into community solutions. If the apocalypse/revolution we'd all been waiting for was here, we better get good at caring for each other.

I've never been offered as many gigs to talk about care collectives as I was in 2020 and 2021. And the surge in interest in collective care was amazing. But I couldn't help but notice, in so many of those webinars and panels and talks, when people asked how we'd live after the cops and the medical industrial complex were over, I'd see panelists pause, then throw out the word "Interdependence!"—usually looking both uncertain and a little frantic. Everybody would nod, but I could tell they were also thinking, *Yeah, but what does that actually mean?* It's as if "Interdependence!" was this superhero who was going to fly in and fix everything, but the details of exactly how—the nitty-gritty of what it looks like to give and receive care well—well, there's not a lot of time to tell those winding stories of a million moments in the five minutes left for Q and A at the end of a webinar. In the absence of specifics, it's easy for a concept like interdependence as magical and simple to take hold, a kind of fairy tale people really want to believe is true, that "community" will just magically come together through the power of love to help you when you're in need.

But the thing is, people know better. They know that care is so much more complicated and painful and weird than that.

Bob Dylan (yes, I know) said, "To live outside the law, you must be honest." One of the foundation of DJ as I know it is honesty. I have experienced it as a movement of multiply marginalized disabled people being really real—more real than a lot of abled or white disabled people can deal with—about both the real deal of our disabled Black and brown lives, and the real-ass complexity of what happens when we try to build community and organize. We don't do ourselves or the futures we are building any favors if we start to pretty things up or make them out to be simpler than they are, and that includes when we talk about care as the world ends. (To be clear, I don't think disabled people are doing that: I think we're being super real about the intricate work of creating collective care. But I think a lot of people do fudge it, because they're scared or unsure how to talk about the specifics.)

As I did care web workshops, and as I lived in a small community in Seattle before and during the pandemic—a community that traded-off errands, food drop-offs, and housecleaning for each other—as I got deeper and deeper into figuring out my own care and access needs, especially around being autistic and plural, as we more and more dive deep into the waters of this thing called interdependence, I wanted to write more specifically about the real deal of what it is. Because your questions and cliffhangers, you are not alone in having them. Because the world is still ending and care is not simple and we deserve to hear the stories of how we are caring for each other anyway.

WHAT THE HECK IS INTERDEPENDENCE?

In April 2019, I was at a crip gathering, a really wild one, part of the *I wanna be with you everywhere* DJ art festival in New York, where disabled people took over part of the Whitney Museum for a day. I couldn't believe we were actually in there, drooling, eating snacks, and staring out the window looking weird. Disabled queer activists Akemi Nishida and Eli Clare did a presentation entitled "What The Heck Is Interdependence?" the title glowing from the screen behind them. They kept the workshop really simple, just asking us to get in small groups and talk about how we did interdependence as disabled people. Me and Neve and Syan, disabled Black and Asian femmes, went in a corner and talked, one of many small triads and duos of disabled people sprawled on the floor and sitting in our wheelchairs in the corners.

We were all so hungry for this conversation. And we kept getting stuck. This was stuff we thought about all the time, but the words came out halting, like water out of a rusted pipe. In that way that happens when you think about something all the time—it's the bones of your life, care—but never have a chance to talk about it, and when you finally do, it's like opening the door to a vault that's been rusted shut. You can't quite believe you've got permission to talk about it.

But people had questions about care. In that workshop, and in every care workshop I've thrown or been a part of. Did they ever. Questions like:

How do you care for someone and not, like, lose yourself?

What if there is literally nobody around to be interdependent with?

What if your "disabled community" is three people and one of them is your ex who hates you?

Uh, what's a "need," anyway? What if you have no idea what your "needs" are? What if the number one way you've survived your life so far is by not having any needs? What if you got so punished for having needs as a kid—period, or certain ones in particular—that when someone asks you what your needs are, you go blank and can't think of any? In a traumatic amnesia way?

What if asking for help with the things you actually for-real need is incredibly difficult? Like, you can ask for stuff that's not super risky—picking up milk at the store, say—but asking someone to be there when you're really losing your mind, or to come over and clean your house when it's really gross, is so vulnerable you'd rather live in filth forever?

What if someone you helped was an asshole to you? Even if they are disabled? (Maybe especially then?) What do you do then?

What if you were raised in an abusive and/or alcoholic/addicted family to be a caretaker, to know other people's needs before you know your own, so you always default to caring for other people and never ask for care? And you're so good at it, so people ask you for help all the time? And automatic caregiving and being so good at it feels good, and is also a way you don't have to feel the gaping holes where you need stuff, because you can just volunteer for more tasks and shove the feelings away?

What if the person you are trying to support in one month blows through the whole 20K you raised from the GoFundMe and then there is no money?

What happens when everyone in the care web is sick and tired at once?

What if you're sick of only being asked to help out? What if no one ever asks you to just hang out?

What about when those people yell "interdependence! rest!" but they still want to work you to death and underpay you?[42]

What if the sick, tired, and busy ones are still the only ones who answer the urgent text message on the group thread?

What happens when it's crisis/pandemic times and the "super crisis" times are lasting like YEARS and people are so bled dry they got nothing left and, yet, it continues?

These are just a fraction of the real-deal questions about care that lie beneath when someone patly exclaims "Interdependence!" They are the math problems of care in real life that we are trying to figure out how to solve.

---

42 Thank you to Bianca Laureno for this thought.

CARE IS PAINFUL: THINGS THAT HAPPENED IN CARE WEBS WORKSHOPS, 2017–2021

A little while after *Care Work* came out, in one of my periodic revisions of what the hell I do to make a living anyway, I thought, *When places ask if I do a workshop, I'll tell them, yeah, I can do a workshop on Care Webs*! I heard all the time from people who felt alone and like no one was around who could help them with their or a loved one's care needs, they had no one to ask for help—maybe at the end of this two- or three-hour workshop, they would've made a whole care network.

I thought, *Great! I'll throw these workshops and people will know how to do it without it being a disaster!*

Things didn't exactly pan out that way.

I was used to people feeling good and like they'd gotten something concrete and satisfying out of workshops I taught, for the most part. But a lot of the time at the end of the care webs workshops, I felt like a failure.

I wasn't expecting the level of pain people shared in those workshops.

I wasn't expecting people to name a bunch of needs in the chat window, shoot down every suggestion about how they might be cared for, and then say the whole workshop was bullshit.

I wasn't expecting people to say, "Sorry, could you repeat the question?" three times when I was like, "Think about a situation where you need care, or someone in your life does. What are their needs, what conditions need to be there for them to be held well?" I would be doing the workshop, talking about care, being charismatic, telling stories, showing stats about unpaid care labor, everyone would be nodding. And then I'd get to the part where we actually had to try and do it and everyone would freeze.

I knew that care is a subject that people have a lot of pain around. But having been in disabled community for over a decade, I had mostly been around other disabled people who had some experience and willingness to try figuring out care with each other—and a sense that good, loving care was possible, because they'd had lived experience giving and receiving it with other disabled people. Because of the ways disability communities are so siloed and invisibilized, there are a lot of non-disabled QTBIPOC who have never experienced that. They've been the one person caring for their mother while everyone they ask to help out says no, you do it, they're silently taking care of their care needs on their own and feeling embarrassed anytime it's not possible to hide their diaper or they're late ten minutes because they had a body thing happen. Their friends are still rolling their eyes, calling them "flakes" and "needy" or "too much" behind their backs. I had been in cripple world for a while, and I wanted to bring the gifts of cripple world to the rest of the world, but I was not quite prepared for the level of built-up grief, pain, bitterness, and anger being in a room with a whole bunch of people who had rarely or never experienced giving or receiving good care.

That pain came from many places. People had pain from doing unpaid or badly paid care labor, sometimes for generations, in their families—as immigrant, women of color personal care workers or nursing assistants or cleaners, but also from just being expected to be the unpaid cleanup squad because *hey, you're not a cis boy, that's your job*. The levels of pain BIPOC not-cis-men had from being expected to be a caregiver available 24-7, who never got to say no, or be asked first (or ever) if this was a good time, just being dumped on. The ways so many of us had been raised to survive by never having needs. I knew this because it's my story too.

The thing that I wasn't prepped for, the first few times I did the workshops, was people's sense that there were not and had never been any times where people—BIPOC, disabled, queer, trans people—had given or received care well, without abuse. That stunned me. I would think, *No one ever gave you a cigarette at a bus stop when you were shaking, no one ever cracked a joke to make you laugh at the food stamps line?*

I'd been embedded pretty solidly in disabled community for a while—by which I mean, not some kind of cripple Disneyland, but a bunch of circles of people who had been trying out this thing of caring for each other as disabled people: "collective access." But while disabled/disability justice community is growing, there's still plenty of people who have never accessed disabled community or friendships before and have no lived experience of disabled people offering each other care. Or, they have, but they don't believe that their experience counts. It was a big lesson in how internalized ableism has taught us that *it's not possible for disabled people to do anything, and the things we do are not real*.

When we open the Pandora's box of care, when we say *check on your strong friends* or trumpet *community care!* we have to also expect, and attend, to the well of sadness and rage that's waiting inside. All the years and generations where we were a dishrag wiping up after someone else, where there was no help, no care without abuse, we have to be ready for that before we can begin to make care plans. Otherwise, people just stay frozen in their pain and grief about all the generations where they were used for care but never cared for and loved. Otherwise, it's hollow.

CODEPENDENCE VS. INTERDEPENDENCE

The first time I got asked, "What's the difference between interdependence and codependence?" in a workshop I was like OH YEAH. And then I was like, *Good question! I don't really know the answer though!*

Part of it was that I didn't know what codependence was. Wasn't that a kind of dusty, '80s mom support-group kind of word? I had used it, I dimly remembered, when I was getting out of a relationship years ago, a romantic and sexual partnership that had felt like "queer family," but where I had been unhappy for the last chunk of it and felt like I was losing myself. Like the price of being "family" was that I could never just go for what I wanted, that I had to get her approval for everything, from what I wanted for dinner to big things I wanted for my life (i.e., grad school), and I could never say no to her calling me eight times in a row or knocking on my door when I'd said I was working. It felt like we were one person, but we didn't have enough oxygen for two people to breathe. Wasn't that the price tag that came with finally having "queer family" as someone who didn't have birth family because of abuse and estrangement?

I hadn't thought about codependency much since then, so I googled. There are many definitions of codependency, but it's a term originally created to describe the behavior of family members of people with alcoholism or addiction who often feel like their attempts to support their loved one end up making things worse for both of them. "A codependent person is one who has let another person's behavior affect him or her, and who is obsessed with controlling that person's behavior," according to Anne Beattie, author of *Codependent No More*. She goes on to describe some of the characteristics of codependent people as including "feel[ing] responsible for other people's needs, feelings, thoughts, behaviors and well-being ... Feel[ing] almost forced to help others, regardless of whether they actually want to help ... Saying yes when they really mean no, doing things they don't want to do ... Don't know what they want or need, or feel their wants are unimportant."

Her definition mirrors (just without a race, class, gender, or disability analysis) a lot of more modern language I see on the healing justice neighborhoods of the internet, talking about appeasing and automatic caretaking behavior as ways people survive traumatic families, and the automatic caretaking femmes and feminized people, especially Black and brown people, are urged to act as a way to pay for our right to exist in the world—and punished when we set limits around it or stop doing it.

Here's the thing: I may not 100% know what codependence is or if my definition is the "right one," but I don't think it matters. The people who were asking me what the difference between codependence and interdependence was, they weren't reading from a book or an official definition. They were asking, *How do I care for someone without totally having my boundaries blown past, never feeling like I can say "no" because someone is in an emergency, being worked to the bone and feeling like I'm falling back into generation patterns of being a BIPOC femme caregiver without consent?*

Because there's this thing that happens in queer/disabled/ BIPOC and other oppressed communities. Often, we're not wrong in believing that we are the only ones who keep each other safe or save each other's lives. And our lives often are in dire situations that need saving. Including dire situations the abled world may not have the knowledge to understand as dire. When a friend calls me and says, *My ex is still my power of attorney, I need to write a new one without them on it immediately, can I use your printer?* I get it right away and if I can, say, *Yes, sure, come over.* Not everyone gets that, but I do because I too have had to draft wills and POAs in the middle of night to keep the abusive assholes away.

In crip world it's not uncommon for us to have maybe one friend who we can call when shit is really ultra hard, one friend who we trust with our specific hard stuff. And when we are that friend, we can feel like, *How can I say "no"?* when the call comes and we're about to go to sleep, or just watching TV. When we are the person calling the one and only and they say "no," it can feel like, *How can I accept their "no" with anything but rage?* They must not love us. They've let us down, like all the rest.

"Ride or die." "My rock." Crip loyalty. All of those things are lifted up in our communities. I've done it. They're not always bad. They can be places full of richness and love. But they're bad when we stop feeling like we have a choice.

When we escape abusive family, sometimes we lift up loyalty-till-the-end to our chosen family. But we may not have gotten much of a crash course in what not-fucked-up loyalty looks like. Or what the difference between showing up hard for someone and sacrificing yourself is. That it doesn't mean sacrificing yourself.

And the existing stuff that's out there that talks about care doesn't have an understanding of disabled reality. The reality of crip community scarcity and that needs happen all the time in disabled life, not just once a year. Health and wellness website Verywell says: "*Occasionally* depending on others—and allowing them to depend on you—for help and support is perfectly valid" (emphasis mine). *Occasionally*. HA! Crip life often has a lot more everyday emergencies than abled life. And you want to be there for each other. Out of love and care and in general, but especially when you have been raised to be a caretaker automatically, like as a brain-stem function, and as the only way you are valuable. So you're there. Dropping everything. Responding to everything like the sirens are going off and you are the only ambulance.

The thing is, sometimes not everything is an emergency on the same level.

And it is totally untenable for you to be the only ambulance.

Even when we live in a racist, ableist world where you might be the only ambulance, we have to be building structures where that's not true forever, where there's more than one ambulance.

And also, not every need or moment or crisis is on the level of a heart attack, needing an ambulance.

We don't always have the community, the crip peers, to talk our way through that exchange. We have panic, the parasympathetic nervous system shutting down and THIS IS THE ONLY WAY OR I WILL DIE coming online. But those skills of nuance and discernment and slowing down and asking yourself, *Can I do this? Is there another way of doing it?* are crucial ones to practice, that each of us can practice. Building and improvising disabled networks where there is more than one option is a crucial part of the work we are building.

"Enmeshment" is another one of those codependent-no-more words that I've had a hard time finding a good definition of, but I am choosing to define it as: the place where you are so enmeshed in someone else you don't know what you want or need but can feel every single thing they fucking feel before they feel it. And feel like you can't breathe or scratch your ass without their permission, and everything becomes a consensus decision. Versus this wild healthy relationship idea where you know yourself, you attend to yourself, and you ask for, receive, and give help, and when you can't give it or get it, you figure out a Plan B.

Knowing yourself and your crip boundaries is a big deal, when the "forced intimacy" Mia Mingus writes of has made it so we're often in a position where survival and getting our access needs met means having no boundaries. Or where masking of many kinds has made us know that survival depends on there being no needs, nothing to see here. Or where we might know our needs, but we only ever feel safe attending to them by ourselves, in utter private.

CARING WITHOUT SAVING

When I finished *Care Work*, my friend Dori asked if she could send me an electric toothbrush. You know, you might have one, the Sonicare kind that vibrates all your plaque off and massages your gums. The kind a lot of us fuckers over forty are supposed to get becauae our gums start to fall apart and brushing with the regular bristle tooth- brush both does nothing and fucks them up more at the same time. I had been needing to get one for a while because my gums had gone from periodotinitis to actual gum disease and I was having to pay to get the deep clean every three months and getting dire warnings from the dentist that I really needed to fucking go to Costco and get a Sonicare if I wanted my teeth to not all fall out. But I didn't have a Costco membership, and I felt bad spending the money on myself and it always fell off my to-do list.

Still. A toothbrush?

She said, "I want to get you a present, the way a parent would, to show you I am proud of you and all your hard work."

I cried then. And then the toothbrush came in the mail, and it's still on my bathroom sink three years later, and I use it every day and my gums stopped getting worse, and I have all my teeth.

Dori wasn't trying to Save Me or my gums or endlessly agonize over this is a CRISIS, LEAH'S TEETH WILL FALL OUT or being Captain Save-a-Crip. She just noticed something nice that would help and sent it to me.

And since then, I bought my friend, also an orphan of assholes, a similar toothbrush he would never buy for himself, when he graduated from rabbinical school after ten years of working five jobs to put himself through it.

A lot of my old ways to care maybe valorized sacrifice and always being there. It is OK to not always be there. And to be there in a very different way.

Caring for me these days feels like:

Notes in the mail

Hey do you need anything from the grocery store, I'm going?

You're finishing your book? Yay, you! Can I send you thirty bucks so you can buy a pizza?

Do you want to go on a slow walk without talking?

I have extra soup I made, can I drop you off some or leave some on the porch? bc I can't talk right now

Are there things that would feel supportive?

I need to take a break from texting / have non-verbal time right now

Can I clean your tub? I need to scrub something and it would feel good

Do you have ten minutes for me to vent?

These are all pretty autistic/neurodivergent things. And things that are less transactional (i.e., I do endless unpaid, unthanked emotional labor) and more "care where it feels good for both people / they both get something out of it / they stop when they get depleted." It's people practicing being real and offering what they can without trying to magically fix anything.

A SMALL CAST OF IMPERFECT DISABLED CHARACTERS

When my friend of twenty-five years Graeme Bacque died in September 2021, I wrote on Facebook about meeting him in late '90s Toronto psych-survivor community and how he and that community was a big part of what kept me alive. Not because they "fixed" anything, but because it was a space where we didn't try and fix each other. It was just okay to be nuts and weird, and no one would call the cops on you. A younger Mad brown friend asked, *How do I find a community like this?*

I told them: when we met in 1997, it wasn't perfect or a utopia at all. It was like a couple of Crazy people who put up fliers at the coffee shops where other Crazy people hung out and had meetings and worked on a project and annoyed the shit out of each other and had conflict and triggered each other and stormed out of the room screaming. And also, managed to create space where we could be there for each other, imperfectly, and not tell each other not to be who we were.

Living in Seattle during the Trump administration and the pandemic, with an imperfect, small cast of characters of sick and disabled Mad and autistic people, imperfectly taught me almost everything I know right now about practicing interdependence. About what was really hard, what was really beautiful, what I knew, what I realized I didn't, and what I learned along the way.

Living in Seattle during that time was a weird series of juxtapositions. I think people thought I had a more glamorous life than I had, that being unexpectedly indie successful and visible as a disabled writer had propelled me out of disability—like success had made me abled.

But my daily life was very ordinary, private, and slow. Disabled quotidian. I make tea every morning and do my dishes while I'm waiting for the kettle to boil. I make a lot of lists to try and corral my executive function into working. I get sick. I manage my medical appointments. My guts explode. I go to the co-op. I text friends. I am pretty invisible in Seattle, and even though it's been an ongoing struggle to feel so disconnected from how I've lived in community for most of my adult life, there are ways it has worked out for me. I had private space to figure out autism and neurodivergence in my forties, and private space to figure out care. Nobody gives a shit who I am, and I can just get coffee and go home.

And in the midst of it, I had a small circle of friends in and around Seattle who would talk on the phone, text each other, check in, say, *I'm going to the grocery store, do you need anything?* say, *I am having a* hard time, *do you have support spoons for me to call you?* Sometimes we say no. Sometimes I get irritated when someone asks me. Sometimes I answer when I'm a little stretched. It's not perfect. Sometimes I get mad and then am like, *We can still text about whether or not everyone's surviving this heat dome/blizzard/wildfire* OK.

They are people I can call when I get my incredible steal of a $49 Cyber Monday sale Joybird couch home from the Southcenter Habitat for Humanity thrift store in the back of a rented U-Haul van, and realize belatedly that it's not IKEA furniture—it's made of actual wood, and it's heavy, and there's no way I can even push it out of the van, let alone get it into the house single-handedly. And I'm already halfway towards a meltdown because driving a big van on my own stresses me out and so does night driving, and I'm supposed to get this goddamn U-Haul back before the place closes at 7 p.m. and the lady who works there already told me I should probably be there at 6:30 because she goes home on time, and it's 6:45 and I'm definitely going to be getting a late charge.

But the small, imperfect disabled network I have, and the ways I've been haltingly practicing saying what I need for a few years now, means I have the intimacy to call a friend and say, in autistic short form because I barely have words at that point, *I am in a jam, I need help figuring out a situation.* And they say, *Hey, my friend is on light-rail to come to me—would you like it if he gets off at your stop and we meet you and figure it out?* And I say yes, and I come over and together, step-by-step, we figure out how to get it into the house. Step-by-crip-step. Their friend falling over on the stumps of the cherry tree my landlady has placed by the fence. Us stopping and pausing to assess how we're doing and what angle the couch can get up the stairs, checking in if it's OK to pull down a mask for a second to drink some water, my friend saying, *I'm OK, I can hold it, don't patronize me,* when their friend starts to talk over them.

"Check on your strong friend" and "Don't be afraid to ask for help!" are well meaning, but such inadequacies. The language of interdependence is intricate. Is code. Is built step-by-step, in all the tiny steps we take to know each other, the brief moment of eye contact (or not) that says, *Can I trust you?* The moment where you throw a ball to me and I catch it, or I let it drop but I pick it up, or I ask someone to do it for me.

Sometimes when people say, *Where is that community, how do I find it, how do I make it?* I sigh inside, throw up my hands, say, *There is no place where it is waiting, ready-made.* There is what we make. With a small, imperfect disabled cast of characters. With people who piss each other off and fail each other and make mistakes and don't always know the right thing. Who draw a damn boundary when someone is a jackass, and drawing that boundary is huge work, takes courage. With people who, little bit by little bit, practice knowing what we need, and saying what it is, and negotiate receiving or giving it. With people who are assumed to be passive recipients, not creators of care, proving it wrong.

LEARNING OUR AND EACH OTHER'S CARE LANGUAGES: A DANCE OF A LIFETIME WITH MANY SMALL STEPS

Learning our own and each other's care languages is a dance with many small steps and moves, unfolding over a lifetime. The work of learning how to give and receive care means being in a practice of knowing what our needs are and what conditions need to be there for us to receive or offer care well.

This might sound simple, but it is deeply not. It is a practice that is often part of a recovery process from being denied the right to have access needs, or any needs, as disabled people and particularly as disabled BIPOC people. Many of us have been taught not to listen to or trust our bodily sensations—at times very overtly, as with autistic people who are taught to mask and ignore our somatic sensations of pleasure or distress within ABA (Applied Behavioral Analysis) programs. And at times, we are taught this non-overtly, but omni-presently. Many disabled Black and brown, working-class, and poor people have survived by learning to "not be too much trouble" by "making it work"—essentially, by taking up as little space as possible with our disabilities, with these bodyminds that are already hyper visible and targeted by racism, that have been punished for needing anything and for whom having needs can seem like both a luxury and something that makes us even more of a target.

Part of our process of learning to love ourselves and each other and to practice care means doing the incredibly risky work of tapping back into the disabled body/mind we have been taught to suppress and abandon, to learn what our boundaries are, and what we want, need, and desire.

This is a big deal. And the work of a lifetime.

Learning our own and each other's care needs and access realities is a daily practice that views needs as not fixed, but an open-ended spiral of discovery and experimentation.

When I think of the care webs I am a part of that mostly work, they are a complex moment-by-moment dance of figuring out what we need that is a lot like consent negotiations in sex. Raw embarrassment, messiness, confusion, working through shame at needing something (or anything), figuring out what I might need to even begin to ask for That Thing—all are part of the real deal of negotiating care. A dance made up of moments of asking, automatic denial / *I'm fine*, softening, *well ... if it's not too much trouble*, panic and shut down, guilt and release, peace when I brought someone chili, or we hung out without speaking, or they took out my compost when I couldn't lift anything and it felt nice.

Mia Mingus's conception of access intimacy, which she first wrote about in 2011, has been incredibly important to many disabled people attempting to think about and create disabled intimacies, care, and collective access. Mingus defined access intimacy as "that elusive, hard to describe feeling when someone else 'gets' your access needs. The kind of eerie comfort that your disabled self feels with someone on a purely access level. Sometimes it can happen with complete strangers, disabled or not, or sometimes it can be built over years ... Access intimacy is also the intimacy I feel with many other disabled and sick people who have an automatic understanding of access needs out of our shared similar lived experience of the many different ways ableism manifests in our lives."[43]

Mingus's invention of the term "access intimacy" was a pivotal disability justice moment. Learning about Mingus's term felt to me like an opening, a softening, an exhale. It made words for a disabled

---

43 Mia Mingus, "Access Intimacy: The Missing Link," *Leaving Evidence* (blog), April 5, 2011, https://leavingevidence.wordpress.com/2011/05/05/access-intimacy-the-missing-link/.

experience I and many others both had and longed for, but not had a name for. It made new space in disabled relationships and disability justice community and movement building, for access intimacy to be a central part of how we built with each other, and a demand we had the right to make of spaces we inhabited.

However, a caution I have felt about access intimacy lies is in the part where Mingus names it as "an *automatic understanding* of access needs out of our shared similar lived experience" (emphasis mine).

It's not that this kind of instantaneous disabled-to-disabled understanding of an access need or reality doesn't exist, or that I haven't experienced it (and loved it). It's that I am very cautious about the idea of instant, automatic intimacy and knowing. I have witnessed many times in disabled and disability justice communities where, sometimes based on people's interpretations of Mingus's term, we make an assumption that people are going to automatically get our disabled experiences, our access needs or realities, and it bites us in the ass—personally, and in terms of movement and community building. People with similar disabilities may have identical access needs and realities, but it's also true that two people with the same disability may have drastically different desires and needs about access and care. As crips we might know what "pain face" looks like, but we don't all automatically know all of each other's shit! Making the assumption that "I know what you want/need because I have the same thing" is dangerous.

I've witnessed people's understanding of access intimacy becoming a kind of magical thinking, and an assumption that if other disabled people love us enough, they will *just know* what our access needs are, and if they don't automatically know, they're bad/wrong/

failing us and disability justice. But in crip spaces and in particular in mixed disability spaces (coalition spaces where people with a lot of different kinds of disabilities, neurodivergence, Deafness are trying to work together and build relationships), the truth is that we *don't* automatically know each other's access needs, realities, and cultures. I've been a Mad person in physically disabled community who realized abruptly from a comment that people had stereotypical ideas about neurodiverse people, or didn't know about mental health advance directives or what a 5150 was—things I culturally knew from being in Mad community for many years. On the other hand, I've been a Mad person in a particular Mad, mostly able-bodied space where I realized through someone's comment or confused look that thinking about wheelchair access or chronic pain was new to people. There are a million examples, but at the core, if we want to build cross-disability communities, being committed to a practice of learning each other's care and access languages is a crucial skill if we're going to be able to trust each other and work together. That learning takes work, and is not automatic.

The emotional weight of concepts of automatic access intimacy can lead us into territory of crip loyalty, trust, and betrayal where it's easy for people to get hurt. The concept of automatic access intimacy can set us up for the idea that care and access realities[44] are things one "just knows" and, by implication, if you don't "just get it" you'll never be able to learn it. I would like to instead advocate for the idea that access and care intimacy are learnable skills that everyone

---

44 NEVE, "Access Realities," Access-Centered Movement Facebook post, March 5, 2021, https://www.facebook.com/accesscenteredmovement/posts/new-term-and-graphic-from-accesscentered movement-specifically-nevebebad-has-neve/2782500555295797/.

can practice. Viewing access and care intimacies as learnable and practicable, not automatic, means that disabled people aren't failures or betraying each other when we don't automatically know each other's stuff. It makes room for us to make mistakes, learn, and make repair—which creates space for more resilient disability justice community and movement building, where there's room to come back from a fuck-up instead of feeling forever betrayed because "they were disabled, I thought they would understand." It also makes room for the idea that abled, neurotypical, and hearing people can learn access and care skills too.

Don't get me wrong: I think we can and should celebrate the bliss of moments of crip eye contact and instant knowing of each other's access intimacies—because they *are* magic. I just want to lift up a practice of disabled intimacy as an ongoing practice of learning and sharing our access needs and realities, and learning about others'—as an active process, not an automatic assumption. I want to advocate for this particularly because if we want cross-disability/mixed-ability community and coalition building, learning about each other's disability and access cultures is something that makes cross-disability community possible. When I learn about the histories, access needs, and realities of little people, or Deaf folks, or folks with a neurodivergence not my own, I am showing respect and creating the conditions for mutual trust and understanding.

A decade after Mingus's foundational article, still in conversation with her concepts, I want to add to the conversation by talking about *care linguistics* and *care fluency*, concepts my friend and comrade, chronically ill, neurodivergent, nonbinary, queer, transracially adopted/Korean adoptee, writer, artist, and academic Teukie Martin is working deeply on, and which we discussed recently on Facebook Messenger. Martin's working definition of care linguistics is:

> Coming from an understanding of access and care as a dialogical process, where both the asking and offering of care is iterative and cyclical, I am offering "care linguistics" as a way of understanding this emergent practice amongst and between crips. Care linguistics honors multimodal forms of communication, including tics, stims, and facial expressions. It also highlights processes of translation and translanguaging (i.e. I might describe what would support my access in a particular scenario as a framework for you to determine your needs based on our overlaps and departures) and the ways in which learning the care languages of others shifts and expands our own care vocabularies. I may take on something I learn from you, you may transform something you learn from me. Through this process we develop a "care fluency" as both providers and recipients of care. Every care interaction is an opportunity for deeper learning and understanding—we become more skilled and confident in navigating our needs and the needs of others.[45]

Martin's definition of care linguistics is incredibly rich and important for so many reasons. They lift up neurodivergent ways of communicating—tics, stims, and facial cues—that ableist and allistic society often bashes and dismisses as "not real communication" and "defects" to be corrected. Instead, Walleroo advocates for ways neurodivergent people communicate all the time as valuable and perfect as they are. Walleroo also emphasizes that care linguistics and the process of becoming fluent in our own and each other's care

---

45 Teukie Martin, Facebook Messenger conversation with the author, March 22, 2022.

linguistics is a collective process supported by being in community with other disabled people.

When I think of examples of care linguistics in practice in my life, I think of how I know a friend will make a joke or deflect five times when I ask them how they are, and if I can hang in there and joke back and then go, "OK, but how are you really?" they'll let me know how they're doing the sixth time I ask. Or how another friend (or me) loses some of their speaking capacity when they're in pain and can only talk in short, very direct sentences, and how I know that isn't rude, it's them having five seconds of speaking oxygen. Or, for myself, the language to know and communicate, "I'm exhausted and in pain and could use help, but am not up for talking and being social," and a friend offering, "I could just drop some ginger beer on your porch without talking, you don't even have to come out," and my deep relief at both the conversation and the offering of *you don't have to talk or be social to get some sweetness dropped off, and I won't be offended*. It is our internal landscapes of what kinds of care we need, what conditions need to be there for us to care and be cared for well, and the ways we communicate about all of it.

Intimacies of all kinds—our intimate relationship with ourselves and other people—that are held well are not static. They are always evolving and changing, because we are always growing and changing. As disability justice and collective care practices continue to grow and bloom, I want us to be in a practice of curiosity, of continually learning who we and others are, as we change and evolve—including about our disabilities, Deafness, and neurodivegences as they change and evolve through aging, body/mind changes, and time.

This abundance of disabled intimacies is the polar opposite of the ableist care rationing of the world. I want to swim in its deep sea of care possibilities.

A DIVERSITY OF CARE TACTICS

Figuring out our care languages, becoming fluent in ourself and each other is the work of a lifetime. It is a collective work, and a work of decolonizing ourselves from internalized ablism. It is a gorgeous cross-disability dance with many small steps. I want to be here for the crip dance party of it.

As both the promise of disability justice and the failures of state systems to help us survive pandemics push us to build collective care on a scale more massive than we have done before, I want us to have patience with ourselves and each other as we learn to dance this giant ballroom dance of care. I also want to advocate for a *diversity of care tactics*.

"Diversity of tactics" is a term I first heard of in radical and anti-authoritarian struggle to describe a strategy framework that believes in hitting systems of oppression with everything we've got. Diversity of tactics is what's going on when some people physically fight Nazis in the street, and some people who can't take that risk safely have a legal protest. It says that electoral politics, safer legal protests, cultural work, and direct action are all ways for people to fight against oppression and build power. It's a way of organizing that says creating alternative clinics *and* fighting for patients' rights within traditional hospitals are both important. A diversity of tactics creates options.

A diversity of care tactics means I believe that, yes, we all need to practice our care skills so it's not just the same mommy or couple of overworked disabled Black or brown femmes doing all the care in a community. I believe in care collectives and care webs, networks of often unpaid people caring for each other through disabled mutual aid and collective care. And I also believe in the need to create societies where everyone who needs it has access to care that is safe and skilled, whether or not they have relationships or community— because many disabled people do not have many relationships or community. Community care offers a lot, and I've also witnessed mutual aid and disability justice organizers buckle under the strain of being expected to do it all, especially after two years of a pandemic. This does not have to be a failure: it can be a place we learn from.

I want a world where paid care workers are highly paid, skilled employees with workers' rights, time off, training, and good pay. Not what you see right now, where Seattle, for example, has a minimum wage of fifteen dollars, and you know who's exempt from it? Personal support workers: the Washington state disability agencies pays care workers twelve dollars an hour. This has lead to a care crisis, where lots of PSWs have quit their jobs, because you can make eighteen dollars scooping ice cream in Seattle, work that is intense but involves less direct physical care labor than personal support work. As we get curious about growing care, I am drawn to ideas of care cooperatives, care banks, systems that allow everyone to get PCA care, and/or a variety of forms of care, not based on popularity or being in relationship/community. I am excited about the work of organizations like Hand2Hand, bringing disabled people, elders, and care workers (many of whom are also disabled!) to fight for disabled and workers' rights, together.

A lot of people think of care as only a certain kind of soft, allistically empathetic "how are you *doing*?" type of thing. Care that is often visualized as very personal/one-on-one, only done for someone you love or are very close to. Care can be that individual act to an individual person, but it's also about creating systems that benefit everyone collectively. When I or someone else shovels the snow on the sidewalk so that everyone, especially disabled people, mobility device users, elders, and people with kids in strollers or granny carts of groceries can use the sidewalk accessibly, and there's a community norm that "of course we shovel the sidewalks so people can get by" and there's support—paid workers who shovel the snow, equipment available to make it happen—that's an example of collective care and access that is a system.

As we figure out what the heck interdependence is, I want us to dream and build multi-fanged systems of interdependence and care. Systems and "let me pick you up some seltzer?" conversations, strong and flexible enough to hold us all, and always keeping in touch with what's real. Interdependence is indeed not some superhero that's going to fly in and fix it. We—with all our unearthed care lineages, desires, boundaries, and care languages—are the very messy, beautiful, everday care heros building the new world.

I leave you with some homework, some questions:

What is care to you?

What are your care lineages?

What were you taught about care growing up?

What roles did you play?

What kind of roles do you fall into when you give or receive care now?

What do you need in order to receive care well? To give care well?

What new skills do you want to learn around giving/receiving care?

What do you want to unlearn? What do you want to lean into practicing?

What new ways of giving and receiving care do you want to grow?

"THERE IS NO DISABLED COMMUNITY HERE"

But, you know, there's no disabled community here ...

They always say that. Every single city, people always say that. Not the abled dismissing us, but us, the disabled. Detroit, Philly, Portland, Iowa City, Burlington, Atlanta, small-town Pennsylvania. *You don't want to move here, it's so inaccessible. You don't want to move here, there's no disabled community here. Oh you know, it's an old city, it's not accessible. Oh you know, it's a small town, nobody talks about it. Oh you know, it's a West Coast city, everyone's so "healthy."* Toronto with its bathrooms in the basement for no reason anyone understands, NYC with its Hunger Games endurance runs of just getting from point A to point B or finding groceries, Oakland's broken BART elevators, the Seattle Freeze isolation and ubiquity of an all-REI wardrobe, "staying active and healthy" lifestyle. These cities are not an exhaustive list, just a few places I have lived.

Believe me, I get it. I get how hard disabled community is to find or make. I get disabled isolation. I may look like I live in a wonderland of crip community, and I am very conscious of the riches of the sick, disabled, and autistic community I have—that did not just appear out of a poof of dust one day, but was consciously made, text-by-text, moment-by-moment. Before this last decade of my life, I lived in inaccessible buildings, up two flights of stairs on a flare, stuck, without kin who got it. But even after a decade and a half of all this all disability justice–building all the time, I have a very small number of people I actively see or hang out with in person where I live right now.

For the past six years, I've traded off what's accessible about where I live—newer West Coast city with accessible transit where there's an elevator that (usually) isn't broken, the ability to have a car, not a food desert, relatively clean air when the woods aren't on fire, some of the greatest housing stability I've had in my adult life (wow, another year and we're still not evicted, a miracle)—with the sadness of living in a city that has an overall incredibly white, northern European, middle- to upper-middle-class culture, thousands of miles away from the people I've known the longest and love the most. There is a small but mighty crip community here; it's not a city where nobody thinks or talks about disability ever, but I've still spent the past six years missing having brown non-Christmas in Goldstone Noodle Restaurant, laughing and bitching with my T'karonto friends. Disabled people make trade-offs like this all the time.

And yet: implied in the sentence *There's no disabled community here* is the idea there is some place out there that's magically accessible and abundant in disabled community. And I don't believe in that. There is no place that is perfect like that, waiting for us. There are places that are more and less survivable for each of our specific access needs, realities, and desires, more and less what we need and yearn towards at any given time. And there are only the places we make and carve out, for ourselves and together.

Saying *there is no disabled community* erases the disabled people and communities that are already there, everywhere. We leave notes for each other on the walls to mark safe zones, pass messages to each other, carve out hours and moments, blink and touch on a screen. We are that community that is not supposed to exist. We may not look like what "community" is supposed to mean, but we're still there. We may not say "disabled" all the time, but we and our disabled and sick experiences are still there. Most of the people in my hometown who are all sick with something wouldn't call themselves the D-word, and yet their rust-belt sickness makes us a disabled city.

My Deaf white poet kin teaching two hours west. My new friend who says, *There's one flight, is that OK* and invites me to use their erg chair when I get to their apartment. My crip art femme friend and comrade in town for a hot minute, we sit on the benches loud-talking, eating bún, and it's the healing I need. The kid with the cane who side-eyes us and wants to say hi but doesn't know how to yet. My friend's wheelchair-accessible new-construction elevator building apartment. Me helping my friend drive their car, together through their city, our spatial difference support and cheerleading. His friend who's on a new tier of the prison she's in chatting on a forty-minute video call scheduled two weeks in advance. The Deaf queer zine I remember from six years ago. All community, all messages, notes and caches for each other. All carving out space in a world that works every day to erase and kill us, surviving anyway.

I understand the need for explicit proudly Disabled organizing and culture. Trust. I understand the need for more, the ache when we don't have. And I also want us not to shortchange or dismiss what we have. I want us to know the crip community we make is real, wherever we are, however big or small it is. We make disabled community simply by existing as we are. And it counts.

POD MAPPING FOR MUTUAL AID

By Rebel Sidney Fayola Black Burnett

Mutual aid can look many different ways. Those of us who are sick and disabled, Black, Indigenous, multiracial, and people of color, poor, working class, immigrants, queer, trans, two-spirit, and more, probably already practice mutual aid and may not even know it. Mutual aid is that random person from the internet bringing a hot meal when you can't get out of bed, it's cleaning or spiritually cleansing the home of someone who's too severely depressed to do it themselves, it's staying up late talking to that suicidal friend, helping unpack an apartment after someone moves, giving rides to chemo, visiting or writing letters to folks in prison, walking someone's dogs when they can't walk them themself. It can also look like sharing coping skills, survival skills, job-search skills. Mutual aid can be sharing medicine, making medicine, helping sift through allopathic doctors to find a good fit, or referring someone to that awesome working-class naturopath you know. Mutual aid can also be fighting to change the structural causes of oppression so that everyone can be more free.

I'm writing this as COVID-19 is taking hold in my region, people are talking about social distancing as a form of survival, and I'm thinking about all the people who are already housebound and having a hard time making ends meet, getting needs met, and who need social support to survive. I'm thinking of my houseless and elderly neighbors, my immunocompromised friends who may need food but also protection from any germs I may be carrying. I'm thinking about how we survive together rather than apart. Even if together means Zoom hangouts, texting, leaving groceries on the doorstep, and not coming in to say hi.

Mutual aid can happen between two, twenty, or 200 people (or more!). A good place to start, though, is with your "people." Whether that's your one best friend, some folks from church, or the handful of acquaintances you never hang out with but who came through that one time when things were really tough, it's important to assess who would show up for you in a crisis or emergency, and who you'd do the same for.

This is where "pod mapping" comes in. Originally developed by Mia Mingus for the Bay Area Transformative Justice Collective, pod mapping is a tool specifically for accountability and dealing with harm in communities. However, it can also be adapted to help you assess who you can rely on in a pinch—who you'd turn to for support and who would turn to you. These groups may or may not overlap. You may also have different pods for different situations.

A "pod" is a microcosm of "community." Since it's more concrete, it's easier to get organized—to connect, make a plan, and follow through if and when it's needed. There may be certain qualities you look for in the folks in your pod(s): maybe they're really reliable, well-resourced, generous, committed, kind. Maybe they have certain skills that you don't and need. Maybe they live nearby.

Here's what the pod mapping worksheet looks like.[46]

In the center circle, write your name.

---

[46] See Mia Mingus's pods and the pod mapping worksheet at https://batjc.wordpress.com/resources/pods-and-pod-mapping-worksheet/.

The dark circles are your pod. It's important to write specific names, as well as what supports they can provide. Is it a neighbor who has a generator that will charge your wheelchair when the electricity is out? Is it someone who can buy and drop off groceries? What about a friend who will take care of you when you're sick? Talk to your people and ask what they feel able to provide. Then ask them what they need from you to be in their pod, or let them know what you can offer. (Mutual aid is mutual.)

The dotted lines are people who are movable—they could become part of your pod if you have some conversations and build relationships.

The larger circles on the outside are bigger community groups, networks, organizations, etc., that could be resources for you. Here's my pod map as an example.[47] I don't have everyone's skills written down because I still need to have those conversations. As I have more information, I can continue to fill it in.

Like, "Do you want to be part of my disaster survival mutual aid pod? OK cool, what do you feel like you can contribute? I can bring meals and groceries, provide emotional support, and have a couple extra inhalers. We have a safe place where you can come and stay in our guest room if you need it."

Use this tool in the way that works for you. And don't forget where it came from—this is a resource created by BATJC to designate who could be a support in being accountable for harm, holding someone else accountable for harm, or who could help you if you witnessed harm.

Honor where it came from and who created it.

---

47 See Rebel's pod map at https://batjc.files.wordpress.com/2016/06/batjc-pod-mapping-2016-updated.pdf.

CHAPTER 3

Disabled Grief Technologies: Disability Justice Future-Building in a Time of Mass Grief

'Cause it hurts, 'cause it hurts like the end of the world.
—JAMES BLAKE

Let me start with grief.

My new therapist asks on the intake form: *Have you lost anyone to death recently?* I say *oh, yeah.* Two of my closest friends, the sister and brother God gave me when I didn't have any. My father. Two long-term friends and comrades from the psych survivor days, who are some of the reasons I didn't die when I was twenty-one. Disabled people I didn't know personally but whose lives move through mine and make it possible: Mel Baggs, William Peace / The Bad Cripple, Elandria Williams, Carrie Ann Lucas, Engracia Figueroa. The number of friends-of-friends are too many to count. Every day there is someone else. I woke up and Lee Maracle was gone. Two weeks later, Greg Tate and bell hooks die in the same week, and my friend Gabe reminds me that Lee just passed a couple weeks ago. I stare blankly because it feels like a year. "It's grief fatigue," he says. He's right.

I spent a lot of 2020 on a half-busted orange Ektorp couch, crying. It wasn't "bad." It wasn't good. It was what needed to happen, to hold the space to honor the losses. I did the bare minimum I needed to pay the bills and survive and went back to crying four times a day. My eyes look wrecked in every Zoom recording from April 2020 to maybe this fall.

I didn't know how to get through. And: I bought the binder I'd wanted for years. I bought a "skin-care system" so my over-forty skin could glow, sort of. I went and got ice cream once a week and sat on the park bench after everyone went home, discussing life and death with a friend from six feet apart. Summer 2021 was the warmest climate change summer on record, which is fucked but it meant you could go swimming in Lake Washington without wanting to die from the cold, and I did. There were plenty of other people doing the same. Some swimming, but I think so many of us were letting that big water hold our huge grief. Watching the sunset, looking at Tahomah / Mount Rainier watching over us. In the big huge silence holding our big huge losses, the ones that are too big to really understand, and that we are not supposed to hold alone.

Grief is political. Grief is an epidemic in the middle of the pandemic.

Cripple grief is a specific kind of grief. It's one of the million crip things not really talked about.

And I've felt a lot of it in my life. And in these past two years.

And so have you probably.

So I'm going to talk about it. As a thing we live with. A tech we learn. That might have deep implications and uses for how all of us are going to survive the damn pandemic and the end of the world and what comes next and how we live out the whole rest of our lives.

I'm going to start with the big one. It might be yours too.

#STACEYLOVEDME

On May 19, 2020, I woke up to a text of three broken heart emojis and a tear from my friend Max. I thought it was a mistake. I was still rumpled in my bed, trying to get up to be together from the neck up for a Zoom I had complex feelings about in thirty minutes. I texted, "Is this for me?" In one of those before-and-after moments in which your life is completely transformed, Max called me and told me that my soul sibling, my work wife heart friend who had been there since the beginning of my entry to disability justice, Stacey Park Milbern, had died that morning, the morning of her thirty-third birthday.

She had gone in for a long-delayed surgery to take out her kidney cancer. We had all been excited: her prognosis, we thought, was great, she was going to be cancer-free, and we were all going to move forward with our amazing lives and plans together! Stacey's life was on fire when she died. She was a year into buying her house in east Oakland through a massive community fundraising campaign and had turned it into the Disability Justice Culture Club, a resoundingly non-NPIC[48] disability community center and hangout zone. She had co-authored Bernie Sanders' DJ platform and co-created the online experience for *Crip Camp* and been shouted out by *President Barack Obama* on Twitter, to mention just a few things. She was working on her first book and we were texting each our our dreams about about co-writing a disabled queer BIPOC romcom script for Netflix.

And then she died instead.

And the world ended.

---

48 Non-Profit Industrial Complex.

I was no stranger to grief. I grew up surrounded by other survivor kids who killed themselves, were killed by the police for being Mad in public, or danced with the risk of both. In my early thirties, friends in Toronto started dying from cancer and suicide and the by-products of being poor. From 2015 on, I lived through the suicides of many femmes in my community, deaths that rocked femme and queer communities on their hinges and made us start talking about madness, mental health, and suicide more. I have lived with suicidality for years, as a survivor of child sexual abuse and complex trauma and an autistic person who survived years of allistic abuse as a child. In the Trump pre-pandemic years, so many people died—not just the 2016 ones people remarked upon, like Prince and Carrie Fisher, but many students, acquaintances, friends, loved ones, kin—car accidents and overdoses and just not waking up. I ended a friendship with a white disabled friend when they laughed and said, "They always annoyed me, so I really don't care," when I asked them how they were doing in the wake of a working-class Southeast Asian ND friend's recent death in a car accident, and seemed confused when I was offended. That person later sent me a message "inviting me to explain my relationship to death." I wrote, but didn't send, many letters that all said, *My relationship to death is that I am living in a war, and every time one of my kin is cut down, I feel like we're losing it.*

But this one undid me. Upended me. Ripped my heart open and kept it there. Altered state. Silent scream. Loud scream. More tears than I'd ever cried. My girl. My sib. #TeamTaurus. The reason I no longer live in poverty. The sis who was there when there were just ten of us, it felt like.

And the knowledge that she wouldn't be the last. And then the reality that she wasn't.

There's no sympathy card for this.

A CRIP'S CRIP: LOVING DISABLED PEOPLE WHEN YOU KNOW MANY OF US WILL DIE

I am a disabled person's disabled person. Almost all of my close kin are disabled, sick, neurodivergent, Deaf, or Mad. I love us the best. I think most abled and normal people are really fucking boring.

But in the months after Stacey's death, a horrible realization started to hit me. Even if I won the game and evaded the forces trying to kill me in the WSCCAP,[49] like suicide and ovarian cancer: I might outlive all or most of the people I love. I might watch all or most of the people I love die of medical neglect, abuse, ableism, racism, fatphobia, and transphobia, in systems that don't see their lives as worth living or fighting for.

The thing about being a disabled4disabled, crip4crip person was not just all of our magical disabled joy and brilliance. It was living with the knowledge that the people you love the most, who are the best people in the world, that there is a strong likelihood that they will be murdered. And that the world doesn't have language or a framework to understand the tragedy of their deaths. The world is more likely to tell you "Oh your friend is in a better place," when they die, to tell you, "At least she's finally free of her wheelchair." The world doesn't understand that disabled communities and kin networks are

---

49 "The white supremacist capitalist cis-sexist ableist patriarchy," a term created by Femme Heartshare Circle Toronto in 2012, growing from bell hooks's phrase "the white surpremacist capitalist patriarchy."

a thing. That we are disabled in the next world. That our wheelchairs are beloved friends. That we are wanted and loved here.

How would I live with that knowledge, I thought to myself? And what does it mean for our movements and communities, to live and organize with that knowledge alive in us? I had spent a lot of my twenties and thirties fighting frantically to keep us alive—and thinking that if we just organized hard enough, it could happen. I still believe in that possibility, and in the need for that fight. But in my forties, I now understand that with this love comes this particular kind of loss, some of which may not be preventable.

And what does it mean for the development of our movements, our relationships as disabled people, when all of us are vulnerable to death from ableist, racist medical abuse and neglect, albeit in different ways, but some of us have been told for years we will die young, and some of us are told that just maybe with enough turmeric and anti-inflammos, we can live to a sore and creaky old age? How does that affect our movement choices, where some of us go hard and don't stop, because you never know when you're going to die, and some of us move slower, rest easier?

Would this knowledge make me go numb, or shut myself off to closeness to other crips?

Would it make me reach out more fiercely to hold my loved ones close?

Would I know how to do that?

I reached out to Corbett O'Toole on Facebook one late night when I was having a really, really rough time facing this abyss of potential disabled loss. The moment I was experiencing reminded me of second-wave queer feminists of color I knew who had also watched their comrades—friends and lovers, giants they'd birthed a movement with—die of cancer and diabetes in their forties and fifties, and how mad from grief they sometimes went. Just a more intentionally disabled version. I was feeling like I could become them. Corbett is an older disabled white dyke I know who is one of the original feminist and lesbian disabled activists from the disability rights movement. She was there as a young white crip dyke at the Section 504 occupation onwards, she was one of the people who created so much foundational queer and feminist disability organizing. And she had watched so many of her comrades—women like Laura Hershey and Carrie Ann Lucas—die young.

She said, "Just a bit of elder advice: The weight of secrets and deaths continue to grow as you age. So plan more quiet time for yourself. You'll need it."

She continued: "About deaths: find people who get it and talk to them. We can't get through it without each other, and folks outside our world don't have a freaking clue what we're going through. Like the weight of knowing the enormous resources that crip mentors put in so that Stacey's generation could get mentors and opportunities, and how many of them have already died. We die because we don't matter in the nondisabled world."[50]

PANDEMIC GRIEF AS CHRONIC ILLNESS

Recently, I was in a text message exchange with one of my oldest friends. We had been playing phone tag for a long time, and I texted her, *I didn't hear back from you last week when you said you wanted*

---

[50] Corbett O'Toole, personal Facebook conversation with the author, July 2020.

to talk, do you still want to? She said, *Sorry, friend, I knew you were stewarding grief.*

My reaction in the moment was, wow, is she viewing the grief avalanche of the past two years in a similar way to the ways abled people view chronic illness—through the lens of a temporary illness, like a cold or flu? *Rest up, call me when you feel better?*

It turned out she didn't, but it still turned my thoughts to this truth: *Pandemic grief is more of a chronic illness than a short-term virus.* And chronically ill strategies of managing and living within chronic illness are going to go a long way towards helping up living within this pandemic, anthropocene grief.

Crips know. When you first go down with your chronic illness, many people around you will tell you they hope you "feel better soon." When you never "get better"—when this is your chronically ill life— you have to learn new strategies in how to live it. It's common in sicko communities for people to talk about learning pacing—how to break tasks into small steps, and doing them bit-by-bit, resting in between. I basically don't have abled people in my life anymore (lol), but when I did, I used to get admonished/tsk-tsked when I'd talk about slowly doing email or other work when I was having a flare—finger wagged that I should be "Resting and getting better!" I felt so lonely in those moments. Those people didn't understand that my chronic illness was not a weeklong flu or a daylong migraine (though I have those too), but that I would have flares and fatigue all my life, and if I waited until I was "well" to work, I would never get anything done.

I saw similar skills in grief stewardship in COVID. I had days and weeks of acute grief, where I wept for seven hours on my couch, where everything was overwhelming, where I felt closer to the dead person than the living. There are death anniversaries where I need to make time for open space, for candles and ceremony, but also mostly to hold space for the fact that anything could happen. Yet, I also have days and weeks where grief is a more everyday presence. The tears that spring up are not an emergency, but a regular visitor.

I wrote my friend back, saying, "The thing is, I am at a point where there is almost never not going to be someone dead, someone I am grieving or doing death work around. Sometimes I might be nonverbal and need to be alone. But that weekend, I did yoga, went for a walk in a park I love, went to a bookstore, hung out with a friend—all of those are ways I also hold my grief on a daily basis." My grief was not a short-term thing to "resolve" with a week alone—it is a daily presence that ebbs and flows and whose manifestations alter.

If we listened to the skills created by chronically ill people to acknowledge pain and fatigue, reorient to a disabled, slow, sick body as "normal" and everyday, and build life rhythms and patterns, strategies and survival tools and relationships, around that sick sad bodymind—would that open new doors for all of us living within a chronic grieving self?

Is it already happening? Yes. The pandemic has created new formally organized and informal spaces for grief stewardship. Online communities like Radical Loss: We Grieve Together, founded by Black liberationist and media justice activist Malkia Devitch Cyril, who has written powerful essays about Black grief and intergenerational trauma and healing, like "Grief Belongs in Social Movements: Can We Embrace It?"[51] and the private group a friend started for

51 Malkia Devitch Cyril, "Grief Belongs in Social Movements: Can We Embrace It?" *In These Times*, July 28, 2021, https://inthesetimes.com/article/freedom-grief-healing-death-liberation-movements/.

"adult children of dead abusive parents" normalize and create containers to hold long-term grief. There are more BIPOC-specific grief resources out there than I've ever encountered before. We might need more disabled-specific ones, but a DJ knowledge infuses many of the spaces I know, and disabled people hang out, listen, watch TV and witness each other through this.

Grief stewardship is not just about the individual skills of holding grief and loss. My beloved disabled Roma friend mentioned that they were going to a program that trains people to be death doulas. I told them I was intrigued, had thought about becoming a death doula for a long time, but wasn't sure if the work would be too intense for me. They said, "Don't you think you're already doing it?" They were right. I—along with many disabled people I know—had also spent the pandemic doing the active work of death care. I had helped plan memorials, archived my friends' writing, helped give away their durable medical equipment, and reached out to their friends to ask if they wanted to get a piece of clothing, jewelry, or a book of our friend's. Many other disabled people have worked on Zoom to ensure non-local people could be at the memorial, organized ASL interpretation and Spanish translation, got the flowers and did the spiritual care work of placing herbs and flowers on our loved ones' bodies. I have messaged friends reminding them when the Zoom memorial was and offering to text with them during it, and we have hung out together online remembering them and planning the tree-planting to happen for them in the spring. When a friend's body was composted, friends worked together to make sure their compost was given to anyone who'd loved them who wanted some.

Enrollment in death doula programs has skyrocketed during the pandemic[52] because of the millions of people—5.65 million at the time of this writing—who have died from COVID worldwide. "For the first time in a generation, everyone is experiencing the possibility that death may touch their lives—not someday, but now," says Ann Burns, president of the American College of Trust and Estate Counsel.[53] This is knowledge disabled people have often lived with for most of our lives. Disabled people have particular skills we have honed to remember our friends and do the work of stewarding their end-of-life accessibly and from a crip place. Again, we have skills the world needs, and we share them.

"DEATH COVIDS" AND DISABLED GRIEF ACCESS INTIMACY

Every single BIPOC person I know had an incredible number of people in our lives die during the pandemic. A lot of us weren't strangers to death, we'd lost people to suicide or gun violence or cancer before. But the past two years of COVID and the triple pandemic have meant we've often lost more people, more quickly, than ever before. I know friends who've planned seven funerals since 2020, or lost four people they loved in one month.

And it's been my experience that a lot of even my white disabled friends were uncomfortable with this kind of mass death faced by their BIPOC disabled friends. They lost people too, but it wasn't quite at the same level. And they didn't know how to deal with it when we did.

---

52 Melissa Chan, "Death Doulas Used to Be Rare. The COVID-19 Pandemic Changed That," *Time*, January 26, 2022, https://time.com/6128469/death-doulas-COVID-19-pandemic/.
53 Chan, "Death Doulas," https://time.com/6128469/death-doulas-COVID-19-pandemic/.

I lost a lot of people I loved to death during the pandemic, but I also lost some significant white friends. Usually this didn't happen with a big explosion. But, when they asked me how I was doing and I mentioned that someone else had died, they just didn't know what to say—besides "Wow, that's intense." And then they withdrew. I could tell they were freaked out at just how often someone in my life or community died, from COVID but also from suicide brought on by how horrible the world was, from overdose, medical gatekeeping or lack of access to medical care because of pandemic shortages or fear of going to a hospital.

Some of them, not knowing what to say, might be honest. But I couldn't help but see the difference from my BIPOC friends who also were living with staggering losses, and their ability to say "Hey, I see you," or "I know there are no words, but I am so sorry," or "Thinking of you," or just silently mailing me a huge GF Southern caramel cake in the mail. When those white friends said "Wow, that's intense" and left, it felt very similar to the "Feel better soon!" responses of abled people to me or another chronically ill / disabled person mentioning a chronic crip body moment we were having.

The phrase "Feel better soon!" is often a source of eyeball rolls and sarcasm in disabled communities. It assumes an abled-bodied and -minded normalcy, that disability and madness is a temporary and unfortunate stop on a disabled life. It shows abled squeamishness around crip and Mad realities. It is also often paired with a "Let's hang out when you feel better" that says intimacy and social times are reserved for the abled and normal—that only when you can lift your head from the bed, shower, and talk in complete sentences is your body/mind tolerable and worthy of intimacy and friendship, of witness.

Not all of my white friends did this. My friend in New York who's a hospital chaplain, who held a million iPads up to dying intubated people so their families could say goodbye; my friend in New York who is a long COVID survivor and teacher doing nonstop mutual aid work; my friend in Seattle who worked night shifts as a CNA (certified nurse assistant) in a hospital emergency room the whole first eighteen months of the pandemic—they got it. We had "pandemic intimacy." My CNA friend said to me, as we hung out on my fucked-up leatherette-with-all-the-leatherette-peeled-off porch couch one day, blowing bubble wands and staring into space, "I have a hard time hanging out with anyone who didn't have a 'death COVID,' you know?"

"Some people had another kind of COVID?" I asked.

"Oh yeah, some people had an 'art COVID' or an 'I'm bored COVID,'" they said. We both snorted. I'd forgotten that anyone might be coasting through this without the sirens going off all the time.

We had a different kind of intimacy—the long-term autistic, disabled death-witness intimacy. We knew not to ask "How ARE you?" But we checked in on each other. We texted even when we didn't hear back. We remembered deaths and death anniversaries. We said, hey I'm thinking of you. We didn't force each other to answer, "How ARE you?" when there were no words for the amount of bodies piled up.

There are crip and ND/autistic intimacies that keep us alive, where we mention it or don't mention it. Understand death as everyday. Allow people not to talk about it. Don't need words to know. Have skills around not trusting people. (An abled friend was surprised when I said, *Oh I never trusted people before this—I know they lie about how sick they are or where they've been. I was never surprised when people lied about their exposures.*) And some of them are about a deep ability to let our messy grief be witnessed, without makeup or good lighting.

As time went by, the world got more crip, even for us crips: the ever-present jokes about daily sweatpant-wearing, getting weirder and weirder at home, and wearing a button-up and underwear on Zoom. But it also opened up a disabled Zoom cosmology of mess. I let myself look sick and messy and tired on Zoom. I figured out how to have nice lighting but less as "normalcy" and more as a gift to the people watching me: to see my cute outfit and hot pink bedroom walls. But I also had celebratory hangouts of disabled people where we got to revel in the intimacy of Zoom in my friend's lap as he makes pasta in his wheelchair while talking to us; the low lighting of Zoom in the bedroom of my friend's RV, where they have relocated from their long-term home—decimated by wildfires—to a friend's rural land, where they live out the pandemic in isolation; my friend's small studio apartment that takes their Section 8. There is courage and crip intimacy when all of our spaces are not blurred out of embarrassment.

We let each other see our disabled lives. We let each other see our disabled grieving faces, our unashamed tears. We pace ourselves. We break the tasks down into small steps for the spoons we have. We make room for grief at the table. We listen to her. We make our movements, our hangouts, our lives, our futures assuming grief is a permanent compassion, and teacher.

This is a place of cripple healing, in the middle of all the loss.

ROSEWATER FOR CRYING EYES

The summer of 2020, the first pandemic grief summer, I cried so much, so many times a day, every day, that my eyes and tear ducts were continually swollen and inflamed. My friend Tala passed on this recipe. Rosewater has been used by many peoples as a cleanser, heart healer, and something that just helps the swelling go down. I had already been using rosewater as a cheap and delicious facial toner for years, but I am thankful to Tala for sharing her wisdom that it could also be a piece of my brown femme grief stewardship.

METHOD

You really, really don't need to make it yourself at home from scratch if you're all fucked up from the loss of your loved one and have been sitting on your couch staring at a wall for nine hours, and you also do not have to spend twenty dollars at Sephora or the organic store on some fancy varietal either. Go to your local halal / South Asian / Middle Eastern / African grocery / section of the supermarket / immigrant food warehouse. (I am mostly thinking of BIPOC folks. If you're white, maybe go to the hippie store or online.) They will have multiple bottles on the shelf starting at two to four dollars. If you can't make it out of the house, Vitacost and other online sellers sell it too. Buy one that speaks to you, go home, and pour some on a clean cloth, paper towel, or cotton ball (but the first two are best IMO, the cotton ball shreds everywhere). Lay it on your eyes for up to ten minutes, but a little is better than nothing. Allow your eyes to soak up the soothing. Doing this two to three times a day is fine. Thank the roses for their help.

If you want to make it yourself, go find yourself some pesticide-free roses. If you're lucky, you have a rosebush in your yard or a friend does, or there's some bushes down the block. They might be blooming in spring or summer, but in the Northern Hemisphere where I live, it's not uncommon for me to see a rose or two hanging on in fall. Go when it's early-ish, before it gets super nuclear hot out, but on a dry and sunny day. Sit with the roses a moment and take some breaths and just hang out with them. Notice, yes, they are pretty and smell good but they also have thorns. You might want to offer a little bit of your hair you cut off or pulled out of the comb in the shower, or something else for the plants before you harvest, and ask their permission. Gather some roses: four to five heads, or more of the smaller kind, can be enough for a small amount of rosewater, enough to use before it goes bad.

Take them home. Rinse them off if they look dusty at all. Pull the petals off the bud and place them in a non-reactive pot (ceramic or stainless steel or glass, but honestly use what you've got) with enough water to cover. Bring to a low simmer with the lid on for thirty minutes, then take it off the heat, cool it, strain off the solids, maybe add a little vodka if that's safe for you and if you want it to keep longer, and put it in the fridge. Or, you can put a lid upside down on the pot, put some ice cubes in the lid, and do the slow simmer for thirty; the lid will catch the condensed rose water.

Either way: give yourself honey, rest, and sweetness. Soothe your hardworking, grieving eyes.

CHAPTER 4

Nobody Left Behind and Wanting to Run Like Hell: Disabled Survival in Climate Crisis

Hello fan. This is the shit, hitting you.

In summer 2020, I wrote, "We're in a real fucking moment, comrades."

Firestorms and firenados. Toxic smoke. Mixed in with the coming coup in the US; Proud Boys and cops often the same thing, running rampant beating the shit out of or murdering people; police murder of Black people that just went on and on with impunity; and our nerves about the coming presidential election and the likelihood Trump would try and steal it and install himself as a dictator, the results of which possibly presided over by a post–Bader Ginsberg Supreme Court that has Serena Joy on it.

But most of all, on the West Coast, the fires, worse than we'd ever seen them. The "West Coast super smoke storm" brought AQIS into levels never seen before on earth—and definitely not here. We were used to 200 or 300 being bad, but we were seeing AQIS of 500, 600, 800. At least 1,200 people in California died from toxic air from the West Coast "super smoke storm" of September 2020 may have been a factor in up to 3,000 deaths, according to one Standford study.[54] The numbers are probably much higher, and millions more people are going to be dealing with long-term impacts, a heightened risk of death, or our chronic health conditions getting worse. The week after the two-week smoke storm passed, everyone I knew in Seattle was nauseous and migrained-out, but there was nothing in the news, and public health kept chortling that there were "no long-term side effects." We'll get sick and/or die all the same.

The West Coast smoke storms of 2020 were an important moment in disabled history. A lot of the disability justice communities of the United States were thinking about moving away from the West Coast, where many of us are located and where many of us increasingly can't breathe. Our disabled climate crisis activism—our mask distros and box-fan filter builds—have been heroic and saved lives. But the storms of 2020 were so severe that it left many of us questioning whether box-fan filters could be enough to deal with this. We knew: the fires were not going to get better. They're really bad, and they are going to get worse.

I witnessed masses of people talking about moving—after lifetimes or years—from the West Coast, because they cannot survive a smoke season that now lasts months every late summer and fall. Where the smoke is beyond bad (300 AQI? Try 600, 800, 900), but almost just as bad is living in a constant state of fear that your home is going to burn down and you are going to have to flee for your life with whatever you can grab and put in your car. I also saw friends exploring what it would take to emigrate to Canada or Belize or honestly

---

54 Lisa Fernandez, "Stanford Study: Smoke from California Wildfires May Be Factor in up to 3,000 Deaths," KTVU, September 23, 2020, https://www.ktvu.com/news/stanford-study-smoke-from-california-wildfires-may-be-factor-in-up-to-3000-deaths/.

anywhere—including places in the Global South with robust public health infrastructures that had crushed COVID.

It was the Great Disabled GTFO of 2020. And yet, moving is not that simple. We've spent the last five to ten years, or our whole lives, building robust interdependent disability justice communities. Sure, plenty of these aren't in the meat world—they are are virtual or diasporic, flung geographically all over the place—but plenty of them are based in a specific city, town, or area. I don't mean that there's some place where 100,000 disabled people are all friends and united. No— we are much smaller, fragmented, and disagreeing with each other than that. But I mean the sense that there are a bunch of disabled people in a city, and my network might be me and three other people I depend on, who also depend on me.

When people say "Just leave!" or say that staying and not abandoning our people is "martyring ourselves" or that "you can't do anything for anybody if you're dead," trust me, I think those feelings are absolutely understandable. I get it. I don't want to fucking die, and I have Klaxons going off in my head to GO NOW.

But they're missing an important point. We're not thinking about staying to sacrifice ourselves, or out of codependency (at least, not necessarily). As the Black feminist writer Mia Birdsong wrote, "Leaving is just not an option for most people. And the people who have the resources to leave will be leaving others behind who will be less positioned to fight back. There is no country on the planet for Black people. And I mean all Black people—women, queer, disabled, etc. As James Baldwin said, 'The place in which I'll fit will not exist until I make it.'"[55]

55 Mia Birdsong, Facebook, September 13, 2020.

As disabled people, we know we are interdependent with other people. Even when facing isolation, we built these webs of support that took years to create. The friends who you have built up enough trust and shared language with that when you are really sick, you can call them and ask them to buy you groceries or help you clean your house. My mostly accessible house with the fragrance-free washer/dryer, the deserted park I hang out in when I'm a certain kind of over-stimmed, the one good doctor at the clinic. None of these came easy. None of these are guaranteed to be found elsewhere. None of these are something we can automatically uproot and take with us.

This is something many abled people do not understand, not one bit. When I finally left Toronto in 2007 to move back to the US for grad school after two years of debating it, some people in my life were exasperated at how long deciding to leave had taken me. *Why was it such a big deal? Just go!* They didn't get it: all the disabled work I had put in for ten years to finally get to a place where I felt kind of like I had various layers of survival hacks that could keep me alive and the rent paid if I had a big flare for two months. It had meant years of building up relationships and flexible work gigs and places I could make $100 doing a focus group if money was tight, finding the one nurse practitioner who was okay at the local community health center. It was a big fucking deal to think about risking that delicate crip survival web for something amorphous like California.

I'm not just thinking of the individual webs we create. I'm also thinking of policy, of the secret crip maps that come out of geographi-cally specific laws and policies. For example, it's not a random accident that so many disabled people live in California. Sure, people live there for the mild climate, sure, and Black/brown, gay-ass places to live. But there's also a lot of disabled people in California because California Medicaid is some of the best in the country, and pays for home and community-based care attendants, adaptive equipment, and more. I have beloved friends in California with roots in North Carolina who love the climate and community in NC. But North Carolina doesn't pay for in-home and community-based care, and didn't sign on to Medicaid expansion. One of my friends had to leave for California in order to get in-home care paid for by Medicaid so she could come out, which she couldn't do when her loving-but-fundamentalist-Christian parents were her caregivers. Another friend got a grand total of twelve dollars in food stamps when she was desperately ill and poor and disabled in Durham. These are disabled maps of where we can survive, and their cartographies are tricky, and known by us.

I have friends living right in the middle of fire zones who would leave, except they have a whole web of lifesaving medical care that took them decades of searching and fighting to find, paid for by Medicaid. Our disabled communities grow in ecosystems, some of whose roots are state laws that enable our lives, and some of which are delicately pieced together quilts of tiny places of care. We do not have the abled luxury of picking up and leaving them easily.

COLLECTIVE MOVES FOR COLLECTIVE SURVIVAL

As disability justice people, we've built webs of mutual aid networks, survival centers and DJ collectives where people ask for and give help to each other. We are a collective movement and have built power collectively. But most of the stories about escaping fascism that are easy to access are individual. I have stories in my head of Jews and

Roma and queers and Black people and political radicals (and all of the above) who saw the signs of fascism in Europe in the 1930s and '40s and got out early—mostly by themselves. They were the one kid the family got a visa for, the one person in a community who was able to marry someone to get papers.

There's no country with socialized medicine that will sponsor your entire pod or crip village to come migrate. Migration is limited to the individual—student and work visas—or the Western-defined biological nuclear-ish "family": two partners who are married, or your grandmother or child. Not your poly pod. Not your whole extended non-blood chosen disabled family. There's been a lot of times during the current interregnum when I've joked, "If Trudeau ever legalizes poly marriage I'll marry all of you and help you get across the fake border!" but it's spoken to something deeper. I am not married, except to the movement. I am estranged from my non-chosen family because of their abuse. I have a rich and robust family I have chosen and made. And I want to bring all my folks with me.

One of my foundational ancestral stories is about how my Sri Lankan grandmother got out of Malaysia when the Japanese invaded during World War II. She fled on the last boat out, with nothing but the clothes on her back, her year-and-a-half-old son, and two books of photographs. Her story lives in the core of my bones and has been part of the survival strategies I've plotted since I was in my early twenties. When I was twenty-one and moved to Toronto, I did it for love, but I also did it because I had Appamma and *Parable of the Talents* in my ear. Get as many passports as possible, she hissed. Always be ready to go someplace else if you need to. Enjoy where you live for as long as possible, but always be ready to flee. Don't be stupid. Don't relax. They're always coming.

After Trump got elected in 2016, the nudges started up again, hard. The literal equivalent of President Steele Jarret in Octavia Butler's Parable books had taken office. Clearly, this would be a great moment to GTFO. As things got worse, and worse—Nazis, curfew, pandemics, and more—my friends north of the fake border increasingly asked when I would be showing up to quarantine in their spare room. My sister especially did not mince words, "I'm worried about you. Very worried. I just want you to be safe."

It's not that I don't, or won't move. But when push comes to shove, the people who don't leave aren't just willfully in denial. Some of us are broke. We also love our homes. We love our cities and towns and country places. We love this specific ecosystem: that pho place down the hill, this garden. And we love and are invested for survival in our other, disabled, people: our friends who themselves maybe can or cannot leave because they have a medical team they can't just up and find elsewhere.

I have thought a lot lately about whether there were people my grandmother left behind, that she loved and mourned. That her life depended on, and that she never got to see again.

I have thought a lot about how, even though she got out on the last boat, her kid, my uncle Jeremy, died of "bomb shock" at twenty months. How she got pregnant, probably not fully of her own free will, six months later with my dad, and how the trauma of losing a child in the midst of war and invasion and being expected to quickly get pregnant and replace that kid marked her for the rest of her life—including her relationship with my father.

I have been thinking about moving, but not as an individual solution where I get the hell out and turn my face away and have an OK life and count my blessings while the people who have made me and save me burn.

I have been thinking about a diversity of disabled tactics.

I have been thinking about the organizing of coastal Indigenous North American nations, like the Makah and Quileute, fighting to get more land inland to move to in the face of climate change's rising oceans making their coastal land dangerously unstable to inhabit. How it's not just two people leaving and buying a condo on a hill, but the whole community organizing to move, together.

I have been thinking about how many nations have specifically ablest immigration laws prohibiting crips from migrating legally. Canada "liberalized" its disabled immigration laws in 2018—after forty fucking years of denying legal immigration to disabled people under the guise of "medical inadmissability" because our access needs "would be a drain on the welfare state," neoliberalism kicked in and said, *Hey, some of these cripples, they have small businesses—they* CONTRIBUTE, *they're worthy, not useless eaters! Let's let them in—but only if their access needs costs less than $99,000 over five years.* So it's not like crips can just get across the fake border super-duper easily anyway. Especially crips who can't hide it.

I am thinking about how maybe we can think about:

If we move: how do we, in the words of Sins Invalid, move together, with no one left behind? How do we plan to move a pod, a squad, a network to safer ground? I know individual Black and brown disabled folks who, pre-pandemic even, relocated to Mexico or other parts of Central America when where they lived got too expensive.

Can we hook up with our folks there? Can we ask them for a place to crash and help figuring out where to set up?

International migrant rights organizing and Indigenous justice organizing is a part of all this. Uh, there's a lot of migrant justice organizing in Canada (just to give one example I know the most about) that's been fighting for years to open borders, allow crips, asylum seekers, and poor/BIPOC people in—way before masses of American folks started actually thinking about leaving in more than a "I'm going to Canada, man!" way. We can't talk about moving without talking about linking up with our folks there who are doing this work, to ask them to push and keep pushing (and how can we support this pushing) for all forms of migrant justice.

While also pushing for treaty rights, Land Back, Indigenous sovereignty, and being in right relation with the folks whose land we might be coming to as an uninvited guest. When people talk about moving to (fill in the blank place), I don't care whether it's urban or rural, somebody else owns it and is already there. Whether it's Black folks, disabled BIPOC folks who were doing organizing just fine before all you Californians showed up, or Indigenous people in the middle of a protracted struggle to keep their land claim. We can't just panic-move and not think about existing land claims and Indigenous and local communities who have been there.

If we stay: how do we build together so that people continue to have what they need? How can these groups communicate and share resources? During the last four years of smoke and fire hell on the West Coast, there's been a thing developing. When California was on fire, Seattle crips sent air purifiers, money, and masks to our friends down there. When we were on fire, the same thing happened in reverse. This time around, there were some examples of us sharing resources even though the whole damn coast was smoked out. Can we who might make it north or east continue to spread the word, fund-raise, and provide stops on a route out, or respite / safe-haven space?

There's also the reality that most people can't or won't move, and somebody has to stay and be Starfleet Command and fight to save this part of the world from total fascist bestiality. Can we use and share existing community safety guides, and make new ones as conditions evolve?

What do we learn from other diasporas about survival and communication? About going back? There's an article I love about living through the Sri Lankan civil war from a Sri Lankan perspective, how brutality and normality live side by side, and the very deep parallels to what it's like living in the US today.[56]

It also made me think of the different eras of diaspora during and after wartimes. People went home. Some, during the war, during a lull, or not. Some chose to move home during the worst of the white van abductions—journalists, ordinary people disappeared by force—the murder-city of it all. I remember one activist aunty leaving Toronto for Colombo at the height of the worst shit, all of us thinking she was nuts, and her saying, "I'd rather be home and be able to actually organize than just be sitting angst-ridden here reading *Al Jazeera* and wringing my hands for the next ten years."

And no matter how fucked we were and still are, people moved back after. To see, to rebuild, to try and re-create, to fight for accountability,

---

56 Indi Samarajiva, "I Lived Through Collapse. America Is Already There." *Indi.ca* (formerly *Dirty South* blog), September 25, 2020, https://gen.medium.com/i-lived-through-collapse-america-is-already-there-ba1e4b54c5fc/.

to be home. And people sent money, letters, traded information, got the word out during the worst of times. No matter what happens on each presidential election, each heat dome, wildfire, flood, or freak winter storm, all of these choices will happen here too.

I would also like to encourage people to ditch the "Oh, let's go make a huge compound in the woods!" vision as the only solution. Great idea; I'd love it. We also may not have a lot of time, and often we don't have enough spoons to pick up takeout, let alone do construction to build a million accessible tiny huts. Also, we all don't get along that great, and in the Parables books, the Acorn compound gets smashed by Christian American rapists. I'd settle for us getting an accessible apartment building, or living with Aunt Monica someplace. Also, many disabled people don't want to live in the woods. We want to live in a place where there's food delivery, and sidewalks, and a place that repairs durable medical equipment. The woods can be great, but they have to be accessible too. Not leaving each other behind means not abandoning cities, where so many disabled people live.

I didn't have the answers, so I decided to write down the questions and the panicked midnight thoughts. The problem of surviving climate change as disabled people is not an individual problem, and because of this, there is no individual solution that will be enough to save us. Life as the only crip who survives may not be worth living.

In the immortal words of Sins Invalid, as disabled people, we are committed to a politic and practice of "we move together, with no one left behind." When I read those words for the first time, and since, I know that they are not a simple description of reality. There are plenty of us who have been abandoned to die, who have been left behind. But we know that as disabled people, we are some of the only ones of us who slow down and move at the pace of the slowest of us, call the nursing home over and over demanding to know if someone is OK, sit in the hospital ward letting the staff know people care about our friend who is sick. That phrase / those words, are an assertion and a challenge, to disabled and abled people alike. What strategies come to us at the slow back end of the march? The place where we leave no one to die?

As disability justice folks, we're gonna figure out the answers to surviving climate change together, with all the disabled ingenuity and creativity we've shown for our whole entire lives. We already are. We will not leave our people behind, and not slowly die with our disabled roots ripped out in strange soil.

CHAPTER 5

Cripping the Resistance:
No Revolution without Us

I feel like the revolution is happening and I'm missing it.
I feel like everyone in the streets might die and us who stayed
home will be the people who are left to keep the revolution going.
I actually just feel like we at home are going to die too because
immunity is collective and everyone in the streets comes home
to people with varying levels of risk.
—CAROLYN LAZARD
(ACTUAL QUOTES FROM MY BRAIN AND ALSO OTHER SICK
AND DISABLED FRIENDS)

May 2020 will always mark a crux of death, heartbreak, and resistance for me.

On May 19, 2020, disability justice organizer Stacey Park Milbern died unexpectedly, breaking all our hearts. Two days later, police officers murdered George Floyd by kneeling on his neck for nine minutes, twenty-nine seconds. In the days and weeks that followed, a level of mass resistance to anti-Black police violence exploded at a scale that has not been seen in half a century in the United States.

In response to the murders of George Floyd, Breonna Taylor, Tony McDade, and many, many other Black people by law enforcement, people filled the streets. They took over police stations, turned hotels into homeless shelters and neighborhoods, burned down youth jails, and toppled racist monuments. We were demanding things at a scale I couldn't have dreamed of a year ago: the defunding of police and abolishing of prisons, creating community-lead fire safety and community self-defense squads. After protestors took over ten blocks of downtown Seattle for a month, turning it into CHOP—the Capitol Hill Organized Protest—Seattle City Council voted to defund the cops by 43 percent. Webinars on transformative justice and abolition had hundreds of people attending.

Things were also terrifying. The National Guard and the Feds came to the streets kidnapping people in unmarked vans.[57] Trump threatened to use the Insurrection Act to deploy the military on protestors. White supremacists showed up with guns and bombs. Many of us feared martial law and fascism arriving in an absolute way.

And it also felt like revolution might be here. I was texting "Abolition in our lifetime?????" to friends. I was feeling so many things. Blown away, and realizing how I'd started to not believe we could actually win, even after twenty-five years of being involved in disability and transformative justice activism.

At the same time, I was feeling incredibly frustrated. As a disabled person with a compromised immune system, I had been self-isolating to keep myself safe from COVID-19 for five months. My central act of resistance is to keep myself alive. The extended community I love are all immunocompromised/disabled and we are grappling with the same questions of safety. Many are also vulnerable to medical eugenics because of being fat, elder, Black or brown, poor, or living

<hr>

57 All Things Considered, "Federal Officers Use Unmarked Vehicles to Grab People in Portland, DHS Confirms," NPR, July 17, 2020, https://www.npr.org/2020/07/17/892277592/federal-officers-use-unmarked-vehicles-to-grab-protesters-in-portland.

and working with those of us who are. If I get sick, I could get my whole disabled community sick.

So, I didn't go to CHOP. For the first three months of the pandemic I went to a grocery store exactly once, and it was at eight a.m. during immunocompromised hour. I wipe down all my groceries and quarantine my mail. How the hell can I be in the streets with thousands of people chanting for hours? Even if they all wear masks, the risk felt so high—especially since the police themselves refused to wear masks. Also, I've avoided tear gas at protests for twenty years, because of my multiple chemical sensitivity (MCS, a condition where chemicals used in "everyday" products, smoke, and toxins make you sick), needing to keep my toxin exposure down to manage my fibromyalgia and asthma. How the fuck can I be in it during a pandemic?

I kept feeling like I was staring out the window at the revolution. And so many of the "home front" resistance activities we've often practiced as disabled people—creating safe houses, inviting people over for food before or after an action, doing childcare—are inaccessible right now because of the need to keep our homes a safe germ pod. And much as I love home front forms of resistance—teaching, writing, listening, organizing—I couldn't ignore a desire to also go fuck shit up in the streets, crip style!

I know I'm not alone. I am one of many other disabled, sick, parenting, caregiver, elder, fat, and/or medically vulnerable people wrestling with these same questions.

I want us all to live, especially BIPOC disabled people, to survive both the pandemic and the ways we might transmit it on the streets. I also don't want us disabled and sick BIPOC people to be cut out of the revolution. As my friend and comrade, Black disabled trans organizer and artist Syrus Marcus Ware said recently, "We need to fight back against any idea that the revolution could be here without us. If we—disabled BIPOC people—aren't part of it, then it's not the revolution. Activists need to be more creative now than ever to create responses that allow for us to all survive this in the end."

CRIPPING THE RESISTANCE: THE CRIP REBEL ALLIANCE FIGHTS BACK

People throw around the word "strategy," or don't even use it at all, but don't always define it. However, long-time transformative justice organizer and movement strategist Ejeris Dixon says, "A political strategy is a plan containing a series of goals and campaigns, placed within a defined and intentional order to move towards our vision." (Please read her whole Instagram post series breaking down the fascist playbook and what our competing vision and strategies are,[58] it's really good.)

Sometimes during the fascism/COVID/racism/ableism quadruple pandemic, it's hard for me to think about what my goals are because I'm frozen in fear. But when I stop and can feel into my core, my primary goal as a disabled queer person of color is to survive and to work to keep my disabled kin and communities alive. "To exist is to resist" is a saying many of us say: all the ways we survive a world that wants to kill us as disabled people is resistance.

But I want more than just survival. I want to transform this world so that it is not run by a death cult that wants to murder the land and

58 Ejeris Dixon (@ejeris), Instagram, August 15, 2020, https://www.instagram.com/p/CD7JLz 9Ah_w/.

most of us. I want to defeat fascism and racist ableism and create a world where care, access, pleasure, and human creativity get to flourish, where everyone has enough and no one has $50 billion, and none of us live under the constant fear of being murdered by cops and doctors. And I want to do so as spoons allow, joyfully, creatively, alone sometimes, and with crip kin and allies at other times.

One of the foundational principles of disability justice is that nothing has to be the way it is. And there is no law saying that protests always have to be thousands of people in the streets chanting.

I believe we need to keep using our disabled creativity to crip the resistance. To keep creating crip strategies to fight to win.

As disabled people we have always cripped resistance, and we have so many models to draw on:

- From Carrie Ann Lucas pulling out the wire control of her power wheelchair to use her body and chair as a barricade because the cops didn't know how to turn it back on (she said, "You can google it"), holding the cops off for hours at a Colorado sit-in against Trump's proposed cuts to Medicaid

- To disabled protestors bringing chairs and beds to protests, as fat and disabled protestors did outside the ICE office in San Francisco in August 2019

- To the Capitol Crawl and Mad Pride Bed Pushes

- To Deaf protestors at the Section 504 Protests using ASL to communicate without the cops being able to understand what was being said

- To disabled youth incarcerated in youth lockup and psych wards smearing shit on the walls as one of the only means they have of protest and sneaking in hugs to each other.

Making forms of protest that are accessible for our bodies and minds are just the beginning—we in our cripness create new forms of protest the ableds could never imagine. The recently revised (and always amazing) "26 Ways to Be in the Struggle beyond the Streets" by Ejeris Dixon, Piper Anderson, Kay Ulanday Barrett, Ro Garrido, Emi Kane, Bhavana Nancherla, Deesha Narichania, Sabelo Narasimhan, Amir Rabiyah, and Meejin Richart, lifts up ways we can organize without being in the streets, through teaching, making art, posting, fundraising, and educating. There are some amazing protest guides with harm-reduction suggestions, asking people to self-quarantine after protesting, mask at protests, and make hand sanitizer available and wipe microphones and bullhorns between speakers.

No solution is one-size-fits-all. Black and brown disabled people are often heavily targeted by the police as "threats" and can't depend on being seen as "helpless" or "invisible" to do certain actions. However, I firmly believe all of us have disabled ingenuity from our unique community/personal situations we can use to figure out ways of protesting that work for us, that the powers that be might never see coming. We are all needed to kick ass all the ways only we can to make this NEW WORLD OF DISABLED POWER, JOY, AND FREEDOM THAT IS COMING.

So, some things I am thinking about (with some additions from crip friends I asked) ...

- Banner drops, wheatpasting, painting murals and slogans on public streets, or projector art? These are all things that can be done alone, sometimes from cars, or in small germ-podded groups. You can just write some words on a sheet and tie it to something! What if a bunch of disabled people did a whole bunch of banner drops in different areas, at the same time?

- Helping organize protests and speaking at them via Signal or Zoom, projected?

- "Walking at night wheatpasting or stickering up propaganda when no one is around? Art of all kinds. And documenting it!" (Syrus Marcus Ware)

- Drawing, graffitiing, or making a memorial to our dead in many ways: dropping sculptures or painting a slogan or names in big letters on a sidewalk or street, also alone or in small or socially distant groups?

- Using the ways some of us might be seen as "helpless cripples" who aren't a threat to sneak into places or do things in plain sight, like lockdowns, wheatpasting, banner drops, occupying offices, or much more?

- Using our mobility devices to block entrances, lock down, and be the "Antifa Tank Division" disabled Fat activist group Fat Rose speaks of?

- Doing sneaky small actions far away from the big ones, when the police are distracted?

- Protests that are not just six feet apart, they are SILENT? Using our righteous rage and nonverbal skills to bring the righteous wrath of pointing a silent finger at the powers that be? I am thinking as an autistic person especially of the power and access of silent protest.

- "Making food and medicine to distribute to folks post-demo, left in jars in a no-contact cooler on a porch or stoop.

Or coordination of rides, tinctures, etc. Who needs what where?" (Eli Clare)

- Car caravans as COVID-safer alternatives, like the Anti Police-Terror Project's caravan that stretched for eight miles. Offering the option for folks to participate in foot marches from within our cars.

- Doing ritual and prayer in the streets or at home. Spells binding the police from doing harm! Spells asking the empire and prisons to crumble! Candles for the goddesses of transformation! Whiskey for the ancestors and the murdered! The Instagram action #TurnUpAtYourAlter was a great example of this.

- Getting N95s to protestors: working with makers to make mass masks plus face shields available. Early in the pandemic, when there was panic buying, the mass advice was to not wear masks, let alone N95s. This has now shifted to a mass ask of people to mask up, with cloth masks, as a harm-reduction effort. Protestors—from protestors facing tear gas in the 1960s to protestors with MCS—have long used respirators to protect ourselves from gas and other toxins. If we tried to mass-produce and mass-distribute N95s and respirators at protests, we could go a long way towards making protests safer for everyone, but ESPECIALLY for those of us who are immunocompromised.

- Using noise makers, not voices, to stop vocal spray. Playing mixtapes. Pre-recording voiced chants at home and bringing along to play loud (or sending these recordings with someone who can be there IRL if we can't be there IRL). Could edit these to higher volume OR go silent and modulate them with infrasonic sound waves (sound that isn't audible but can be vibrationally felt). Could place these under cars or other infrastructure like wheelchairs or even brick and play on transducers. Heavy and could probably get broken but maybe could be auxiliary to main protest or installed elsewhere. (Tina Zavitsanos)

- Double masking. Masking plus face shields. Making propolis or salt-spray nose spray for self-protection. Distributing these.

- Running HEPA purifiers while masked during indoor events. Opening windows. Having all events outside. High-ventilation events.

- Using social distance to spread out protests and make for a wild rumpus in the streets that is decentralized but harder to control.

- Using hacking, targeted flooding of social media (as K-pop fans have done to destroy Trump rallies and flood right-wing spaces), projecting images or solo lockdowns as socially distant ways of disruption. That's something you can do from a couch.

- Creating tools. Teaching online about abolition, de-escalation, transformative justice, and fighting fascism. Making those tools accessible, through image descriptions, captioning, ASL, and audio description. Creating guides for how to do online access well.

- The complexities of crip time. Sometimes we are very good at using spoons skillfully, doing something quickly. Sometimes we cannot be caught up in the "urgent immediate response" action cycle the same way abled people can. Case in point: I started working on this article in early June, and I thought it would be published quickly. Instead, I was moving slowly, because of grief and depression and some mental disability crisis. I worried that this piece would be "dated." Maybe it is— but it also gained more depth and evolution as time went by.

— As a neurodiverse person, I think a lot about the power of actions that are not public, not on a 10K Instagram feed. Secret actions. Private actions.

Dubian Ade writes,

> It's a real shame that most activists aren't interested in underground work bc they can't post about it on they Insta, snap, FB, or Twitter. It's pretty damn sad because some of the most vital, tangible, and insurrectionary activity must be done underground. Some of the most impactful rebellions we owe to nameless people who labored in the shadows. In an age where many of us will have to go underground as repression increases, we need to reclaim the clandestine legacies of our ancestors and shake off the celebrity activist culture that is very quickly becoming a burden to our movements.[59]

This rang true for me, and made me think about, while I do have a public presence as a writer, how as a neurodiverse person, I am not comfortable with being all out on front street all the time. I think

59 Dubian Ade, Facebook, August 1, 2020, https://www.facebook.com/dubian.campbell/posts/3428879683829663.

sometimes people are surprised my Instagram isn't like an activist brand with lots of infographics. And I'm like, no, it's private and it's a LOT of pics of my cats and THIS TOO IS THE RESISTANCE. Part of resisting accessibly for me is doing things that never become public.

— Creating spaces for disabled joy, rest, and healing.

MAKE CRIP RESISTANCE SOUP

I understand it can be easy to think that we can do nothing, or that nothing we do matters. That somebody else is the brilliant organizer, someplace else. But I'm going to leave you with a story.

A week or so after Stacey died, I had a dream where we were hanging out. I was telling her, *Stacey, you're gone, who's going to make the hand sanitizer to distribute via the crip mutual aid network now?* (Or the homemade air purifiers, or the number you could call during the power shutoffs to get hooked up with a generator, or any of the other 5 million brilliant crip survival organizing ideas she spearheaded.) *I can't do it, I only got two bottles of rubbing alcohol before everyplace sold out, I'm afraid to leave the house. We're fucked.*

She looked at me and said (I swear to god, I am not making this up), *Leah, you don't have to make the hand sanitizer. You have three chicken thighs in your freezer, right?* (She knew me. I always have three chicken thighs in my freezer.) *You make soup. That's what you're good at. Make soup.*

The point I took from this wasn't that we should all literally make soup. I took it to mean: use what you've got. Make crip resistance soup out of whatever skills, resources, tactics, and brilliant wild crip ideas you possess. For me, that includes writing essays and poetry and tools. Checking in on my friends, cracking jokes, and being there to witness. Doing things that are often underground and not "visible" on social media. Prayer and ritual. And believing in us.

Our possibilities are endless. And we are needed—all of us. All of our disabled brilliance is needed if we're going to create the liberated, abolitionist, disability justice future we need.

Let's get to it.

Postscript: Thank you to Eli Clare, Carolyn Lazard, William Maria Rain, Syrus Marcus Ware, and Constantina Zavitsanos for reviewing and giving feedback and suggestions on this essay.

RECIPE

STACEY SOUP

(created May 3, 2020, made over and over again through the pandemic)

From my small online recipe-sharing-during-COVID-group, posted in spring 2020:

I'd wanted chicken soup last night because I had a tickle in my throat and I realized I'd fallen off my hardcore medicinal cooking spree and was eating a lot of cheese and crackers and some pickles lately.

So I took three chicken thighs, bone in and skin on, out of the freezer this morning, and let thaw.

Then I chopped up and sauteed:

one onion

one and a half yellow carrots

two celery

thumb of ginger

three to four garlic cloves

half a big sweet potato or two smaller sweet potatoes

in the big pot, in olive oil. Sauteed for around five to eight minutes till soft.

Then I added the chicken and let it brown a bit, stirring it around.

I didn't have Thai or Madras curry paste, which is what I was thinking of when I started thinking of the soup. But I did have berbere, and some harissa in the fridge. I added one tablespoon of berbere to start and a big glob of harissa, adding and tasting as I went.

Then I added:

small quart of chicken broth I made last week, from the freezer

four dried shitake mushrooms from the cupboard

one teaspoon salt

Brought to boil so as to thaw out the frozen stock, adding a little water from the kettle to help. Turned down to simmer with lid that's too big but I couldn't find the right one, half on, half off.

After around forty minutes, I added a can of thick coconut milk. Turned it to low, simmered for ten.

Went out to the yard and picked some of the bok choy that is the earliest usable vegetable here (collards or kale are all great). Found the green onion that overwintered that I'd pulled yesterday and then couldn't find. Any greens would've worked. Brought 'em in, washed well, chopped, added these last. Simmered for five.

All this went over the top of some very week-old semi-frozen fridge rice that perked right up with hot soup on it. Lime would've been good but I didn't have it.

There you have it. Medicinal, warming, stretches three chicken thighs, lots of veg, and I could save half the coconut milk for a next thing. Probably has three big servings in it.

Make soup of what you have, out of what you need.

CHAPTER 6

Still Dreaming Wild Disability Justice Dreams at the End of the World

Remember back in 2019, before you survived, when you got cancer and we were all afraid you would die, either from the cancer or from the surgeon's medical neglect killing you when you were on the table? Remember when it was 2018, the first year disabled people built a network that gave out 80,000 masks in one month during the wildfires? The first time you heard the term "large-scale air emergency," but not the last. Remember the first time you saw disability justice listed as a section in the library, Audre Lorde and Leroy Moore's faces next to each other on the shelf Dustin Gibson created? Remember when guaranteed annual income went through, when subminimum wage got lifted and people on benefits could keep our income for the first time? Remember the medical abuse reparation payouts? Remember when the Judge Rotenberg Center and the last forced-treatment facilities for autistic youth closed and we had the mourning and celebration ceremonies? Remember when you first were stockpiling masks, water, and gas, before you had the whole crip of color elder farm we live on and roll through now? Remember when we first built the memorial for everyone we lost—Carrie Ann Lucas, Steve, all of them?

In the spring of 2019, Alice Wong of the Disability Visibility Project asked me to write a follow up to my 2017 essay "Cripping the Apocalypse: Some of My Wild Disability Justice Dreams" for her anthology *Disability Visibility: First-Person Stories from the Twenty-First Century*. I said yes. And then I had a very hard time writing it. It's hard to dream when you're terrified, and these were and are terrifying times. The nonstop repeat blunt force traumas of the last three years, of Trumpism, the horrors that are often beyond the worst we could imagine that just keep coming and coming, have put me and so many people I know in a deer-in-the headlights state of freeze. From the concentration camps to the public charge rule, Brett Kavanaugh's ascension to the Supreme Court to Muslim ban number three, forests on fire on all sides of the world and ice melting on both poles: it turns out that the end of the world is easier to read about in a book than to know how to respond to when it happens in real life.

The past year, as I've been on tour with my book, *Care Work: Dreaming Disability Justice*, I've often worn disabled queer Latinx activist Annie Elainey Segarra's T-shirt that says "The Future Is Accessible" to speaking gigs, especially on college campuses. I have this trick during talks where I ask audiences to stop for a minute, close their eyes or go inside and imagine that future. As disability justice movement people, we know that access is just the first step on the way to a liberated disabled future: it's the ramp that gets us in the door to be able to make the future, but it's not the whole of that future. But when I say, "OK, what did you come up with?" there's crickets. They get stuck. The best they can imagine is maybe not dying in a concentration camp.

But as disabled people, we know that one of our biggest gifts is the Mad, sick, disabled, Deaf dreams we are always dreaming, way beyond what we are allowed to dream. And no, I don't mean the inspiration porn, ableist-imagination way that's the only way many ableds can imagine disabled people dream, of "not letting disability stop us!" You know, wanting to walk, to see, or be "normal" above all costs. Being a supercrip or an inspiration, but never human.

I'm talking about the small, huge everyday ways we dream crip revolutions, that span from me looking at myself in the mirror, messy hair and old sweatpants and hurting on day five of a major flare, and saying, *You know what, I'm not going to hate myself today*. To making disabled homes, disabled kinship networks, disabled ways of loving, fighting, and organizing that not even the most talented ableds could dream up in a million years.

And despite all the ways we are in hell, we are still dreaming right now. As I go to three care network meetings a week for friends facing cancer, kidney surgery, and ongoing psych disability needs. As I finally, finally take a deep breath and ask for the care I need most from my friends, and am able to do this because of the collective work done to make accepting that care safe and possible. As I begin to become the disabled middle-aged artist I was afraid of turning into, as I stop flying so much and learn to write and speak and share my work without traveling to Nebraska or Maine, in a community of other disabled writers and artists who are cripping the ways we produce and live excellent disabled artist lives.

We're dreaming brilliant disabled responses to the violence of climate change. Mask Oakland gives out 80,000 free masks during the large-scale air emergency of the fall 2018 California wildfires, and #PowerToBreathe, a network of twelve disability justice organizations, unites during the Kincade Fire of 2019 to create a network of accessible "survival hubs" with generators and air purifiers by and for disabled people organizing to survive PG&E's life-threatening power shutoffs. We're creating Black and brown disability justice public cultural space, as Pittsburgh-based Black disability justice activist Dustin Gibson builds a disability justice library within a neighborhood public library.

Out of our fear, grief, and rage at UnitedHealthcare's denial of a $2,000 antibiotic murdering beloved disabled queer Latinx fat femme activist/lawyer Carrie Ann Lucas, Health Justice Commons establishes the first-ever Medical Abuse Hotline. Disabled sex workers, disabled migrants, disabled prisoners, disabled people who use Medicaid and SSDI self-organized for survival in the face of Trump—and are the reason why Medicaid and the ACA still exist and Trump's "public charge" rule does not.

New disability justice collectives are popping up everywhere, from the Disability Justice Network of Ontario to Detroit Disability Power to Fat Rose. My sibling, queer Korean disabled organizer Stacey Milbern buys and makes accessible her home in East Oakland—the Disability Justice Culture Club—with $30,000's worth of twenty dollar bills sent in on the first five days of the month from disabled community across the world. And 200 disabled and fat and elder people hold signs that say *irreplaceable* and *#NoBodyIsDisposable* at the Crips and Fatties Close the Camps protest in front of the ICE office in San Francisco—part of a month of daily protests in August 2019 against Trump's tortuous ICE concentration camps—created by fat and disabled people drawing connections from our experiences with being locked up in psych institutions, nursing homes, and back wards with immigrants (including disabled immigrants) being locked up right now.

I am writing this to remember and remind us. Even and especially when we are frozen with fear, we are still collectively dreaming disability justice futures into being.

REMEMBERING THE PAST TO DREAM THE FUTURE: WE HAVE ALWAYS FOUND EACH OTHER

"You know the kind of disabled person who just wants to show up for other disabled people, doesn't ask for any credit, just wants to do the right thing?" my friend Lenny says to me on the phone. Of course I do. I don't tell him, but Lenny's always been that kind of person to me.

Back in the day in Toronto, we were the two houses with homemade ramps on our block. Before gentrification finally triumphed in West End Toronto, our block was full of poor people and comfortably half-broken porches. Years before the modern disability justice movement, Lenny's house was a space where poor, multiracial, queer disabled people would hang out, support each other, plot, and laugh. For years Lenny held "Friday night dinners," where anyone could come over and eat. Lenny would always talk to me about how important it was to him to center the least popular crips: the ones who were cranky, angry, "difficult," crazy in ways that even other crazy people shied away from as "too much." Lenny wanted the people who had the least community, because of all the ways ableism kills through isolation, to feel home.

A couple of weeks before that phone call, I'd been giving a workshop for a local QTPOC community center on care webs: how to create mutual aid networks as disabled people, how to get and give care well. It had gone well for the first half; I'd talked a lot about how much unpaid care work people do, how hard it is to ask for care as sick and disabled racialized people because of all the ways we've been forced to do that work for free, and been punished for needing it. All the ways we are told that good daughters, that queer kids, just show up. All the words about being a burden.

But it got rough when I said, "OK, so think of a need you have and take a minute to brainstorm what you would need to get it met well!" People said, "I'm sorry, can you explain again?" a couple times. The temperature in the room dropped ten degrees. I did the facilitator thing where I said, "Hey, I'm noticing some tension, do people want to talk about it?" And they did. They were pissed because they thought I was giving them some fairy tale about something they'd never seen happen: care. Some of them said they didn't believe that disabled people had *ever* received good care.

Standing at the front of that sad, angry, triggered-ass circle of people, I felt a lot of things. I felt really fucking sad. I felt stupid. Like, how had I somehow not remembered when I was planning the workshop that so many disabled and sick people have no experience of care without being treated like shit? And a part of me was also incredulous, frustrated, and pissed off. Inside, I was like, *C'mon, no one ever gave you a cigarette when you were in line at the food-stamp office, no one ever brought you some takeout when you were sick? I had my own poor person, where is your hustle?*

But I also got it. In the past fifteen years since the term "disability justice" was invented by a small group of intersectional, radical disabled people, we have done so much, found each other, changed the world. We've made it so that there is a disabled movement that is not white, male, and cis, where disabled issues can be the police murder of disabled Black and brown people and the desirability ableist Olympiad within QTPOC community. We've created deep disabled communities and ways of thriving. Of course I had so many examples of disabled care webs, imperfect, and beautiful. I have a decade of archived, lively chat threads from Sick and Disabled Queers[60] (SDQ) on my computer, memories of the times we fundraised to get my friend a wheelchair-accessible van that we wanted to also be a community-based Access-A-Ride or when people mailed pills to total strangers who'd run out. All flying under the abled radar, all unfunded, except by us. And more than the fundraisers and care collectives: the ways we have hung out without trying to "fix" each other, gone to visit friends in nursing homes and played board games, creating friendships and community hangouts disabled at the core. We saved each other's lives. And yet, if you weren't there at that exact right moment in 2013 on SDQ, that world could still be so invisible if you didn't know where to find us.

As disabled people, we're hyper visible and invisible at the same time. Stared at and unseen, our work and lives erased. I think some of our strongest power lies in what a friend calls "revolutionary obscurity." We organize in ways unknowable to the abled, so we slide under their radar. You don't join disability justice by paying dues to some national DJ organization. Disability justice exists every place two disabled people meet at a kitchen table, on heating pads in bed talking to our loves. Anyone can be a part of disability justice if they organize

---

60 Sick and Disabled Queers is a long-running Facebook group founded by Mizrahi queer and genderqueer disabled activist William Maria Rain in November 2010 as an online disability justice space centering disabled BIPOC queer and trans people. It became a locus for disabled community, relationship building, thinking, resource building, and organizing.

from their own spoons, their own bodies and minds, their own sense of what their communities need.

Foundations are starting to figure out that "disability justice" is the hot new thing they want to fund, and while we could use money, we certainly know what that usually does to movements: that the nonprofit/foundation industrial complex has a long and storied history of investing in and then destabilizing and defanging movements. Pitting groups against each other, often giving money to the whitest and the lightest, the ones with the most degrees and 501(c)(3)s. The money is so complicated, and not complicated at all—but tempting. We rack our brains trying to figure out how and what kind to take. I don't think there's one right answer, or that the money is even the most risky to us—but the pull we might feel as DJ gets bigger and people who aren't us think it matters, to move away from the ragged, fully horizontal movement of nobodies where anyone can have an idea, anyone can lead, that we have been, to one where only the crips who have the degrees and the words that make sense to those in power are anointed as stars.

I firmly believe, as I have since I was a young radical studying guerilla warfare, that our power is the strongest when we employ a diversity of tactics on our own terms—tactics that build our strengths, that strike where the enemy is weak or has a gap. We do best when we fight to win on our own disabled terms. Don't compromise. Make something disabled and wonderful.

When I fear loss of everything, I remember that before we had a word for ourselves, we still found each other. In Lenny's house, on our janky homemade-ramped front porches. And in nursing homes, in jails, in psych wards, and yes, in camps. I know that no matter how dire the circumstances, we will always keep finding each other. We always have. We will always find each other whether we are exalted as the flavor of the week or targeted for elimination, or both.

WILDER, LIKE WILDFIRES

I keep talking about wild disabled dreaming, so here's some wild-ass disabled dreams for some of what might come next:

As our networks, people, collectives, and cultural groups grow, do we want to imagine a loosely organized network of communication between us? Do we want to come up with principles of how to act in solidarity with each other when foundations or systems of power try to make us compete? For when harm and power struggles inevitably happen?

Disabled radical people—particularly BIPOC, queer and trans, and other folks—are going to keep writing, creating, and making art. What structures do we want to create to build with each other?

Social media has been a huge tool we've used to connect and break isolation over the past decade-plus, but Facebook, Instagram, and most social media sites increasingly choke-hold and shadow ban so many of us from being able to post, or be findable if we do post. What if we made our own social media communication network?

The old disability rights guard is angry at disability justice people because we've actually succeeded in getting more people to buy into being disabled, because we aren't racist and we're not just focused on policy work. We're focused on building homes, building a million weird little groups and actions and projects and Instagram hashtags and media and stories and rampshares and MCS-toolkit lending-libraries and housing projects and sex parties. So what happens if we can take over the Centers for Independent Living and the disability studies programs—or make something entirely new? An Interdependence and Independence Center, not a Center for Independent Living?

We've got twenty-five years until BIPOC are in the majority in the United States, and one of the wins of DJ is that more and more younger BIPOC are less afraid of disability—claiming it or integrating it into their activism. What do we do with this potential?

As we're pushed out of coastal cities due to hypergentification and rising sea levels, what new disabled homes and communities will we build in the exurbs and wastelands? What crip homespaces will we build in the islands that were Florida, in the rust belt, and on the rez?

What happens if we crip the Green New Deal? What if all those promised green infrastructures and jobs centered disability justice from the beginning?

As we both push to maintain Medicaid but know that existing structures of paid care attendants are underpaid, abusive, and difficult for many of us to access; and as we grow collective care structures but know that for many of us, they are not accessible due to our desire to have someone other than our friends wipe our asses, a lack of friends / social capital, or our knowledge that even if we have those things, people get exhausted: What are our dreams of a collective mutual aid network, of a society where free, just, non-gatekept care is a human right for all? What if we could make a society-wide care mutual-aid system based on disability justice principles? I'm thinking of something like the society in Ursula K. Le Guin's *The*

Dispossessed, where the anarcho-syndicalist *moon* had housing, work, and storehouses of needed items available for all. What if everyone had access to care like that? What if the right to care and access was in a foundational document of any new government? What if there was a Care Act in local Indigenous, city, state, or bioregional areas?

When she wrote the text for her housing fundraiser, Stacey Milbern said, "Disability justice dreams are what got me here and I'm going to keep banking on them."

Sure, maybe we'll all be dead in five years because of all the climate change–fueled wildfire smoke circling the planet. But I know we have continued through total adversity before. And I know this:

We have what we always have had, and more.
We know how to mourn
to pray
to persist
to find resistance in the smallest of spaces
to find each other and make homes, alone and together
to lay down in the middle of the road and keen with grief and rage
and block traffic
to crip innovate
to do some shit that no one says is possible
to do something wild and unexpected under the radar
to keep going.

THE FREE LIBRARY OF BEAUTIFUL ADAPTIVE THINGS

I'm browsing through my email when my eye falls on an announcement from my local library that they are rolling out their new Library of Things. I am charmed and read on. At the Library of Things[61] you can check out birding backpacks, fishing tackle and boxes, musical instruments, light therapy boxes (it's Seattle, we have no sun for six months of the year), and—wait for it—adaptive devices, or "Aids for Better Living for Individuals with Disabilities," as the website calls them.

I click the link and the website explains, in a big, accessible font and plain language, what everything is and what kinds of disabilities it might be useful for. There are all kinds of Things: adaptive controllers for Xboxes, playing cards with enlarged numbers, grabbers to help someone reach a dropped item, rose- and yellow-colored glasses to help people with migraines and TBIs use screens for longer, basic AAC (Augmentative and Alternative Communication) devices for nonspeaking people, utensils with soft foam handles for people who have a hard time grasping, and utensils with weighted handles to steady hand tremors.

I'm blinking back tears. The Library is so beautiful. And I'm forty-six years old and this is the first time I've seen anything like it. It's so

---

61 In case you too want to check out this lovely program: https://www.trl.org/library-things. Libraries of Things are a growing program—start one in your community!

much easier to find information about right-to-die legislation push-ing euthanasia for disabled people than an adaptive-device library that might help make your life rock.

There are many times I could have used The Library of Adaptive Things to Help My Disabled Life Be More Awesome: to try out a new device without paying for it, to use it for a little while if I only needed it temporarily, to not have to pay for it when I was poor, to be able to access it without having to have a series of arguments with my doctor or insurance provider that I should be able to access it. It's so hard for many newly disabled, or newly disabled-in-a-different-way people to try a wheelchair or a jar opener—because of lack of access to money and medicine and because shame and internalized ableism tells us that using any of those things is pathetic, but also because it's so hard to find information about adaptive technology at all. Have you ever tried to research using a new adaptive device? Was the info about it easy to find, and was it easy to find devices that were cute and affordable? Or were you hesitantly googling, getting overwhelmed, and putting your computer down, defeated?

And how often, if ever, have you had a doctor who was positive and encouraging and well-informed and offered you information about different adaptive tools, access hacks, or crip tricks? Mostly never, right? I have so many stories in my head of times when practi-tioners from community acupuncturists to rheumatologists reacted with shock and barely concealed disgust when they noticed my cane. They've said things like, "How long have you been using ... that?" or "Well, we'll have to get rid of that ugly thing as soon as possible!" When I've subluxed my joints, it was other disabled people who offered that using forearm crutches or a wheelchair would give me mobility and take the weight off my knees, allowing them to heal—not doctors, who literally gasped when I asked if using a wheelchair might allow my knees to heal. I have a robust disabled community who can remind me that adaptive devices are super cool friends, but I still feel shitty after those encounters with doctors. I know it lands even more harshly on disabled people who don't have that kind of community, often delaying them from trying out a mobility device for months or years. These encounters shape people's whole experiences of disability, turning what could be a neutral or joyful experience to an onerous burden.

The Library creates space for a more playful, curious, and flexible space to explore disability and changing access needs. One where disability is a matter-of-fact everyday reality, and of course here is this publicly accessible free library of tools that can help you live it well.

I want one in every neighborhood.

CHAPTER 7

The Future Is Disabled (with Karine Myrgianie Jean-François, Nelly Bassily, Sage Lovell, Sarah Jama, and Syrus Marus Ware)

As disabled people, we're told in a million ways we're lucky to even be allowed to exist. But our disabled lives are luscious and we are dreaming new futures into being all the time. I see it in places like @Disabledpersonals, the disabled personal IG account where so many disabled folks are building love and connection with each other, or in the life of queer fat femme Latinx disabled lawyer, activist, and mom Carrie Ann Lucas, described by her friend Amy Robertson as maybe "the only wheelchair-using Latina with a bumper sticker reading 'just another disabled lesbian for Christ,' dressed in camo, driving her trak-chair into the wilderness in search of the perfect photo."[62]

Dreaming not just what we're against, but dreaming what we're for, is just what's needed right now. Lucky thing that being unapologetic and brazen, and living wild, magic disabled lives is something disabled folks are great at. I asked some disabled writers, artists, and organizers who are doing incredible work in Canada to tell me

---

62 Tina Griego, "Disability-Rights Advocate Carrie Ann Lucas, 1971–2019, a 'Bad-Ass' to the End," *Colorado Independent*, February 28, 2019, https://www.coloradoindependent.com/2019/02/28/remembering-disability-rights-carrie-ann-lucas/.

their wild dreams of a free disabled future. What will it look like when we win?

KARINE MYRGIANIE JEAN-FRANÇOIS AND NELLY BASSILY, DAWN (DISABLED WOMEN'S NETWORK) CANADA

A future where disability justice won looks like queer, trans, Black, Indigenous, folks of colour, and women, girls, and nonbinary humans are living in a world where disability is the norm, and where access is no longer a question but a *fait accompli*. Gone are the days where our disabled bodies and minds are compared to the able-bodied and able-minded. We've flipped the script. We still like our non-queer, non–people of colour, non-disabled friends and we'll have them at our fully accessible dance parties (which include comfy chairs and couches for our aches and pains, subwoofers that make you feel the vibrations, active listeners, and personal support workers, so we can fully enjoy our time out, and plenty of room as well as fully accessible bathrooms for wheelchair-users to dance, dance, and dance as well as pee with ease, and no stairs in sight and clear paths to sway or rest as we please).

Because, please, did you really think this could go on, this able-bodied and -minded domination? It's not that we've flipped the script to exert power and replicate oppressions on our able-bodied and able-minded friends, they just over time learned to not take up so much space and not be offended or feel left out if we don't organize with them in mind. Actually, in our accessible/disabled future, binaries are broken. We fully live on and in the spectrum of possibilities of non-stigmatized minds and bodies. In this spectrum, we are fully connected to one another, which means that decolonization has happened and is still happening and that patriarchy has been toppled and much more. This interconnectedness that we now live daily means that sometimes our able-bodied and able-minded friends are learning every day, including from their mistakes, and are understanding in how many ways our differences and disabilities manifest. This also means that we have collectively built this future and thus have learned and understood differences and disabilities, and all of us are still doing that important work even when it is hard because this future world is ours!

SAGE LOVELL, DEAF SPECTRUM

When thinking about making a more accessible future for d/Deaf folks, I could think of many ways to create this accessible world, and I'm going to mention the main ways to do this.

First of all, we need to ensure that d/Deaf children have access to sign language to prevent them from experiencing language deprivation, which can have disastrous effects on our development and well-being. With language acquisition, d/Deaf children have a better chance of obtaining a prosperous future. Having a language means Deaf folks would be able to gain access to education and future employment opportunities.

Now, education needs to become more accessible for Deaf folks by meeting their basic educational needs. What does accessible education look like? Having sign language and disability education being part of the K–12 curriculum because we need Deaf and disability representation, which would normalize Deafness and disability.

Accessible education also means free education for those who would like to attend Gallaudet University or National Technical Institute of the Deaf and providing interpreters for any of their educational needs without limitations.

Currently, the unemployment/underemployment rate for Deaf folks in Canada stands at around eighty percent. Only twenty percent of d/Deaf folks earn enough to maintain a sustainable lifestyle without scarcity. In the future, I hope that more job opportunities open up for Deaf people that include positions such as teachers, actors, politicians, doctors, lawyers, interpreters, and more. Having Deaf representation working in positions of power can significantly shift how mainstream society perceives us Deaf folks because, unfortunately, oftentimes we are perceived as unintelligent, weak, and helpless. Having Deaf folks being part of the decision-making process for all levels of government would lead to creating changes through legislation.

Lastly, but not the least: we need more Black, Indigenous, people of color (BIPOC) working as interpreters, as the number of BIPOC interpreters is at a disproportionally low rate in comparison to white people. Deaf BIPOC communities need interpreters that represent them; to have BIPOC interpreters understand what it's like to experience racism; and to minimize the racist experiences that Deaf folks have with white sign language interpreters.

To wrap up, the four main things we need to focus on to make a more accessible future for Deaf folks are: language acquisition, accessible education, job opportunities, and BIPOC interpreters.

SARAH JAMA, THE DISABILITY JUSTICE NETWORK OF ONTARIO

The Disability Justice Network of Ontario is working toward a world where people with disabilities are free to be. We aim to build a just and accessible Ontario, wherein people with disabilities have personal and political agency, can thrive and foster community, and build the power, capacity, and skills needed to hold people, communities, and institutions responsible for the spaces they create.

For too long, conversations around disabled people have circled around our need to participate in society, predicated on our ability to achieve certain milestones: go to school, get a job, raise a family, have sex, or travel to faraway places. But these conversations always stop at the tip of the iceberg. What happens once we are in school, are employed, start building a family, or express our sexuality? Are we safe and supported along the way? Or is each milestone enough for society to wash its hands? What about our comrades whose bodies and minds are too radical for today's conceptions of employment, or too radical to sustain nuclear families, or who don't fit in any of the boxes that we keep on being shoved into?

We want to see a world where people are free to be, regardless of their ability to fit into capitalist institutions that say we are nothing if not the right kind of fodder for the system. This looks like: universal basic income, dignified and accessible housing, free health care and pharmacare, and health care systems that treat us like we have value even after we turn eighteen. This looks like an education system that fosters collectivity and passion and deeply rooted love for those around us. This looks like the abolishment of our prison systems, police, and the RCMP (Royal Canadian Mounted Police), all of which have colonial roots and have been created to eliminate bodies and minds that aren't controllable by the state (hundreds of people with disabilities have been killed by law enforcement in Canada, many of whom were racialized, simply because their disability was seen as a danger). A world that has disability justice is a world where we are all free to be, regardless of race, religion, geographic location, sexual orientation, age, or disability.

SYRUS MARCUS WARE, BLACK TRANS DISABLED ARTIST AND SCHOLAR

My disabled future is Black. Black like the holes at the centres of every galaxy. Black like the sticky tar on every piece of cracked and broken asphalt in every working-class hood. Black like a million crips strong, finally finished our fight for disability justice and freedom. Black like the night sky when we can finally rest, lying on blankets in the hot summer night waiting for the Perseid meteor showers to fall.

My disabled future is accessible. Accessible like everyone is self-determined. Accessible like hot and sexy as we want to be. Accessible like being able to wake up and live a free life, in charge of our own destinies. Accessible like we all make it.

My disabled future is trans* with the stardust asterisk Marquis Bey describes. Trans* like everything and anything is possible. Trans* like we're still fucking here, in the words of Miss Major. Trans* like crip gender magic.

My disabled future is life, as long as I want it, and death when I want it.

LEAH

There is no one disabled future. But in mine, there is guaranteed income, housing, access, food, water, and education for all—or money has been abolished. I get paid to write from my bed. The births of disabled, Autistic, Mad, Neurodivergent, Deaf, and sick kids are celebrated, and there are memorials and healing and reparation sites on every psych ward, institution, nursing home, youth lockup, and "autistic treatment center" where our people have been locked up and abused. Anyone who needs care gets it, with respect and autonomy, not abuse. Caregivers are paid well for the work we do and are often disabled ourselves. Disabled folks are the ones teaching medical school students about our bodies. Schools have been taken apart and remade so that there's not one idea of "smart" and "stupid," but many ways of learning. There is a disability justice section in every bookstore and a million examples of sick and disabled and Deaf and autistic and Mad folks thriving. I have a really sick lipstick-red spiral ramp curving around my house.

Because it's beautiful. Because I want it. Because I get to live free.

PART II

THE STORIES THAT KEEP US ALIVE: DISABILITY JUSTICE ARTS IN THE INTERREGNUM

The function of art is to do more than tell it like it is—
it's to imagine what is possible.
—bell hooks

No one can stop Change, but we all shape Change
whether we mean to or not.
—OCTAVIA BUTLER

CHAPTER 8

Twenty Questions for Disability Justice Art Dreaming: A Winter Solstice Present

My experience with being a disabled creator/writer in 2019 is a trip, and definitely not everyone's. I'm that weird, rare thing: a cranky, middle-aged brown, queer writer who is sick, autistic, and crazy, doesn't have a trust fund or a rich partner, and somehow still makes a living from disabled writing, teaching, and organizing (and occasional tarot-card reading and weird gigs). I'm offered a lot of gigs, which is a mixed blessing—it's a lot better than being offered no work, which has often been the case in my life. But, like many disabled creators, many of my gig requests mean being asked to do things for abled people on their timeline and (limited) sense of things. It's "We totally forgot about access at the festival, could you help us, it's starting in forty-eight hours?" or "Can you tell our whole org everything about DJ in thirty minutes on their lunch break?" All of them want it in the next few days. All the emails are titled "Urgent."

Those asks, they set up a paradigm where as a disabled creator, I am there to Fix It. They're not an invite to stare out the window being unproductive, thinking up a next poem or disabled performance or weird art thing. The people asking me may have learned about me through my writing and art, but that's not what they're paying for. They're not paying for creativity, for wild, well-funded disabled writing and performance art. They're paying for utility, for me providing a service to abled people, on an abled agenda.

I know a lot of disabled artists and creators who also do Access 101 or access audits or DJ 101 workshops or panel discussions, for forever and increasingly as DJ gets more visibility and ableds are like, *Oh, this is something we should do something about*. Weird disabled poems and performance and art things don't pay the bills, and many of us have figured that doing talks and trainings are a better-compensated side hustle that can pay some bills and buy some time to do some art work. There's nothing wrong with doing this.

But it's a fascinating dynamic, because disability justice is so strongly rooted in cultural work—so much of the work we've done has been writing, art, performance, stories—cultural workers are some (not all) of the most visible DJ people abled organizations hit up when they need a speaker or someone to teach them How to DJ. This setup puts us in a position where we're responding to abled need out of both our need for money and our wish to do good, do something practical that makes change: "OK, I guess they need help ... I guess it's an opportunity to put disability on the agenda ... so I guess I'll do it."

I'm not shaming any of us for taking that gig or doing that work. For many of us, any work is something we can't afford to say no to; any offer to do any kind of disabled work is an even richer one. But these offers and their ways of conceiving of disabled art practice can creep in and limit our vision. They keep the reference point the "abled" need, not the disabled imagination. They can eat into both our time and our consciousness, take us away from what *we* want to do—from that groundbreaking disabled cultural work we might otherwise be dreaming up. It's hard to say no to offers to be the paid fix-it guy, and to keep insisting on our "crazy," "unproductive," disabled creative space—on our own agenda, our own priorities.

As disability justice creatives, we are a phenomenal disabled richness within an ableist scarcity wasteland. One that's not often recognized, but I do. We have so many, many amazing things we are creating, dreaming, thinking, and doing, in the midst of a society that is still in the negative balance when it comes to thinking about anything disabled. It is no mistake or surprise that so much of the work and organizing of DJ has been cultural work. Disability justice performance art collective Sins Invalid[63] from its inception has been an audacious disability justice art dream—*of course* you can advance a disability justice agenda and transform the world and people's hearts and minds by creating truly WILD performance art about disability, race, sex, kink, medical torture, desire, and isolation.

There is still critically little space or resources that support us as disabled creatives, period—and even less for making art that puts a crip perspective on traditional art practice and art forms. Our wild disability justice artist dreams, the ways we bend and reshape traditional neurotypical and abled art practices, or with autistic/disabled/sick/Deaf audacity, view them as irrelevant, are way beyond the radar of most abled curators, funders, and the people who hire us. They may never understand or value us. We do it anyway. And, as the disabled dance artist and choreographer Alice Sheppard and I discussed recently, we deserve space to do ambitious, jaw-dropping, huge, and complicated work—not just the 101, not just a "this is what my disability means," not just simple stories of empowerment. We deserve to make big weird complicated ugly confusing work.

63 Sins Invalid: An Unshamed Claim to Beauty in the Face of Invisibility: http://www.sinsinvalid.org.

So for you, the wild and wonderful disability justice artists who are my comrades and kin, I have written this following series of meditative questions for disabled creatives, out of this specific time where we are more on the abled radar, where we are being asked to do things we don't quite hate, but which take us away from the sweet dark disabled places inside, where our weird, honest, disabled, incomprehensible gifts grow. As I write this in winter and the Northern Hemisphere grows dark, many of us have the possibility of turning to what disabled Black and Indigenous queer ancestor Ibrahim Farajajé referred to as "luminous endarkment"[64]—a sacred Dark time, a quiet, inward, bed time. A crip space of creation and possibility.

These questions are a potential deep space of disabled healing. A place where, as we begin to sometimes be more visible to the abled gaze, we can return our focus, our choices, our agenda to ourselves. They are places we can heal the wounding of ableism, by re-centering ourselves, by making ourselves the fuck-normal normal, by honoring all the disabled skills, brilliance, and gifts we have.

So I ask you:

- Where is your disabled existence/experience at right now? What's new? What are you learning, amazed by? What is kicking your ass? What are you bored by?

- What kind of crip art community are you a part of? (One person counts. People you've never met count. Nonhuman beings count. Yourself, alone, with a book counts.) Where are things at with them? How are your relationships with them? What needs tending, mending, real-talk conversations, or celebration?

64 Taya Mâ, "Luminous Dark," *Taya Mâ* (blog), August 7, 2014, http://taya.ma/luminousdark.

- Where is the community at in terms of issues we're facing, internal "isms," big political things impacting us, and dreams for the future?
- What's the latest thing you learned from someone else who is a disabled friend / artist / collaborator / someone you admire / someone who made a meme? The latest thing you were enraged or amazed by?
- Who do you want to collaborate with? How will you build that relationship?
- What do you want to learn next? What new artistic skill, or administrative or organizational skill? How will you learn it in a disabled way? Disabled skill?
- What is the lineage of crip art creation you are rooted in right now, and always? How do you honor, reference, and relate to it? What's the next piece of work you want to add to it?
- When you start planning your art, cultural, whatever project: how are you thinking about disability? From the beginning? Wait, are you?
- Tell me, and yourself, all your secret, internal crip shit. What did you figure out this week about yourself? What do you want to figure out? (I'll start: I figured out I can work only seven hours a day. I know, wild. I mean, of course I can do more—and have done more hours—but this is what works for my body. Also, I will never wake up easily and be at work at nine a.m.! I have brain fog! Why not stop fighting it and just accept that my workday starts consistently at eleven a.m.?)

- How much time, space, etc., do you really need? Like really? How much wiggle room when you get sick, when something falls apart (surprise, not surprise)?
- What are your needs? Wait, I did that too fast—I know, some of you may be saying, "what's a need," again? OK, so ...
- What are the needs you're comfortable-ish stating out loud, and what are the ones you can barely whisper to yourself, and what are the ones you're not even letting yourself dare to dream?
- Can you take a minute to honor all the ways you've survived, quite handily, by having no needs? Shoving those holy sacred disabled needs in the closet, taking whatever you could get and making it shine? Taking care of all your shit on your own, quietly, in the background, where you knew you would get it right and no one would see? We all have done this, we all are in a process of unlearning this, we all still have to do it sometimes.
- What do you want to offer? You, on your own terms? What's the one or several disabled art things that only you can offer?
- What are the skills your disability, Deafness, neurodivergence, sickness give you that abled, hearing, neurotypical people don't have?
- What disabled art practice or project gives you the most pleasure to imagine creating?
- What's your wildest, no-holds-barred, disabled dreaming? The stuff you don't even let yourself think about because there's no way it could happen, it's illegal, it's foolish, there's no way you could ever ...
- What would it take to start making it happen?

CHAPTER 9

I Wanna Be with You Everywhere (And I Am): Disability Justice Art as Freedom Portal

Every time and place we inhabit is crip time, the forms of it are just always evolving. When I wrote this piece, I was living in the kind of crip time that's being in the I Haven't Seen Anyone for Three Months Club of pandemic immunocompromised homelife, organizing with other disabled Black and brown people from a laptop in bed in-between wiping down the grocery delivery. During a global pandemic it's increasingly very hard to remember the kind of crip space/time that was sitting in a big New York performance space with 300 other disabled people.

Yet, in April 2019, that's exactly where I was. I was in New York at Performance Space New York (PSNY) and the Whitney Museum as a performer, coconspirator, and enthralled audience member in *I wanna be with you everywhere* (IWBWYE), "a gathering of, by, and for disabled artists and writers and anyone who wants to get with us for a series of crip meet-ups, performances, readings and other social spaces of surplus, abundance and joy." I was in a room of 300 disabled people flirting, talking, stimming, and resting, coming back night after night to see disabled art and be with disabled people. Featuring performances and readings by Eli Clare, John Lee Clark, Kayla Hamilton, Johanna Hedva, Jerron Herman, Cyrée

Jarelle Johnson, Camisha L. Jones, me, Jordan Lord, NEVE, and Alice Sheppard, the cast was all disabled and Deaf and vast majority Black and brown queer, trans, and genderqueer artists.

The show also featured stuff you don't see every day or, let's be real, ever: five rows of "creative adaptive device" seating in the front, right in front of giant featherbeds called Buffies people with pain (including yours truly) were lying on to watch the show (fuck a chair), a sensory-friendly room designed by and for neurodivergent people with a ton of free ear defenders, pillowforts in the corners where you could recline on bean bags draped with curtains, coloring books, and someone's seashell collection. Killer ASL and captioning of course, but when I say captioning I mean the captions were projected on huge screens over my shoulder as I read, seamlessly integrated into the gorgeous and professional light and sound design for the show. When I tell you there was audio description, I don't mean the kind of terrible and functional robot voice I've often experienced audio description as being, but my memory of one of the audio describers dancing in her wheelchair with joy as she whispered audio description of Jerron Herman's closing disabled vogue jam performance (where the whole crip audience joined in) into her headset.

I mean all the ways I experienced this show as being a kind of opulent yet accessible disabled next-level luxury. A disability justice temporary autonomous disabled zone that showed us what was possible, that was a portal to a disabled future. And that's what I believe the function of DJ art is.

I wanted to write this down, what IWBWYE was like, as part of an ongoing archive of that DJ art work. So you can read about if it you weren't there. Because our disability justice culture spaces, and freedom portals, need to be remembered. Because this could be a handy road map to how you might do something like it, or completely different, in your town.

———

I've been a disabled writer, performance artist, and producer for twenty-some years. I've seen the gamut of disability in performance. I've been there in the years where basic access, let alone disabled culture, wasn't on the radar of the collectives I worked with—where of course the space was up a flight of stairs, or three, and event producers shrugged defensively if anyone brought this up. I include myself in their number. We weren't always being total jerks about it. We were cash-poor, marginalized queer of color artists who every space said no to, taking what we could get. The scarcity we were making art in—of money, resources, event spaces, information—was real, and so was our particular kind of internalized ableism that queer and trans BIPOC people—disabled, closeted disabled, and abled—have. The response I/we often made to access requests went along the lines of, *We could barely pay ourselves, and you want a ramp?* It came out of both complete exhaustion at how hard it was to get any event space, let alone an accessible one, and making shows on a $200 budget, and anger at the gall of disabled people to ask for something.

In 2009 I was incredibly lucky and got hired to be a featured performer with Sins Invalid, the game-changing disability justice performance collective that's one of the origin places of disability justice. Sins was the first place I saw a deep cripping of the arts, and it changed everything about what I thought was possible in terms of both access and disabled culture and realities in performance art. It was where we started tech week (a week, not the two hours I was used to—or, let's be real, more like a panicked twenty minutes before the show started) with an hours-long access check-in. The first thing performers, staff, and curators did was say what our body/mind needs and realities were, and that crip knowledge wasn't a hasty add on—it was the foundational knowledge we built our rehearsal, tech, and performance around. This was just the first instance of some deep crip abundance. *Of course* there was a huge spread of food accessible to everyone's dietary needs. Of course there was audio description, captions on all the videos, skilled ASL interpretation by interpreters who specialized in working with performance, and a huge mobility device–user seating area (not the paltry one or two spots with crappy sight lines wayyyyy in the back that's often the standard in theaters). Of course the access we offered grew each year: fragrance-free one year, with BIPOC ushers we hired for their ability to communicate without shaming BIPOC audience members who have cultural ties to fragrance, including all-my-hair-stuff-is-scented, without shaming us, *à la* "Hey, you smell great! There are some folks sitting here who are allergic / have cancer, would you mind sitting over here?" Trauma-informed counselors hanging out the next year, there if people needed a place to unpack watching a scene that dealt with medical trauma, sterilization, and race. And out of this crip performance abundance, of course the audience and the performers together made a lush world of disabled joy, flirting, talking, signing, dressed up and in pajamas.

Like many other disabled artists I know who got brought in to Sins, I felt spoiled and forever changed after my first run with them. Going back to non-disabled performance spaces that sucked at access and had zero disabled awareness was incredibly hard, after seeing how rich disabled performance could be when access and crip understandings was a cornerstone, not a begrudging afterthought. I wanted everything to be different. I ran smack into a place many crip artists, expecially BIPOC crip artists, run into: being "the disabled one" who becomes the only one talking about access and shouldering the work of making it happen in an arts collective. We do a lot and often feel glad to help, but it's incredibly stressful being the one crip trying to make cross-disability access happen single-handedly, without institutional support.

For years, despite trying to bring accessibility to collectives I worked with, working as an "access czar" for queer of color performance spaces and, with my friend Syrus Marcus Ware, co-founding Performance/Disability/Art (a.k.a. PDA, a small, Toronto-based disability justice performing art collective), it still often felt like Sins was the only game in town when it came to Black and brown disabled queer performance with high production values. The other small number of disabled performance collectives I knew of were either lead by white disabled performers and dominated by whiteness, or were very underresourced disabled BIPOC collectives with great art but limited ability to pull off an ambitiously production-valued show. I was glad Sins was there: I knew there were people experimenting with making DJ art all over; I wondered when there would be more than one large-scale DJ arts group so we could be in conversation. With this show, I felt like we had finally arrived: there was more than one of us. And I was glad. We need and deserve to be many, and to be in conversation.

I wanna be with you everywhere was a big fuck you to the tremulously earnest yet half-assed "inclusion" (one disabled artist in an all-abled show; lots of earnest, "good for them!" abled claps) and "Do you want to *say more* about your disability?" models that are all disabled artists often get when we try and get our work into non-disabled space. By the latter, I mean the assumption that all disabled art can do is a 101 explanation of what sick and disabled and Deaf is to a presumed all-abled, hearing, and NT audience. We want to be able to do work that both assumes we're speaking to a disabled/Deaf/ND audience that is lushly diverse in its experiences of disability and is also steeped in disabled aesthetics, in-jokes, experiences, and languages. As festival organizers wrote in the show notes: "IWBWYE refuses policies of individuation and inclusion in favor of (and in the flavor of) whatever disability aesthetics has in bodymind. We won't know what this is 'til it shows us, but we do know that disability communities don't only make art about disability. ;) (winky face emoji)"[65]

For too long, when we've had space at all, we've been asked in a million ways to tokenize ourselves, accept being the only crip artist on the lineup without question and to represent all disabled people, asked to pay for and do all the work of access ourselves. We're also expected to create artwork that's inspiration porn or a laborious 101 explanation, where the audience is always assumed to be abled. Instead, IWBWYE assumed a space of disabled playfulness, insider language, crip joy, and potential.

---

65 Show notes, "I wanna be with you everywhere," *Performance Space New York*, April 2019, https://performancespacenewyork.org/shows/i-wanna-be-with-you-everywhere/.

A MAJOR SENSE OF EASE

The show notes continued, "Programs and events will unfold across each evening, but there's also going to be a major sense of ease. There's time in between events for hanging out—both in and of itself, and in resistance to the inaccessible infrastructure that so often keeps us physically separated."[66]

A *major sense of ease*. Those words stick with me. So much of the time in non-crip performance, there is a major sense of no ease. Lack of access is as much about the assumption that everything must happen at a breakneck pace, with no shifting to make room for a new access reality (lateness, vomit, a panic attack), and/or an attitude of guilt, defensiveness, and "it's impossible, we can't do that" from producers when an access hiccup happens or people ask about access at all, as it is about what equipment is in the theater. For a sphere that prides itself on pushing the envelope, where nothing is too wild—blood and shit smeared on bodies is no problem—performance and theater are remarkably conservative when it comes to cripping performance. This ableism can infect all of us—including me. It is so easy to fall into thinking that the way it's been is the only way it's possible to be.

For example, when I learned that IWBWYE was having only two or three performers a night—with a thirty- to forty-minute break between each set—I felt that incredulous, outraged reaction: *That's not how you do a show! People will be outraged!* I worried people would feel cheated and not come. I thought, *In order to get people to come out, you*

---

66 Show notes, "IWBWYE," https://performancespacenewyork.org/shows/i-wanna-be-with-you-everywhere/.

have to give them the sense that they're going to get their money's worth,
so you need to have a show with six to twelve performers. I felt guilty and
apologetic when I told my friends about the format of the show, and
hoped they'd still come out.

But when I was actually at the festival, experiencing three days
of performance with just two or three performers going deep every
night, I felt this tentative opening blooming in my chest. *Oh. This is
one deep way to crip performance.* Having a show where each night had
just two or three performers gave disabled artists space to relax, enter
into and expand into doing our work, without the pressure to rush to
fit it all in in ten minutes that we often feel. Having a show with this
kind of spaciousness gave audience members with diverse access
needs more room to be present to experience the show in many ways.
Having two or three artists with a forty-five-minute break in between
stopped me from getting overwhelmed as a neurodivergent person
and checking out after the first performer—something I wasn't even
aware I was routinely doing when I went to a traditional show, until
I went to this one. People had ample, luxurious space between performers to go to the bathroom with an attendant, to go outside and
vape, to sit quietly and take a sensory break, to take longer to get back
to their seat than they thought they'd need.

The sensory room—the only one I'd ever seen at an arts performance space—was a work of art itself, not a shitty little storage closet
with some pillows grudgingly given to autistic people. There were
pillow and blanket forts, many comfortable places to lounge, and an
abundance of stim toys and sensory tools—all without gatekeeping.
There wasn't any questioning about your diagnosis, a need to "show
proof," or policing of how people were stimming, communicating, or

being. There was no guarding over the stim toys and access tools, no system where you had to go up and ask someone to give you one, which many people are too shy or scared of being grilled about why they need it to do. They were just there, on a table, free for you to pick up and try and use if you wanted. I picked up my first pair of ear defenders there, fell in love with how they allowed me to be in a big crowded performance space witnessing intense art without getting checked out or overwhelmed, and took them home with me. All of this speaks to a major access factor: a trust in disabled people by disabled people, an openness to a practice of letting people experiment with access tools instead of locking up access and crip tools and doling them out balefully, one at a time.

This spaciousness with time, this open trustingness and generosity around sharing sensory toys, this whole-ass gorgeous sensory room, are the polar opposite of the crip realities found in most performance spaces. The needs for quiet, stimming, trust, and abundant time are access needs not found on an ADA checklist, and are just a few of the many common and everyday access needs disabled performers, staff, and audience members routinely swallow and deal with on our own. We cramp ourselves down to fit our bodyminds into spaces made solely with abled/NT/hearing bodyminds in mind. Or we don't perform, produce, or come to shows at all. Without having to hurry and stifle our bodyminds, we were able to be fully present with the art in a way we are almost never allowed to be. This created a different kind of crip sacred space in the room. It felt holy and treasured, sitting there with many people able to exhale and be crip-present in a way we perhaps had never been before.

IWBWYE is also the only performance space, disabled or abled, I've ever seen that offered a Travel Fund, making good on its promise to not just create lots of space to hang out, but to financially support the most marginalized crips in getting there. Event organizers knew that not only was the New York public transportation system wildly inaccessible, but that a lot of disabled Black and brown people in New York live on the edges of the outer boroughs—in Far Rockaway or the Bronx—and weren't necessarily going to feel up for taking Access-A-Ride or trying to negotiate the subway for a performance art show, no matter how disabled that show was. Knowing this, and knowing that so often disabled people either shell out money for a car service (if we can find one that will take us and our service animals and wheelchairs, one that will not be heavily fragranced), balance the exhaustion and lack of access of public transit with the desire to see a show, or stay home, the event organizers provided people funding to cover the cost of a cab to and from the show. The organizers also gave every performer a travel stipend, or offered accessible hotel rooms a block from the venue. I stayed with my friends who had a kitchen in Brooklyn, but could take a cab to the show every day. I didn't have to blow my spoons on miles of walking, four sets of stairs in each subway. I'd never seen that invisible crip tax of having to come up with an extra fifty to a hundred bucks or more to cover a car to a show, or deal with the stress and violence of public transit, being named and accounted for by a performance.

Once we were there, the more spacious, crip-timed performance schedule allowed us to relax into hanging out and socializing with other disabled people. I'm used to the giddiness of intermission, as well as the time waiting for the show to start and the time hanging out in the lobby and trickling out to the sidewalk after: the temporary community that's formed during a night of performance. The flirting, the dressing up and deciding what clothes you'll wear, the coming tired after work or school, the decision of who you will ask to go with you, or whether you will—sometimes especially to a space of vulnerable, disabled art—come alone. All of that is as much what the show is. When DJ cultural spaces are some of the primary spaces disability community forms around, people want abundant space to hang out and say hi to their friends, in this fought-for, rare accessible space that organizers have made. Often, that hangout space is squeezed, a tight fifteen-minute intermission, the need to start on time and clear out fast so the producers don't get charged. Here, it was an integral part of the joy of the show.

All this ease took disabled work to ensure it happened. We know that one of the cornerstones that accessible events live or die on is whether it works in practice—whatever the nice language on the website is, will all kinds of disabled, Deaf, and ND people be able to buy tickets accessibly and get in the door easily, instead of being stuck out in the cold? After the *New York Times* featured IWBWYE in its hot picks of the week section, we should've felt great, but we were actually scared that abled people would buy up all the advance tickets, fascinated by the novelty of a disabled show, and disabled people who depend on being able to buy tickets in advance to feel safe going would be left out. We got assurances that there would be no wait list, that anyone disabled who showed up could get a ticket, but one event organizer, who knew that they wouldn't look like a fancy art person to the venue staff, but a "nobody" (a fat, working-class white-cane user)—tested out the theory by caning up to the front window and asking about the show, to see how they were treated.

This disabled ease that came out of all that crip practicality and crip creativity, and the ways it expanded how we were able to present and take in art, is a space of crip possibility, not deficiency. And in that crip art practice space I see new worlds opening up. I see it in moments when I witness a hesitant crip, someone who I get the sense this might be the first time she's ventured to a disabled art show, shyly and semi-apologetically ask where the accessible seating is, probably expecting the usual—that it's three bad seats in the back behind a pole—and being told by a bunch of rowdy crips that its the whole first four rows, and our smiles and body languages are welcoming and encouraging. There's more space for more disabled people to feel welcome and come home when there is more space, period.

Most of all, IWBWYE was pure disabled joy. In Herman's disabled dance jam at the end, the slow way more and more disabled people took up space. Dragged chairs onto the dancefloor and danced in them. Disrupting the binary wall of who was a dancer/performer and who wasn't. Taking up space, grooving together.

I was talking with a friend recently about disabled performance, and how we both believe in the right of disabled people to make art that isn't just basic or functional, not 101 or explanatory, but epicly huge and complicated and edge-pushing and wonderful. Work that confuses us and makes us think, and also expands our ideas of disability possibility. That we deserve that. We talked about how doing that kind of work means that we sometimes need Big Theaters, not community-center tiny stages, sound and tech and lights that cost more than $100. How it's complicated to negotiate that, because it means dealing with big abled theater's staff that might be white or male or not know a damn thing about disability. But how we both tentatively felt like at this moment in time, somehow, sometimes, some of us were turning a corner and were able to push and crip venues to make that work happen there, make that access be held, more than ever before. And I also firmly believe that we can and do make crip art spaces on street corners, in the subway, on Zoom. The common denominator is our abundant disabled creativity. The common denominator is the outcome of fifteen-plus years of disability justice cultural work—the making of crip art that is BIPOC and queer—and also fifteen-plus years of making best-practice sheets and access-in-the-arts guides, building relationships with technical staff, mentoring other crip artists and producers, and badgering the doors to open.

In this pandemic, 2022, moment of crip time that is so often inside the walls of our homes, so fearful and surrounded by people who want to kill us, I am grateful to have experienced those four days of big disabled maximalist possibility. I hold the memory close of the last night, where someone put on Fleetwood Mac, and the whole damn crowd sang and signed along, with such wistful fierce crip yearning: I wanna be with you everywhere ...

Because that's all I/we want, isn't it? To be with each other, our crip kin, everywhere everywhere everywhere. To have disabled art joy and eat pierogies lounging on an accessible giant bed, to be dancing in our bodies. To make and know a disabled freedom portal of disabled joy and cripworld pleasure and possibility, to the place where everything can be different.

As disabled artists, when we make crip art spaces like those, we are making—even if it's just for a few hours—the next world that's possible. That people take home with them.

That's why it's important.

CHAPTER 10

Disability Justice Writing, the Beauty and the Difficulty[67]

On June 19, 2010, me and the great Stacey Park Milbern limped and rolled into Community Art Room 156 at the Allied Media Conference (AMC) in Detroit, MI. We were about to co-throw the first writing workshop we'd ever do together in the next eleven years of wild crip Asian femme friendship, coevolution, and comradeship. In the middle of a disability justice movement being born, that we were a part of birthing. The Azolla Story[68] Queer and Trans of Color Disabled and Chronically Ill Love and Zine-Making Workshop was also the first queer and trans disabled POC writing workshop either of us had ever heard of, let alone thrown. That didn't stop us. We just did it. Crip asian brother femme poetic audacity. If she was being a poet on her secret public blog and a disabled community organizer at eighteen, of fucking course she could co-throw a queer disabled BIPOC writing workshop. If I had been writing and teaching writing workshops I made up out of thin air since I was a sick and nuts twenty-two-year-old, so could I.

But I was nervous as hell. I had been disabled since I was twenty-one, but I was still in the early crip "Do I have the right to call myself

---

67 This title is a riff off of Dorothy Allison's essay "Sex Writing, the Importance and the Difficulty."
68 The Azolla Story was one of those early pieces of disability justice history that has mostly disappeared into the mists of time, Myspace-era internet, and the memories of the people who started it and hung out on it—but it was an old-school online message board that was one of the first spaces specifically by and for disabled queer and trans people of color.

disabled?" zone. "Disability justice" as a term was only five years old and our workshop was part of the first DJ track ever held at the AMC. It felt like there were maybe twenty of us angry radical beautiful disabled QTBIPOC across the US who were doing this stuff. It was such a special time, but it also felt like there was so, so much weighing on us to Get It Right. So much hunger and need and expectation, so few role models. Plus, we had been so busy doing crip grunt work of organizing: getting the AMC to order fragrance-free soap for the whole conference and holding down the three accessible dorm suites where we were all posted up—we hadn't created much of a lesson plan. And I didn't even know if anyone would come. Back in the early 2010s, when I would propose having a QTBIPOC-only disabled workshop when colleges asked me to do a visit, the student organizers would say, "Um, isn't that kind of specialized?" In fact sometimes nobody, or only one or two people, would come. Talking about disability in QT/BIPOC spaces still felt brand new, and frightening.

But people did come. The door opened, and opened again, and the room in the community arts building slowly filled with crips of color. It was really quiet. People didn't chat. You could feel the tension in the room, the weight of people's nervous desire for this kind of space.

Into that quiet, Stacey said, her voice clear, "Hi, everyone. OK, it's really simple. What are the queer disabled POC stories we want to tell?"

Crip after crip walked or rolled up to the blackboard, which slowly filled up: *the Hiawatha Asylum for Insane Indians, my mother's polio, my first cane, being in the ICU, crip sex, sex with someone ableist*. We asked people to pick one and write about it. Our second prompt was, *If your body could speak, what stories would it spill?*

Four years later I would start teaching my Frida and Harriet's Children SDQTPOC[69] writing classes online, and I would start class with the same question: What are the sick and disabled QTBIPOC stories you/we are burning to tell? Posing it to students, most of whom had written me asking multiple times if they deserved to be there, if they were really disabled, if they were really a writer. Disabled writing and poetics has been met with a silence. *Who even is a disabled writer? Oh ... Maybe Virginia Woolf?*

In mainstream literature, disabled people are inspirations, tragedies, monsters, hermits, cautionary tales, plagues, warnings. We are Beth from *Little Women*. We are Bertha, Rochester's mad Jamaican first wife locked up in his attic in *Wuthering Heights*. We are symbols, and we are an absence. Rarely do we get to write our stories for ourselves, be disabled writers writing disabled characters. Our literary traditions are erased, our poets and writers dismissed with a "Oh, did she actually identify that way?"

But the reality is crip writing is everywhere and crip bodies are overflowing rivers full of stories we are burning to tell.

When I think of disabled literature and writing, I can think of a breadth of writing that spans decades and generations, that uses the D-word and does not. I think of Audre Lorde—Black Lesbian poet warrior mother, legally blind, living and dying with cancer, whose work shines with the knowledge she gained from living with bodily difference and fighting the medical industrial complex. I think of and have written about Gloria Anzaldúa, queer Latinx maestra who

---

69 Sick and disabled queer and trans people of color

started her period at age three and lived with bodily and reprogenital differences, living and dying with diabetes. Some of my work as a disability justice writer has been to look at the legacies and work of those foundational second-wave queer and trans feminist writers and creators of color—Audre Lorde and June Jordan, Gloria Anzaldúa and Marsha P. Johnson and Sylvia Rivera, Chrystos and Sapphire, to name a few—and to witness the disability all up in their work, even if they did not use that word because of any number of factors including the whiteness of the disability rights movement at the time. June's last decade of writing was all about her cancer. Gloria's writing had everything to do with her diabetes and neurodivergence and lifelong bodily differences. Marsha and Sylvia were both neurodivergent Trans Black and Latinx activists and creators whose writing, performance, and art was at the center of their lives and activism. Chrystos and Sapphire's Indigenous and Black feminist incest survivor stories and poetry write from spaces of surviving extreme trauma, chronic pain from stripping and cleaning houses, CPTSD, grief, and psychiatrization.

I also think of the deep legacy of disabled writers (some dead, some still living but having done this for a while) who intentionally, politically identified as disabled. Laura Hershey. Leroy Moore. Qwo-Li Driskill. Aurora Levins Morales. Billie Rain. Dani Montgomery. Nomy Lamm. Cheryl Marie Wade. Emi Koyama. Pat Parker. Tatiana de la tierra. Raymond Luczak. Anne Finger. Leslie Feinberg, who died of Lyme disease. Peggy Munson. Beth Brant. Vickie Sears. Writers who are small press, micro-press, self-published, indie press, out of print. Writers I know and cherish, whose names I call when I talk about disabled writing.

We are so often kept apart, we disabled people, and kept from knowing each other's names. We are told not to hang out with the other kid with cerebral palsy, told to deny or downplay our disabilities or Deafness or ND. We often grow up not learning disabled history, Deaf literature, or that those are even a thing. In their essay, "Collecting [a] home for Disability Justice in the Library," Dustin Gibson and Dana Bishop-Root talk about their process of creating a Disability Justice collection in their local public library in their Black industrial neighborhood in Pittsburgh, one where "Audre Lorde's *The Cancer Journals* sits next to Leroy Moore's *Black Disabled Art History Volume* 1, creating a relationship between the two." They refused to use the Dewey Decimal System's limited categorizations because they kept our disabled work apart, putting some of our writing in health, some in Black studies, some in queer studies, a few in disability studies, but never together. White genderqueer writer Meg Day wrote of meeting Laura Hershey at a Lambda Literary retreat and Laura asking Meg why she wasn't reading certain Deaf and disabled writers, saying "these are your foremothers." I didn't know about Laura or her writing until after she died—she'd FB friend requested me but I didn't know who she was.

Yet, as Laura Hershey wrote in her poem "Translating the Crip,"[70] here we are: "thriving and unwelcome, the irony of the only possible time and place." And we are writing and creating our own media whether or not the abled world can see hear read or witness us.

70 Laura Hershey, "Translating the Crip," *Laura Hershey: On the Life and Work of an American Master*, eds. Meg Day and Niki Herd (Warrensburg, MO: Pleiades, 2019), 79.

When I'm talking about disabled writing and the struggle to create spaces for disabled literature—in talks, to other crip writers, to who-ever—I tell the story a lot about the fight I got into with an editor in the last weeks before *Care Work* was going to the printer, where I insisted that the BISAC codes (the codes on the back of books that tell booksellers what section to place them in) on the back read Disability Studies / Disability Justice / Queer Studies when she wanted them to read Social Studies / Health / Queer Studies. The editor's response was dismissive: "Well, we do have to go with the official BISAC codes," (note: there is one for Disability Studies, and has been for decades), "and I've never seen a disabled section in a bookstore—have you?"

Of course I had: Modern Times Books, where I was the events coordinator (and cashier) from 2009 to 2011 had one and was known for it. Third Place Books, Left Bank Books, and Elliot Bay Books—my three favorite bookstores in my current city of Seattle—all have robust disability sections and Queer Disability special displays. Anjula Gogia, who ran the Toronto Women's Bookstore for decades, confirmed that they'd had a disability section since the 1980s and it was always one of their best-selling sections. I fought back, pulled the white crip guy (friend) card, and was like, ELI CLARE HAS DISABILITY STUDIES / ACTIVISM ON THE BACK OF BRILLIANT IMPERFECTION. IF HE CAN DO IT, SO CAN I. I DO NOT WANT MY BOOK NEXT TO THE GOUT CURES. We compromised on "disability studies / queer studies."

Four years later, Poets.org would ask me to curate a disability jus-tice poets folio for their 2022 theme of "Poetry and Disability Justice." It was a wonderful task, and I ran into the reality that Poets.org, like most poetry databases, didn't have "disability" or "disabled poets" or "Deaf poets" as keywords. As with most poetry databases, the closest you get is "illness" or "the body." Something as simple as having "disability," "disabled poets," and "Deaf poets" as keywords or search terms allows us to find each other, to come together, for disabled and Deaf people searching for words to illuminate our experiences and create a community to to find them. In "Creating [a] home for Disability Justice in the Library" Dustin Gibson and Dana Bishop-Root write about disability justice as "a place where we can kick it / a place where we belong," echoing Tupac Shakur's lyrics in his song "Thug Mansion." That resonated with me. More than anything, more than rhetoric, I want disability justice writing to be that space where we can kick it and belong too. The DJ section in the poetry section, the politics in the art section: they can be one of those places to kick it, be with each other, belong.

If you don't see your crip life in writing, you can't imagine a crip life to be. If there is no Black brown queer trans slut asexual disabled poetics, nonfiction, journalism, essays, crip, Deaf, and neurodivergent literary forms, how the fuck will you write them or write your life? With difficulty.

But our literary work is an imaginative space. I thought of *Care Work* as a community in your pocket when you have no crip friends or you are all alone, as so often we are. I have written or co-created nine books, but it wasn't until my fourth book that I started writing unapologetically about disability. It still felt like a risk. As a friend once said, "Everyone wants to write the poem that makes people go *yeah!* and pump their fist at the performance." So much of the time when I'd tried to write, or read, poetry about being disabled, about being chronically ill, the opposite happened: instead of wild clapping and screaming, I got met with the awkward silence, the nervous laughter, the "I'm not sure if it's OK to laugh," the #sadface. If you wanted to be the best, to have people love your work, too often it felt like too much of a risk to write and perform crip work. I was able to finally take that risk and write and perform and publish disabled poems in *Bodymap*, my third book of poetry, because of the collective work in disability justice writing and performance. Because of Sins Invalid and individual disabled BIPOC writers, because there was starting to be a movement of disabled writers and creators, queer and of color, who were creating space to do our work. I could believe there was a audience who was hungry for the work, and I got it. Without that, my writing would have stayed in my journal, stayed in drafts that didn't make it into the books I published.

It's often said that disability justice means slowing down. This isn't wrong, but I think what outsiders miss sometimes is that it also means speed. Sure, we don't sniff "unprofessional" when someone's five minutes late to a meeting or sick three times in a week, it's true. We move as slow as we move. But what I think people miss is how fast we also work. We work fast because we have only five minutes of good energy a day, or five minutes of phone privileges. We also work fast and hard because we know we may not live forever. We don't know how long we have because ableism may kill us.

Two of the people in my life I loved the most, two disabled BIPOC queer people, both died this past year before they could write their book(s). A few months before he died, LL had decided to quit his day job and go on disability so he would have time and spoons to focus on both his writing and successfully fighting for a kidney transplant.

Stacey texted me in late summer 2019, really excited because she was committing to writing a book. She was taking it in when people said that her writing was powerful, that every Facebook note or long comment she shared was epic, things people reposted and shared and asked where they could get more of. And that wasn't even mentioning her essays, talks, teaching gigs, videos, keynotes, and poetry. In December 2019 she created a fundraiser to help support her writing time and asked me if I would be willing to give her some coaching or work with her to support her around her book practice. Of course, being Stacey, she made the fundraiser fifty-fifty going to her writing practice and to Creating Freedom Movements, with a goal of $300 a month, which means she would only get $150 a month. I texted her, "You making your Patreon also into a fundraiser is the most Taurus move ever" to which she texted "Thank you for seeing me lol."

She wrote:

> Many friends have asked me to write a book and have offered emotional support, but I have had difficulty prioritizing writing when it feels like all of us in the Bay are hustling hard to pay the rent and keep each other safe. *Even as a physically disabled person I myself work full time and two side gigs to pay the bills … any time on top of that is spent supporting community/queer fam …* My goal is to raise $300 in monthly donors to support CFM 2020. From Jan–Dec, I pledge to write 5 hours a month if we raise $50, 10 hours a month if we raise $100, 15 hours a month if we raise $150, 20 hours a month if we raise $200, 30 hours if we raise $300. (Emphasis mine)

I'm so proud of Stacey for challenging herself to make time and resources for writing. But five hours a month writing is not a lot of time. I see the ways she struggled to feel OK taking time on her own, just to write. She didn't feel OK fundraising just to be a disabled writer—she had to justify it by promising to work and raise money for the movement spaces she was supporting. When you do the math, you also realize she was paying herself only $10/hour.

The words: *"Even as a physically disabled person I myself work full time and two side gigs to pay the bills ... any time on top of that is spent supporting community/queer fam."* To live in disabled community means that there is always a crisis. Someone is always crazy, in a crisis, or dying, and loving each other means noticing and giving a shit. It also means that you are the one people trust, and you are the one who might have certain skills, from listening to someone in crisis without judging to being the one with the list of medicaid therapists who aren't awful.

Being close to death can push you to write. But when you're sick and in pain and in and out of the hospital and needing to work gigs to pay bills and to keep your job so you can have health insurance, and you're tired, it's a hard promise to keep. This is one of the key reasons why there is not as much disabled BIPOC writing as you would hope. We could die, and in the meantime we are working, organizing, resting, and responding to community need. Those survival needs, of ourselves and our communities, are so stark, we have a hard time believing in ourselves. There are so many very good reasons why it feels like writing is a selfish hobby, not a priority, not as important. Even though our writing and art are the stars that light up the sky for others.

What would change things, besides ending medical abuse, gate-keeping, and violence? Besides creating a world where disabled, Deaf, and ND lives were seen as sacred and worthy of protecting, and that worthiness was supported at every level of society, from health care to housing to education to our right to live long, pleasure-filled lives?

Well, a lot of things that are both separate and intertwined with those big human rights, anti-ableist moves above. There are a lot of things literary and creative communities could do, starting right now.

I want so many things, always. I begin with wanting a cripping literary and creative space. I want accessible writers' retreats. Fully accessible: wheelchair accessible, chemically accessible. Retreats that have electricity so you can run your CPAP or your air purifier, refrigerate your insulin. Retreats that might have Wi-Fi because screen time can be an access need. Retreats where of course your attendant, your service animal, your kid can stay with you. Retreats where the accessible unit is not crappier than all the rest. Retreats that are not always run on the model of being seven miles down a dirt road in the wilderness, but someplace where you can get delivery and there's a durable medical equipment / wheelchair repair place nearby.

BFA and MFA programs are by far not the only way to be or become a writer, but I want accessible MFAs—where access is the baseline, as much as it in the writing classes I teach online, where the access check is the first thing I do. I want MFAs where there is physical access and chemical access and remote access and an understanding of sickness, death, and medical appointments, as well as an understanding of the different ways academic or professional "excellence" or "intelligence" can appear. I want an understanding of disabled life ways, that may be peppered with flunking out, being kicked out, or dropping out, forced medical leaves and the trauma that makes one avoid academia for life afterwards. I want MFAs to be affordable, and when there are dorms, I want them to be accessible. While we're at it, I want major industry conferences, like AWP, to stop shitting the bed in epic access failures every year.

Once we get in, I don't just want us to be barely tolerated. I want disabled BIPOC teachers and staff and visiting artists, not just begrudgingly there and worked to death, but robustly supported. I want disabled BIPOC artists taught at all levels. I want disabled and Deaf and neurodivergent literary forms and histories to be taught. I want there to be many models for what success as a disabled, Deaf, sick, or ND writer can look like, taught and shared among us as we learn our craft. An accessible schedule of reading, writing, and critique—not the read-four-books-a-week pace I experienced in MFA school—would be nice.

Whether or not we get an academic degree, when we come to publishing, I want us to have our own presses and for us to have control and say over our agendas, and as mainstream presses "discover" disability, I want disabled editors, neurodivergent copyeditors, Deaf publicists. I want a cripping and Deafing of what promotion, touring, and publishing can be, and for presses to have disability justice and disabled literature sections on their websites and in their catalogues. I want disabled writers to be paid well, not a $500 advance, and I want disabled, Deaf, and ND publishing staff to have the resources they need to do things well. I want a publishing industry where all writers and staff are asked what our access needs are—for communication, for editing, for performing/touring and marketing—as a matter of course, instead of there being one abled norm.

Right now, much of the bread and butter work of ensuring access is performed by disabled writers. We're the ones checking with venues—physical ones and also magazines and virtual spaces—about access, sharing our access riders, double-checking that venues aren't lying when they swear they'll use alt text on images and that they know how CART and ASL at virtual events work. We provide resources, ask where the 'terp script is, share our favorite interpreters and CART transcribers, tweet at venues when they don't provide image descriptions on posts about events they're doing with us. The onus is on us to do this access screening, and we're often doing that work of negotiation on our own, without the institutional backup of our publishers. I want that to shift. I will, as a matter of principle, not perform disabled writing in an inaccessible space, a strategy I learned from disabled and Deaf writers and performers who have been making it for years. How different would it be if publishers made a public commitment to refusing to work with inaccessible venues? How different would it be if publishers asked all their writers to fill out an access rider as a standard part of the work? It is past time for editors, copyeditors, publishers, promoters, and venue runners to all learn and take on the disabled work of normalizing and ensuring access in literature—not leaving it to disabled, Deaf, and neurodivergent writers to do the second, unpaid shift of access work. This would change literaure and the world.

I want all books to be published in multiple formats: as print books, audio books, accessible e-books, and plain-language translations of books (something that Alice Wong and Alejandra Ospina broke new ground with with *Disability Visibility*). I want the accessible formats to come out at the same time as print books—not a year later. I know the economic realities of so many small and indie publishers (because that's my publisher), and I know indie presses have to wait to see if Audible or Tantor will be interested in buying a book that sells well. I also know we have the power to be creative and put pressure on industries and change our policies and build relationships to make this happen.

Everything in this not-so-modest proposal means making major changes to huge institutional stuctures: to academia, publishing, and the small-scale literary world. Not to mention capitalism and colonialism. They may seem utopic, impossible, or ridiculous. But I have already seen what changes can ripple from something as small and significant as a press or a bookstore creating a disabled literature section, a reading series committing to ASL and CART as they pivot to Zoom during the pandemic. Like many disabled and Deaf writers, I've witnessed disabled and Deaf spaces with modest funding figure out how to offer access as a matter of course at the events we produce. If we can do it on a fraction of the budget of institutions with much more money, they can do it do.

Most of all, I rest with Stacey Park Milbern's words: "disability justice dreams got me this far and I'm going to keep banking on them." I believe in the endless possibilities of smartass cripples, Deafies, and NDs who refused to eat shit and go along with the okey-doke of business as usual. And that includes in the literary world. Especially in the literary world, in fact. I say again and again that a central power of disability justice is we are a movement based on real-life disabled stories, the unvarnished, hard, and beautiful truths of our lives: blowing your ostomy bag during a meeting because you ate something delicious, surviving medical and other forms of torture, living Deaf or disabled in jail, the complete realness of making a care web with a friend who is at the end of their rope and in a serious up-shit-creek situation. We have gotten so much out of sharing our stories—power, identity, tools, community—I don't think we'd ever relinquish our rights to tell them our way.

While I want systems of power to change, I continue to have the most faith in the boundless vibrancy, creativity, and fuck-you of disabled, Deaf, and neurodivergent people to craft creative and political spaces of possibility. If MFAS and the Big Five publishers refuse to change, we will continue to crip and Deaf and ND writing and literature, with or without them.

———

Crip writing is the piece of driftwood I grabbed and hung on to that stopped me from going under, this pandemic two years when everyone died, my best, most-needed beloveds, the ones the world needed the most. By crip writing I mean the crip poetry and writing I read, from PDF online zines and Twitter and blogs and Instagram and more and more and more books every year we made with all our world-changing crip-lit labor. I mean writing it to make meaning out of the rage and empty, the crip bitter and fried of our friends being stolen from us. I mean writing that saves our lives and makes new ones.

Every line I write is a nocked arrow, the string pulled back, the exhale of release, the deep cunt feeling of yes as it hits the mark, as it goes farther than we have before, to the place we knew we needed named. Alexis Pauline Gumbs once wrote, "Our future deserves a present where our truths were written," and we are writing down our crip everyday, and out of that, writing our future.

No more and no less.

Casual.

CHAPTER 11

Autistic Long-Form, Short-Form, No-Form, Echotextia: Autistic Poetic Forms

NAMING OUR HOMES, ON OUR OWN TERMS

Since figuring out I was autistic in 2016, I (as many late-realizing autistics do) have done a lot of thinking and reflecting about what being autistic means for me and how it's played out in my life as an autistic kid, young person, and adult who didn't know they were autistic. Part of this work has meant reflecting on the ways I see autistic communication strategies play out in my life and in my writing: the stuff I've always done without knowing it was an autistic thing, and the brilliant and beautiful ways I witness other autistics creating and communicating. Somewhere along the way, I started using the terms "autistic long-form" and "echotextia."

I am 100% sure I am not the first person to think of or use these terms, and that's an important thing to say. Part of being a disabled or autistic writer is knowing that the ideas you might think are your unique brilliant realization—especially as a newly out crip/autistic—are actually things other crips or neurodivergent people wrote about or spoke about or knew ten, twenty, thirty years ago. This is true throughout the disabledsphere, but there are particular ways this plays out in the autismverse, because so many early brilliant autistic blogs, videos, writing, and cultural/political activism are hard to find—they've been archived, the person who wrote or ran them died or no one knows where they are, and there's a significant gap between how I see people accessing current autistic-made content (on Instagram, Twitter, and blogs, through hashtags like #ActuallyAutistic) and the more underground, more analog Web 1.0 autistic writing of an earlier, numerically smaller generation, All of this is part of the reason I've veered towards being quiet and private in my writing and thinking about being autistic since I came out in 2016, because I have a lot to learn and I didn't want to accidentally play into "New Crip/Autistic on the Block" syndrome, thinking all my Big Realizations hadn't been said and written and thought before.

One of the things I love the most about being autistic and other autistics are the beautiful and multifaceted ways we communicate, and create and use languages. In a world where we are relentlessly punished and are targeted by violence and oppression for all the ways we speak and act and think that differ from allistics, including being nonspeaking, it is not a surprise that so much of our love work has been claiming and mapping the landscapes of the ways we create and communicate. I am held by the work of people like autistic writer and activist Mel Baggs, whose video piece "In My Language"[71] mapped Baggs' interactions with objects thought to be "unfeeling" but known by Mel to be alive and present, and then translated their interactions with AAC, explaining that the way they communicate and perceive the world as a nonspeaking autistic person is a completely different form of consciousness and language than allistic

---

71 Mel Baggs, "In My Language," January 14, 2007, YouTube video, 8:36, https://youtu.be/JnylM 1hI2jc.

thinking, makes me cry with feeling home every time I view it and broke open so many doors for autistic people. More recently, Jane Shi's essay "Reimagining the Autistic Mother Tongue"[72] makes me shout with home-feeling and gratitude for how Shi maps Chinese autistic creation of words and languages for autism. The ways Cyrée Jarelle Johnson morphs language and poetic forms shines with Black autistic trans creativity, wit, and ache.

When we claim and name for ourselves the ways we perceive and communicate reality, we push back on all those who hate us for talking too long or too short or not at all, who try to force us to assimilate into allistic reality, who shoot us for being nonspeaking. We claim our right to exist and the ways we do so joyfully. I am doing a similar form of playful autistic claiming and thinking in this essay, in love and gratitude to other autistic creators exploring autistic languages and communication, and hope it will be a useful part of the conversation.

By autistic long-form, I mean a (not *the*) common autistic communication strategy for some of us of, well, taking the long way home to get to where we're going, conversationally or communicatively. We meander. We are like streams or rivers that wend our way along a course and go our own way doing it. Our communication has its own logic—there are rocks and bumps and deposits to wind around, explore, weave into the communication—and rarely is that logic of a straight line. When you ask us what happened, we have to start at the beginning and stop to have several improvised side-note scenes along the way, that are part of the story, in order to tell it. We have to

---

72 Jane Shi, "Reimagining the Autistic Mother Tongue," *Disability Visibility Project*, June 13, 2021, https://disabilityvisibilityproject.com/2021/06/13/reimagining-the-autistic-mother-tongue/.

tell you this bit for context, which reminds us of this other bit. It's a very anti-capitalist writing and storytelling strategy, in a way—it does not emphasize scarcity or "getting to the point."

Autistic long form is one of those things that gets autistics yelled at à la "get to the point" or "why are you being so annoying?" or accused of "taking up too much space." I still constantly apologize for my winding river. *Sorry this is taking so long, sorry, sorry, long story short, long story long*. I've had people get impatient or angry with me for talking this way. And sometimes there's a point to this—as I heard a friend say once (I'm paraphrasing) they are aware they speak in a way that is the only way, often, they can speak, and that it is also not a way that is accessible for some people, including other neurodivergent people, because it is a lot of words. And yet: here we are. People might bark *get to the point*, and there might be a valid point to that ask: spoons, or time, or the sense that we're taking up so much damn space to the limitation of others. But there's often a rage at the way we talk that does not have anything to do with those things. We feel ashamed of it. We get a lot of microaggressions about it. We get told that no one will read a seven-page letter.

There is a decolonization and a de-capitalization of time when we long-form. A sense that the story, and all its bridges and rivers, is the important thing. That time is not money. That there should be enough time to tell the long story that leads to another long story.

Autistic long-form overlaps with another maligned form, sometimes known as "infodumping." I don't know if an autistic person made up that term, but it's always smacked of shame to me. Dump is not positive and feels one-sided. Talking a lot about something you care about comes from a place of love and caring and wanting to share about it to show as much. When someone mentions a subject, we use what's sometimes known as horizontal empathy, or empathizing with someone and sharing our own experience with something to show that empathy. Both those forms have an abundance of words, an abundance of caring to get it right.

Plainspeaking, or autistic short-form, is another autistic literary and communication mode I come to and witness in others, especially heightened during times of stress or overwhelm or meltdown. Words mean what they mean, like in the dictionary. There are no little heart emojis. We say what we mean, we wish you would too. There's no hidden agenda or trying to be cruel. There's communication of information. Spoken language may be going out the window, and there's not spoons for anything fancy or more. It's exhausting and painful to try and communicate under stress, and then have to deal with the explosive reaction when we are understood as mean or curt or rude.

And then there's what I semi-jokingly call ultra short-form, or no-form. Communication that is ultra dense, condensed, whether it is speaking or nonspeaking, through word, text, or gesture. I come to this often when I am very nonspeaking, which often (not always) comes when I am stressed, down, or in burnout. But I also enjoy this form on its own, on its own merits. I like a good facial expression or resolute staring into space while making a hand gesture. I like a good "Huh!" I say "Yeah" a lot. There are paragraphs in that one word. I am not alone in this.

Echotextia is a word I made up (as far as I can tell and through research; please let me know if you've seen others using it!) for a poetic form where (to quote myself, lol) "others' words echo in our own and are in conversation." The term riffs on "echolalia," a medical term for a communications strategy where a word or phrase is repeated. Echolalia is a very stigmatized communications strategy by the MIC and allistic people attempting to allisticize autistic children and adults; in the most common definitions you'll find, the word "meaningless" is the first thing you'll see, as in "meaningless repetition" and it is viewed by allistic people as both pathology and something autistic people should be punished for using. Autistic people have pushed back on this, arguing that autistic people employing echolalia are communicating, just not in a language neurotypical people often understand.

Learning about echolalia helped me understand an autistic experience I'd often be wordless and embarrassed about, of easily falling into the accent of places I lived, picking up phrases or turns of speech, and having words or phrases repeat or echo in my head with memory and significance. It also helped me reflect on my experience of having certain poems, or lines of poems, stick in my head, and writing poems that included either a direct reference to them, a quoted line or a line that was inspired by or in conversation with it. When I had done this, I often worried if this meant I was stealing another's work, even if I credited the original line and author and explained what I was doing. Learning about echolalia, however, made me curious about exploring echotextia as a specifically autistic poetic form that breaks from the white/Western/allistic poetic norm of individualism, where a poem exists in a vacuum of Individual Unique Thoughts that Have Nothing to Do with Other Poems. Echotextia, on the other hand, might be a poetic form about being in conversation and coevolution with other writers, poems, and people. A literary interdependence. A collective-access poetic conversation.

All of these forms, especially the first three, may seem to refer mostly to non-literary writing. But I believe our neurodivergent communication strategies can and do play out in our writing and creative practice. As a people, we are incredibly diverse, but many of us share a complete incomprehension about binaries and boundaries of traditions. If the gender binary seems ridiculous to many of us, it makes sense that a human-created boundary between Literary Writing and Everyday Communication would also. Of course we would play and fly between everyday storytelling and communication and the words we write—especially for those of us who are most fluent in text.

I am hungry to be in connection with other autistic and ND writers and creators about the ways we are creating autistic ways of writing and art. I am hungry for the conversations we are having and will increasingly have as we continue to turn towards ourselves, and each other, as our own reference point. Often, the ways my neurodivergence has shown up in my writing—repetition, long-form storytelling, or a short, very intent short-form choice—have been red-penned by editors as an error to be corrected. And one of the many things I love about autistic and neurodivergent communities are the ways we are turning away from those who are not us "diagnosing" us, to exploring and naming the ways we communicate, live, feel, and create using ourselves as our own authority and points of reference.

We risk losing "legitimacy" or "legibility" to the establishment when we turn away from the allistic eye and claim our own languages—but most of us never had those things in the first place, and what we risk gaining is everything. Our own brilliant languages, on our own terms.

With all our autistic audacity, we claim our gifts: our kindness, wit, our multiple and brilliant ways of viewing the world and creating gifts out of that knowledge.

We lift up our autistic gifts and languages, not to prove ourselves human or worthy to allistics. We do it for each other, and the world: as people who have always been worthy.

CHAPTER 12

Cripping the Book Tour

This is a story about being a disabled writer without a trust fund. It's a how-to piece, and it's also a mediation on how disabled writers write and get our work out there: a witnessing and recording of some of our brilliant disabled writing skills at getting our work into the world. It's a disability justice dream for the future, rooted in what we're doing right now.

I've toured books all my life as a working disabled writer, back to when my first handsewn chapbook came out in 2005: I made a tiny cut-and-pasted "press kit" in MS Word and took the midnight fifty-dollar Greyhound from Toronto to New York to sell books out of my backpack. I'm no stranger to the joys and stresses of booking a DIY tour, and I've sold and gotten the word out about all nine of the books I've written or coedited that way: asking friends on Facebook to book me and cold-calling venues, grinding out hyperfocus hours online emailing everyone I know about readings. A queer South Asian DJ friend once told me, "Never underestimate the effort it takes to get the community off its ass. You have to promote just to the point of being obnoxious."

But when *Care Work,* my book of essays about disability justice and collective care, came out in the fall of 2018, I had a feeling of dread when I was getting ready to tour plan. The last time I'd been on book tour, in 2015, with my books *Bodymap* and *Dirty River*, I'd pushed my body a million miles past my limit. With *Bodymap*, I hit the road for six weeks straight and did twenty-five different events in a row. It was my first book in four years, I was totally broke and needed to make as much money as I could from gigs, and I figured, going constantly back and forth from gigs to my house for two days, then getting back on the train or plane was hard—why not just live out of a suitcase for a month and a half?

I don't regret the wildness of it, of going from INCITE!'s Color of Violence 4 Conference to reading at Heels on Wheels' femme literary salon in Brooklyn, from being at an all-BIPOC thirty-poet super-reading at the AWP conference in Minneapolis to a raucous almost-all queer crip reading in an old ceramic studio that was the only accessible space the D Center (the disabled and d/Deaf student center at UW) could find. But at the end of it, I was so tired I could barely remember my own name. When I hit the road for *Dirty River*, it was a little less bananas, but I still went on a ten-day East Coast tour, moved across the country and into a brand new city, then hit the road for a West Coast tour ten days later.

I didn't do any of this because I thought it was ideal. I did it because I needed to make money, and because this is the model writers, especially queer/feminist/BIPOC writers at small or independent presses, have practiced for years as how you sell books, get your name out there, and have any kind of success as a cultural worker. You hustle: you hit the road, book your own events, and do a lot of them to hand-sell books and build an audience. Whether or not we're at a Big Five publisher or an independent or a micropress, we are used to being told that there's no promotional budget for our books— either because a small or micropress is legit so small that they don't have promo money, or because as QTBIPOC/disabled writers, we are not seen as being important enough to support. I was mentored by QTBIPOC writers who warned me that my publishers were going to act like they were doing me a favor by publishing me, and either not give me any funding for touring or misunderstand my work and my audience so badly that anything they booked would totally miss the mark—booking me into a white, literary reading series in an Art Bar up a flight of stairs, say. So, it would actually be a better idea for me to book and produce my own events, even if it was a total pain in the ass.

As weird as this may sound, hitting the road for a tour was the model I was taught was the most accessible way for me to make a living as a sick and disabled writer. Disability and ableism have always impacted how I can make a living. I got through undergrad on a wing and a hyperfocus prayer while I was living with Serious Mentally Interesting conditions (think visual hallucinations, depression, flashbacks, and depersonalization), then got chronically ill with CFIDS/ME and fibromyalgia when I was twenty-two. I was poor and an immigrant and couldn't access social services, so I worked off-the-books jobs landscaping, being a flyer girl, and shoveling snow. When I got a work visa, jobs shifted to housecleaning and telemarketing— work I could do in three-hour shifts, even though I still had to rest for a long time afterwards.

And I was determined to be a writer. I didn't have a trust fund or access to any kind of family support because of abuse and estrangement, and it was pretty clear I wasn't going to become a writer *á la* what you see on television, with a big book deal, an agent, and five-figure advance. It was the '90s, and while there was a rich queer and feminist publishing scene (most of which would close by 2005) no one was paying a big advance at Random House Canada for queer of color poetry.

But the grassroots, hit-the-road model I was taught by friends and peers? That was popping. There were tons of readings and slams, and if you didn't like the ones that were out there, you could throw your own. I watched the small number of other sick and disabled writers I know make money via gigs, and I modeled my work life after them. One friend explained that if you called what you did "performance," not poetry, colleges would pay two or three thousand dollars for it! This was a fortune in 2005, two or three months' living expenses. A friend of mine whose sick is like mine told me a piece of secret crip advice that would shape my next decade and a half of work: people like us, who had peaks and valleys of energy, we couldn't work steady jobs where you had to show up, on time, the same time every day, and "sickness" was limited to an occasional cold—we'd just get fired. But we could work gigs, surfing our energy highs and lows, going really hard to make a chunk of money and then living off of it while you were crashed-out recovering (and maybe writing some).

So that's what I did. I took a risk and quit doing my nonprofit rape and tenant crisis-line work as my day jobs in 2005, even when people said it was stupid and I should get an MSW because that was stable, and write on the weekends. All of this is about limited spoons management though, and I knew that as risky as it felt to do what I was doing, if I got an MSW and a "stable" nonprofit job, I'd never write and I'd get some gendered cancer from the stress. I hustled instead. I got Canadian arts grants, I got college gigs, I wrote freelance articles for the local gay paper and *Colorlines*. I kept my cost of living as low as possible. I taught youth writing programs in schools and shelters and the queer community center. I co-founded and co-ran a couple of arts organizations, wrote grants to get us funded, and sometimes got paid for it. I performed poetry for money, and when money was tight, I read tarot cards in the queer club or the park or my bedroom, or taught the pelvic exam to med students or pulled fill-in shifts at the rape crisis hotline. I never got rich, and I was usually broke, but I paid my rent, and I had the real riches: time to write, and time to be sick. I had a writing and money-making practice that allowed me to be disabled. This was a miracle.

My being able to pull this off depended on a few things. Learning from other disabled writers to ask for access needs was a big deal (and I didn't ask for much for years, but just saying no, I couldn't sleep on the floor, was a big deal). But also, I was helped a ton in being able to pull off the hustle by being ambulatory (my wheelchair-using friends risk their chairs being broken every time they fly) and also, by being willing to push myself hard—to fly from Seattle to Flagstaff to Philly to Iowa City and live on coffee while I did it. Being willing to pull energy from the core of my marrow to give a speech at my fourth Take Back the Night in April (Sexual Assault Awareness Month, always a heavy booking time) when I was totally exhausted. I leaned heavily on an underdocumented disabled skill—not the one where you know your limits, but the opposite. The one where you use your skills at dis-association and pain and spoons management to push way past your your body's *no* so you can get paid, and manage the blowback later.

When slightly older disabled artists told me they'd had to stop flying or stop traveling for gigs, I panicked. Gigging a lot, saying yes to every ask to come keynote or speak or perform, had given me some of the only financial stability I'd ever known. It was terrifying to think of not being able to do it anymore, because I could not think of any other semi-accessible option to make a living and write. I told myself it would never happen, that I would be the exception: disabled road-warrioring it on the Greyhound with 800 mg of Advil till I was eighty. When I re-read my essay "Chronically Ill Touring Artist Pro Tips," I both love all the methods I list to survive and crip-hack the road, and wince because I see how hard I was pushing myself and how accessible touring options just weren't there.

When *Care Work* was getting ready to come out in 2018, I was forty-three and in a much different place than I'd ever been. I had some things I'd rarely had before: stable housing, some gigs doing training and education that didn't mean getting on a plane, and a still-tender but growing sense of my own needs around neurodiversity and that it was OK to ask for my autistic stuff to be honored.

I was also an older crip. And what those older artists had told me would happen was starting to happen. The winter after *Dirty River* came out, I had viral pneumonia for three months—I was being offered a lot of gigs and felt like I had to say yes to all of them. There's a lot of March and April 2016 I don't remember (though I do remember asking the doctor at the CVS Minute Clinic who had just diagnosed me with viral pneumonia if I could take "just a short plane ride" to a gig in Southern California anyway). I remember the reluctance of gigs when I tried to get them to agree to a virtual event, their bias that in-person events "were just better" and that virtual events were ones "nobody wanted to attend." Even one disability studies program refused to make a speaking event virtual, their coordinator writing, "Because it's our big event of the year, we have to make sure it's in-person"—despite the decades of spoonies and sickos calling for virtual or hybrid events. Despite all the resistance to slow down the breakneck pace of the abled, neurotypical tour, when I was five months away from my publication date, staring at my website, I knew something had to change. I wasn't going to hit the road for two weeks straight, let alone six, and I was no longer willing to live on coffee with subluxed joints on tour, or be sick in bed for weeks or months afterwards, recovering.

So when *Care Work* came out, I decided to do touring differently, even though this was arguably my "biggest book." I learned from other crip writers, who shared their rules, like "My rule is one week at home for every one week on the road." Or the strategy shared by Aurora Levins Morales of going to one place for a week and having the time and flexibility to rest, reschedule if she got sick, and build deeper connections with people. Or the disabled writers I knew who were just open about their pain and how many ice packs they were going to lie on when they got home—going against the model of hiding our cripness in order to seem "professional" and a "safe bet."

Below are some of the strategies I tried, and that I've witnessed other disabled writers doing:

Do less. Instead of doing one huge mammoth tour, I did three shorter tours, in the northeastern US, Toronto and Montreal, and the Great Lakes region. I built in a lot of downtime: I let myself sleep, soak, and hang out with the door closed. Instead of going to a different city every day, I did a thing where I went to one city and stayed for a couple of days to a week. I prioritized the kinds of gigs and media I really cared about and could do, and I worked really hard on practicing saying "I wish I could, but I can't" to the rest. I still had the voice in my head that says, "You're reading poetry/writing to people, how hard could it be?" But I also got more practiced at being real about how being on stage in front of a lot of people, performing, answering questions, talking about people's intense shit, and holding them as they cry, etc., is emotionally and cognitively exhausting. It's not the same thing as lying on a couch eating bonbons.

Your spoonie-ass fan base are your friends. You can't make it out to all the events you want to go to, right? (Or like, any of them?) Great, neither can a lot of your fans! Plenty of people bought *Care Work* who never made it to a reading, but read it in bed on a heating pad and shared it with their friends. People posting about the book on Instagram and using disability justice hashtags helped spread the word and sold a ton of copies. I got a small number of good reviews, but plenty of mainstream media sites still had no idea that disabled literature exists or how to review a book that's a sarcastic disability justice mixtape. And the book still sold out its first printing in six weeks and was my publisher's number-one US best seller since it came out. Instagram is an access tool.

Your access rider is your friend, and an organizing opportunity. When I was booking my gigs, I made and shared an access rider: a list of both my personal access needs and accessibility I wanted at the event. Mine includes a chair, water, low or natural lighting, downtime and privacy before the event, no stairs, someone to meet me and take me to the space, and a fragrance-free request, but I also ask for access I didn't personally need: ASL interpretation, adequate prep for it and meaningful promo to the Deaf community, childcare, sliding-scale pricing, food, fat-accessible seating. Access riders save spoons and work—you don't have to negotiate and go over every single point of access individually—and they save time, because if you send them when you're first booking the event, either they can provide the access or they can't and you can move on, without any last minute "oops, we forgot."

Since COVID moved all my events to virtual for the last two years, and because of a ton of demands and education about event accessibility by Deaf, HOH, Blind, and disabled artists, organizers have gotten more willing and skilled to provide CART and ASL. I still use an access rider to provide tools and resources around transcriptionists and ASL interpreters I have worked with, examples of well-interpreted events, and specifying that I won't do podcasts that don't have transcriptions, and that people cannot rely on autocaptions ("craptions") amongst other things. Using access riders are a tool that ensures that you're not going to read or perform about disability in an inaccessible environment, and are an educational and organizing tool that protects your access needs and changes the culture of performance, making accessibility more of an "of course."

Get help. After years of either straight-up not being able to afford it or grinding my teeth about whether I could and then deciding I should just keep doing everything, I hired a friend to help me with the administrative side of gig booking. Not only does he handle the onslaught of emails, working with him an hour a week is a huge support to my executive function and a condom around my impulse to say yes to everything—helping me figure out that, no, I could not get from Portland to Atlanta in three hours—and also helping where I would've frozen and not been able to answer emails and frozen some more. I wouldn't have always been able to afford this, but when I was able to afford a couple hundred bucks a month, I made it back in the gigs I didn't lose and the time I saved having someone who can write in ten minutes an email that would have taken me an hour.

Charge more sometimes. This one was hard for me. Of course there are some gigs—a lot of them—that I do for free, or for a hundred bucks, at bookstores and community spaces, that I really love to do. But I depend on college gigs that pay for a lot of my income. It's very hard to figure out what to charge for college gigs—there's no union or rate sheet or guild, just, if you're lucky, checking in with other people about what they charge. I've never wanted to bankrupt a gender studies department's program budget, and for years the idea of getting any money for doing this work was magic, so I undercharged. However, booking performers when I worked briefly at UW, getting real that inflation goes up and so should our income, and hearing stories of what people charge, gave me some insight into how wildly what people ask for varies. There are people I know who I consider my elders, who have written and created books and projects that are absolutely vital, who are regularly being underpaid by colleges. One was being asked to do complex work for a few hundred dollars; another confessed to me that "I can't crack 2K"—and that was for a full day or two of readings, meet-and-greets, workshops, and more. On the other hand, I know a handful of people doing the college activist speaking-gig circuit who charge around 9K, plus travel. Almost none of these people are disabled. Viewing the range and getting some insider knowledge about how much money actually floats around universities helped me feel better about raising my rates for universities with money and sticking to those rates. This also meant that I can make more money while doing fewer gigs, thus cutting down on wearing myself into the ground with exhaustion.

It's also a not-so-uncommon occurrence where a white cis abled woman (always) asks me to come to her university and do five things for $800 ... or for free. There's the time when an Ivy League school asked me to come fly across the country to speak about disability for no money, just a free plane ticket (wildly ironic considering how sick flying across the country and back would make me) or the time the white women's center director at a Seven Sisters school contacted me to ask me to keynote for queer month, then—without asking to see my rate sheet or asking how much I charge!—said, "Never mind—I've heard what you charge and it's way too high." It is an open secret that many of the most elite universities routinely ask multiple marginalized writers and speakers to come work for free, crying poor and saying we should be honored to even be invited. But community colleges and state universities, all of whom have less money, never hit me up asking if I'm available without having money available!

Disabled people, particularly disabled femmes of color, are asked to do an incredible amount of work for free. I think it comes from an ableist racist idea that we're not doing anything, anyway—we're lying around, living it up on our state disability checks, right—so we should be flattered to be asked to do anything; we should be flattered anyone even cares. There's a specific rage I and other disabled BIPOC femmes have faced when we asked to get paid or are matter-of-fact about the fact that, yes, we do know things, have written books and made films, been organizers, and our work and knowledge is real and deserves compensation. It's garden variety racism, sexist, ableism, and homo/transphobia; us insisting on being paid also flies in the face of structures that say, "It's a big deal we even let you bitches exist, now you demand respect and money?"

Zoom as an accessible, equal alternative, not a cut-rate version of a live reading. In the era of COVID, this line, written in 2019 for the original version of this essay, feels both quaint and prophetic. It also doesn't feel over. Prior to COVID, there was incredible resistance—including from some disabled venues—about doing virtual events. Disabled people remember how utterly most venues refused to even consider doing virtual events for access pre-pandemic. This includes conferences and venues that absolutely had money and internet access.

In 2019 I was invited to present at a major annual academic conference, being held in a big-city Hilton that definitely had Wi-Fi, conference rooms, and a budget. That was the year I had subluxed both my knees and my achilles tendon *and* injured my left wrist, and as none of my injuries were healing and I was living with extreme pain and difficulty walking, I had reluctantly admitted that I needed to scale way back on the amount I was on the road. When I told the conference organizers that it wasn't physically possible for me to do a six-hour flight because most of my joints were in Level 9 pain, but I would love to Zoom in, I was met with total refusal. "I just don't know if we have the capacity to do that ... and if we let you do it, everyone will want to do it."

In the end, of fucking course, I Zoomed in because another disabled person flew to the conference with a projector in their backpack, other disabled people of course knew how to do Zoom and made sure it happened—but all the normals eyed us aghast, like we were doing some kind of obscure ritual. Four months later, I was laugh-crying in crip bitter as I saw how every single not-disabled venue swiftly made

Zoom events and remote work de facto available for their white-collar workers. When the ableds needed virtual, of course it happened.

As of this writing in spring 2022, the book launches and readings I attend or present at are still all virtual, and we seem to be at a place where people are no longer saying, as they did in the early pandemic, "Let's hold off on booking a reading—maybe we'll do in-person when things are back to normal." It's been two years and writers with books coming out seem to be matter-of-factly booking a raft of virtual readings with bookstores and venues, because of COVID safety, yes, but also because they've realized they have hundreds of people attending a reading they do from their house! I know that the US feels in some ways increasingly divided between people who have decided they're "done with the pandemic" and the rest of us who wish we could be, but can't. I've seen some events rush back to in-person-only in a nostalgic rush for 2019 that leaves the rest of us behind. I see disabled person after disabled person point out that in-person events were largely inaccessible before the pandemic, and they are even more so now that gathering inside in large groups can kill you.

I don't want everything to be virtual forever. I miss in-person, accessible events. I miss being at parties and bookstores and in-person big accessible gatherings of crips—as hard as they are to organize, there's a sacredness about being together that I miss. But I love the intimacies and comfort and access and possibility I've found in virtual events, and I want to stay experimenting and growing the possibilities of the space. I want to keep cripping the book tour through virtuality, and I want to have masked readings outside in the park, with ASL and access copies. I don't want to "go back" to in-person events that leave disabled people home in our COVID immunobunkers forever, pressing our nose against the glass, watching all the happy, oblivious abled having a party without us.

Virtual events have been some of the biggest joys and hopes of the past two years, and they contain so many things I don't want to lose if we "go back to" ableist normal. The online dance parties, sex parties, readings where a thousand people were there. The Zooms and Discords where text-only communication was so much more accessible to me and many other ND people than verbal readings. The use of chat to post links and resources. The use of chat to gather questions and edit out the horrible or offensive ones, rather than just having to deal with them at events. The creativity I see people evoking in making virtual events, the normalization of CART and ASL and the way people have widely learned good practices for those. My knees have healed in the last two years because I wasn't getting on a plane every two weeks. I am healthier and less exhausted because I am no longer in a boom-bust cycle of traveling and recovery. I don't want to give any of these things up. I do want real addressing of the digital divide and the cognitive exhaustion screens cause. But I don't want to go back to the road-warrior, permanently exhausted life I clung to before as a touring artist.

In cripping book tours, before and during COVID, we are modeling new disabled ways of being, of sharing culture and communion that are gifts for everyone. I remember being on tour when "sustainability" was a huge movement buzz word, but everyone would still make automatic small-talk bonding over how burnt out we all were—as a badge of pride, of movement warriorness. There was such a sense of "This is the only way to do this," and I know sometimes there's no choice. And I also understand how deeply internalized ableism limits our imagination about what's possible.

I remember running into the partner of a disabled writer at the same conference as me in the bathroom and asking how they were doing, in that crip-to-crip *how much pain are you really in?* coded-language way. They said they were both so tired, because they'd taken a red-eye and said, a little defensively and tough-guy, "Well, there's just no other way for us to do it, it's too expensive. You know how it is."

I did know how it was. But I had flown in the day before so I could go to the hotel and sleep—something other disabled people had taught me it was OK to do. My rest was held collectively when I was on the road, like when I stayed with other sick and disabled femmes who said, *Go take a nap* or *have some alone time in the bedroom*. I got acupuncture in between gigs. I took the train, not the plane, and was so much less anxious because there was no TSA security-theater extended pat-down panic, and I was able to stretch out and eat. When I came home, I didn't go right back to work—I booked days off to rest, be nonspeaking, and do laundry.

Ableism robs us of our ability to see disabled possibilities, even ones that might be relatively small. Think of the boss or professor who snorts and denies your access request for a chair without an attached desk or a wheelchair accessible workspace because "this is the way it's always been done." But there are so many ways as disabled, sick, neurodivergent, Mad, and Deaf writers, artists, and performers we are cripping the book tour, changing the ways touring can be and changing the ways everyone imagines what is possible.

We are creating possibility models that expand the ways disabled writers—and everyone else—can make and share art and culture, on our own terms. When we do that, we all win. But most of all, disabled, Deaf, neurodivergent, and sick writers—we get our chance to shine.

ACCESS RIDER

LEAH PIEPZNA-SAMARASINHA ONLINE EVENTS

(inspired by and with some parts borrowed from Alice Wong's)

Online public keynotes, speaking/reading events, workshops, and panels with Leah Piepzna-Samarasinha are required to include the following:

- **American Sign Language interpreters during the online event.** They must be certified interpreters with experience and comfort working with online events and with queer/BIPOC/disabled/progressive material. At least 2 interpreters for event over 1 hour with a lot of talking, multiple panelists, etc.
- **Live captioning during the online event** by a Communication Access Realtime Translation[73] transcriptionist (not by an app or autocaption, which are inaccurate and do not provide language equity). CART alone does not provide language equity for Deaf people for whom ASL is their first language. Rev.com and Zoom autocaptions *may be* useable for a smaller workshop format.
- After the event, if you also plan to post a video of it online, you **need to include captions and a link to a transcript** (see below).

---

[73] https://en.wikipedia.org/wiki/Communication_access_real-time_translation

- **One option post-event if you cannot provide ASL/CART:** upload a video of the event with captions (not auto-generated ones) on YouTube or another video platform and include a link to the text transcript with the post.
- **One option for writing workshops if you cannot provide ASL/CART:** we do the whole thing in a text-only format like Google Docs. If no one requests ASL and it's a small workshop, I'm OK to go ahead with CART or Zoom captions but no ASL.
- **Adequate prep time and script collection** (no fewer than 48 hours before event does script, including run of show, get to CART and ASL interpreters). This can be talking points, not word-for-word, but must occur.
- **If you are new to online access and events: a brief rehearsal time, separate from the event**, where interpreters, event organizers and/or volunteers are present to make sure everyone is on the same page in terms of where interpreters will be pinned, CART login/assignment, and the use of chat. If you are an organization or media source that does online events all the time and is practiced in making sure the ASL and CART work, this can be a five-minute tech check, but if you've never done this work before, let's book more time.
- An access volunteer or staff member other than Leah must be liaising with the ASL interpreters, CART workers, etc., and ensuring access tech runs smoothly during event—Leah cannot troubleshoot access and speak at the same time.
- **All online events will have security protocols** (registration required, ability to mute participants, no screen share from

participants) in order to limit the possibility of Zoom bombing and harassment.

- **All online events that are interactive will have at least one designated person working as an "access usher"** to answer any access requests or questions from participants and troubleshoot any access problems (CART embed stops working, ASL interpreters disappear, there's a language question from an ASL-using attendee, etc.).
- Personal access request: Leah needs about **5–10 minutes of quiet time** before going live to have their video/audio off and not reply to tech or other questions, as a neurodiversity access need.
- A volunteer/worker other than Leah **collects and screens questions for Q and A for webinars, speaking engagements, etc.**

Example of a YouTube video with human-generated captions (BTW, these are more accurate) and a link to transcript in the description section:

- 2019 Autistic Self Advocacy Network Annual Gala: Keynote by Alice Wong (captioned)[74]

Publicity and media
- Graphics and posts about the event should include info that ASL interpreters and captioning/CART will be provided.

---

74 https://youtu.be/k40okB9yi5Y

- Image descriptions will be added as alt text on social media platforms (e.g., Twitter, Instagram, or Facebook).
- Include an email of a contact person if anyone has questions or accommodation requests for the event.

Radio/Podcast
- Include a text transcript with your post. Access is love[75] and it'll increase your SEO!

Two examples from podcasts about disability and accessibility:
- Contra* Episode 2.10: Contra*Maintenance with Leah Samples[76]
- Disability Visibility Project: Episode 76, Film Festivals[77]

For private, small-scale online trainings which will not be posted publicly: ASL to be provided and paid for if needed by any panelists or trainees. CART/captioning to be provided.

RESOURCES

Media Kit
For social media handles, photos, image descriptions, and bios for Leah Lakshmi Piepzna-Samarasinha: please email X Assistant.

---

75 https://www.disabilityintersectionalitysummit.com/access-is-love
76 https://www.mapping-access.com/podcast/2020/5/25/contra-episode-210-contramainten ance-with-leah-samples
77 https://disabilityvisibilityproject.com/2020/05/04/ep-76-film-festivals/

Best practices for good ASL/CART access for online events: The Revolution Must Be Accessible document from HEARD.[78] If you look at one resource on this list about online access, it should be this one!

Why human captioning is better than auto-generated captions
- Rikki Poynter—#NoMoreCraptions campaign[79]
- The Problem with YouTube's Terrible Closed "Craptions"[80]

Organizing Accessible Online Events
- Zoom and Accessibility, University of California[81]
- How to Make Your Virtual Meetings and Events Accessible to the Disability Community[82]
- Zoom Tips for Deaf + ASL Interpreters[83]
- Best Practices for Effective Video Conferencing, Stanford University[84]
- Enabling ASL Interpretation in Zoom[85]
- Enabling a Captionist in Zoom[86]

78 https://docs.google.com/document/d/1Pl6SWXYmFFg3UJ9HvdDay1FF7oHOyXnVWmHan YD2AqQ/edit

79 https://www.youtube.com/watch?v=QL6yrcq3_BQ

80 https://www.wired.com/story/problem-with-youtubes-terrible-closed-craptions/

81 https://www.ucop.edu/electronic-accessibility/web-developers/productivity-tools/accessibility -with-zoom.html

82 https://rootedinrights.org/how-to-make-your-virtual-meetings-and-events-accessible-to-the -disability-community/

83 https://docs.google.com/document/d/1AP--b_cqvoq9y66w_yogb1fjwZjTAGfy-3mGlzeoTBw/ mobilebasic

84 https://uit.stanford.edu/videoconferencing/best-practices

85 https://wiki.rit.edu/display/ZOOM/Enabling+ASL+Interpretation+in+Zoom

86 https://wiki.rit.edu/display/ZOOM/Enabling+a+Captionist+in+Zoom

PART III

THE DISABLED FUTURE

I hope I dream of disabled ancestors tonight.
—SANDY HO

ADA 30 / DJ 15

It was the summer of 2020: everything was going to hell, I had been inside the house for three months, and my inbox was full. Like every other crip I know, I was getting an endless array of asks to be interviewed, speak on a panel, appear at a celebration, write a think piece or make a comment—all because it had been thirty years since the Americans with Disabilities Act, the biggest piece of US federal disabled civil rights legislation, had passed after years of disabled agitation. Not all of the pieces and events that came out about ADA 30 were bad, and it was an opportunity to get disabled stuff in the media ... but there was also a lot of cringe. Like, a lot of requests by well-meaning abled people who'd never thought about disability before. In one case, I got a lot of "Urgent! Please write me back" emails from someone very nice who I had to tell that the ADA anniversary had actually happened last weekend, so her doing a thinkpiece now would kind of be like writing a piece about Pride on July 5. There were also a lot of asks of disabled BIPOC by white mainline disability organizations to come "represent diversity" on a panel, often with some notoriously racist white disabled person also on the bill. It was a lot.

I'm glad there was coverage of the ADA 30. I'm always glad that there is coverage of disabled anything, and the coverage seemed to be less garbage than it had been in the past. I got interviewed by the *New York Times* by a writer who was respectful, listened, and didn't fuck it up. I also spoke for fifty bucks from my semi-busted burnt-orange couch wearing an "I Love the Disability Young People's Collective" button at a Utah state disability coalition's very sweet ADA 30 online event, where they gave a ton of disabled people twenty minutes each to speak or do whatever they wanted, and everything was captioned and interpreted, with breaks in-between each one.

It occurred to me midway through this Big Disabled Media month that something just as big as ADA 30 was happening that no one was talking about. It was also "DJ 15," something celebrated basically nowhere, but fifteen years since "disability justice" was first invented as a term. From when I got brought into disability justice around 2008, when it felt like there were only twenty of us radical disabled BIPOC weirdos in the world talking about BIPOC disabled issues, collective access, and ending capitalism, to now, when there were tens of thousands, maybe more, radical disabled BIPOC and allies making zines, campaigns, survival programs, hashtags, books, albums, collectives, taking over organizations, writing about pleasure and desire, fighting inside prisons and institutions, saving Medicaid, fighting care rationing, making friends. And most of all: staying alive. We had made a movement. Maybe a series of overlapping movements. We had had a lot of movement moments, twists and turns, we had had one hell of a big chaotic timeline. And no one was talking about it. There were no big thinkpieces, panels, celebrations, gala events. The big *New York Times* article I was interviewed for mentioned DJ— which was big; most mainstream media has a hard time even saying "disability rights"—but they didn't spell out what it was. I wasn't surprised—most media shy away from naming a disabled movement that is explicitly anti-capitalist and created by Black people.

Numbers are weird and time is weirder. But there's still something important about counting the years, marking moments in time.

I wanted to write something, even something small, attempting to mark where we've been and where we are after those fifteen years.

So what do I see as some of the markers / moments / things happening at DJ 15? What's the speech I would've written if it had been celebrated or marked anywhere?

In the early years of DJ, as I said, it felt like there were twenty of us. Because we were so small, it felt like we were wide open—like it was normal to just invite every radical disabled BIPOC you knew to take a leadership role, because there were so few of us. We were building a movement from the ground up, of people so multiply marginalized, including from other radical (often BIPOC) movements, it felt like anyone could jump in, pick a project, and start organizing. That was what made DJ feel so beautiful to me. Other movements talked about "horizontalism," or being a movement without hierarchy, a star system, or leaders. It often felt to me back then like we were the only ones practicing it.

I often felt like some of my early role was as an evangelist for DJ—or, at least, a traveling salesfemme/organizer. I could travel more easily than many people I looked up to in the movement because I am ambulatory and my chemical injuries are not as severe as they are for some. I could get on a plane. So I did. I could go and do my little presentations at colleges and community centers, and draw people in that way. At first, sometimes no one would come ("What do you mean 'disabled queer people of color'—isn't that kind of a super minority?" were words often said by college organizers), but increasingly, the rooms were packed. People were eager for this DJ stuff.

Fifteen years of all that organizing, outreach, conversations, and zine-trades later, DJ is not twenty people anymore. It's tens of thousands of people. There is an enormous base. It's at the point in the movement where it's not quite a big extended family where you know everyone at the community center who's come for the buffet—there are more people doing DJ in some way than I could ever know.

And I see, often, some tension between founders and the next waves. DJ is spread out, fractal, tiny big: we can't control it anymore. The new generation is not waiting for people to give them permission to do disability justice. They are starting projects. Sometimes they don't know all the history, because it can be hard to find. Sometimes they do things differently or have political differences with each other. Sometimes they point out ways people who have been doing DJ work for a while missed something, or fucked up. Sometimes they ask for more than people who've been around for a while do. I've heard people ask why the 10 Principles of Disability Justice aren't in Spanish, why a piece of older disability justice art isn't image-described. I've seen people ask for neuro-accessible space at the shows and get snapped at by other disabled people in an exasperated "We can't do everything!" way. I've seen people want to be paid more than $100. I've witnessed movement old heads bristle, "Just read the 10 Principles!!!" at someone newer to the movement asking an honest question. The 10 Principles were never meant to be catechism. They are a conversation, an unfolding, a springboard for conversation and thinking.

A core part of DJ is that we resist domesticization or scaling up or institutionalization. We've pushed back on the model of "grassroots movements inevitably become 501(c)(3)s." We wanted to be wherever disabled multiply marginalized people are, without the bullshit, because we know that the "nonprofit industrial complex" has sucked the life out of so many vibrant movements, including disabled ones. Yet, what happens as we get bigger and as the need for our work scales up? How do we meet the needs that are out there at the scale of the need, without institutionalizing? And how do we make sure lineage and history are passed down when some of our work is secret, private, in moments that pass so quickly, in moments filled with grief?

We've been an under- or solely grassroots-funded movement for years. No one gave us money or trusted that cripples could handle money, because the history of disabled people and money is all about telethons raising money to cure us, not people giving disabled people money to fuck shit up. But money is starting to be here: funders—mostly small social-justice funds, but some bigger, like Ford—are starting DJ funds. So what do we do with funding? It's common to say, "all money is dirty," and I know we need resources. But how do we resist creating a two-tiered system of funded, "famous" crips, and everyone else?

The older guard of white disability studies/disability rights—often racist, often choke-holding, and perpetuating white supremacy within disabled organizing—is retiring, dying, transitioning out of movement space. How do we interact with the history of the work they did and the harm caused by racism in disability studies and disability rights?

How do we, disability justice BIPOC and allies, engage with this transition? Do we take over institutions, the Centers for Independent Living and disability studies departments? Do we eschew them? Do we continue to organize in our houses for the next fifteen years?

What happens if and when those of us there at the start become the new old guard?

How do we recognize it and hold it well?

What do we do with all the grief we hold from the disabled people we love who we've lost?

How do you timeline a movement that has both been good at documenting itself and existed deep underground, taking place in a million tiny collectives and moments?

How do you get big enough to do everything that's needed and resist institutionalization, all ways?

How do we write these dirty, complicated, bizarre, and triumphant movement moments and stories?

Honestly. Collectively. Crip-ly.

CHAPTER 13

Disabled Secrets

We are so often abused, as disabled people. And something that also happens is that, sometimes, we can become abusive to each other.

There are many more stories of disabled solidarity and love and witness than of abuse. But there are also stories I, and so many crips I know, know of disabled people hurting other disabled people. There are ways this specifically plays out in community, of men and masculine disabled people venting abuse onto women and femme disabled people in particular, and of white and straight and monied disabled folks onto those of us who are not these things. But I would be remiss if I didn't also remember the stories I've witnessed and heard of disabled women and femmes, including BIPOC, unleashing rage and power onto each other.

Maybe we act harmfully out of the specific ways we are abused and siloed and cut out of power. Being denied power means we might struggle to know when we have it, or even more, to want to have power over another. Especially another disabled femme of color who reminds us of ourselves, who asks for things we have been shamed for wanting. Maybe we have the capacity to abuse just like all people.

We don't talk about these things because we have only a miniscule pinprick of space to talk about anything, our communities are small and precious, we are not viewed at all or viewed as pathology. And we are so much more likely to be the abused ones, after all. And yet, these truths don't go away. Even if most disability justice community has more love than fucking each other over. And they affect, deeply, how we are able to organize and build.

This isn't about any one specific situation, if you are wondering, but general musing as I witness disabled people I know (not even ones I am very close to personally) talk about how long-standing histories of sexual and other forms of abuse in their organizations are both sources of pain and barriers to organizing against life-or-death power cut-offs and eugenic policies working to kill us. Or stories I've heard about how the "macho culture" and gendered abuse stuff within disability rights organizations cut people out of the movement. Or within DJlandia, the stories I know and hear, of bitter elders and bitter young ones and us in between, and our rage on each other.

Even in the sacredness of DJlandia, there are stories I hold that I am not able to tell, or only privately in a small group, of harm, rage, of complex hurt that affects me and others. Sometimes, I am one of only two crips on a panel, and I know what she has done. I joke, but it's not quite funny, about writing the secret history of DJ, where it's about joy and miraculous fractal coming together, and then the places we were close fell away or had lines broken. We are bitter young elders, crips who have only been the only one all our lives, crips who have survived by being special and right, and we don't always know how to be with each other as a group.

There are specific ways we are kept from knowing each other. Maybe every oppressed group faces isolation as one of the ways we're attacked, but there are specific ways disabled people are kept from each other: from institution walls to the inaccessible meat world, to not even knowing our names for ourselves. It's hard to find kin when you don't know you are part of a family, or that it has a name. It's harder to know how to be in a family when you've been kept from being in one.

And when we try and organize and build community, projects, something—we don't always, often, know how to love. Sometimes we do a really good job. Sometimes there are moments of blissful first connect that falter at the bumps. Of not knowing each other's languages of disabled reality, of hurting each other inside DJ communities that are so small and precious, so much riding on them, life or death.

When that hurt happens, it's hard to know how to come back.

This week, I was writing in my journal around an anniversary of a particular milestone of getting out of a past abusive relationship, and I wrote, "A red flag for me in relationships is secrets."

It's complicated. Because a lot of the ways I've had crip intimacy in my closest relationships has been around secrets. I've been the one someone trusted with their "no one else knows this secret thing about my body, about my Crazy, I've never told anybody" story in the middle of the night. And I've been the one telling my own secret stories, in a text it took courage to send. We bond this way. We have been there, or someplace close. We build intimacy by sharing our crip wounds, our secret places. We also share a lot things that really do need to stay secret because they could jeopardize someone's Section 8, their food stamps, their Medicaid or their freedom from being locked up if they were found out. Some of our strongest movement places are found in places where we share our secrets out loud. Some of our strongest bonds come from the ways we keep each other's secrets.

Secrets aren't inherently wrong or bad. Shared disabled secrets are such a big chunk of the access intimacy we crave. But secrets get complicated. When I look at disabled community-building, and attempts to build relationships—the ways we are trying to love each other—I see that a lot of how we form relationships can be around sharing and holding (disabled) secrets. The ways a culture of secret-sharing and -keeping become a foundation of how we build movements has big implications for the project of disability justice, for the community and political building we are trying to do, for the internal cultures of our networks and groups. For the ways we come together and what happens when things blow up.

As someone who was raised in certain kinds of radical political movements and communities, like South Asians post-9/11, that dealt with extreme surveillance from law enforcement and immigration, privacy and security culture are core values I organize my life around. As an analog GenXer raised before the internet and cell phones, I value the ability to not be online and exposed 24-7. I love doing work that will never see the light of day, or a million Twitter likes. I know that that work is real. I respect that some things really need to remain very private because people's safety is at stake. I also get this in a way that comes out of my particular kind of 100% bananatown family abuse experience, which included a specific threat of being placed under conservatorship by my parents when I tried to get them to talk about my childhood sexual abuse. If "the whole truth" had hit the courts about just how "weird" I was (i.e., having particular neurodivergent things that might be read as being "unable to function without support"), I might have lost the legal power to control my own life. Because of that threat, I had to keep certain things about my

CPTSD and neurodivergence really private for a long time. The ways I understand people who have had similar experiences of evading capture has stayed with me—in particular, how much we say with our eyes, with a "huh," how much we say by saying nothing.

In disabled community, a lot of people survive by doing stuff that is criminalized, from making money in ways that bend the rules of SSI/SSDI—like getting paid in cash or gift cards or "scholarships" for gig work we do—to doing labor that is criminalized, like sex work or getting paid for stuff on Venmo. It's an unspoken thing that pops up in how we organize—around how we get money, how we get people paid when they're on the system, whether people can travel out of state or the country and what they have to do to do it safely. There's stuff that's unspoken and stuff we don't talk about on email or the phone.

I also really value a certain kind of Mad/disabled intimacy around sharing ND/Mad stuff with each other that we don't share with everyone, that there might be cops or money might be taken away or we might lose access and social acceptance if the information was known. We trust each other with shit that is sacred, that we don't share with most people. One of the first community codes I learned in psychiatric survivor community was not prying or asking anyone intrusive questions about their "stuff." We were people who'd had our most vulnerable places pried into, often as the price in order to access services or support. We were assumed, in the systems and the world, to not have the right to privacy—so we gave it to each other. We could figure a lot out from a look or a glance. And, when someone shared something with you, you often took it to the grave. It was a way we showed respect to each other. Inside this community, where we were often very publicly open about stories of violence that had happened in private spaces—the home, or the psych ward, or the doctor's office—there were really tender things we kept so private.

So I keep a lot of secrets that are shared with me in community, and secrets come easy to me. I've had secret relationships, where no one knew we were dating or friends. And in some ways it's felt so damn comfortable and familiar, because it taps into this feeling of disabled privacy being safe. A small room where we can be free, where we are not being surveilled.

I've agreed to keep really big things secret for people, and a lot of that holding things in confidence has been fine. But I've also gotten into situations where it's been way past that: where I'm the only one holding all of someone's intense mental health disability crisis stuff and a core part our intimacy is built around around me being THE. ONE. AMAZING TRUSTWORTHY PERSON who knows any of it. And that that's the only reason I'm good, and that this is the only way we are intimate. It's a setup, and also something that mirrors my relationship with my parents in terms of me being the messianic caregiver, the One Who Will Save Us (until I am imperfect or unavailable, and then I'm the devil), that I need to avoid.

Often as disabled people we're fucked over and our secrets aren't allowed to be our own, so it makes sense we'd fall into this. But there is a difference between slandering someone to destroy them and sharing something in confidence with a friend because you have no idea what to do with it or need support around it.

Needing to talk about something intense that is happening in a relationship to a trusted friend because you don't know what to do about it is not always the same thing as being the cops or the social workers. There's places where we make our best call and honestly don't know what the hell the right thing to do is.

There has not always been a lot of discernment in there, about how we hold secrets and privacy in disabled communities. There's not a "Can I ask you to keep this secret?" where it's a real question and there's time to think about it and room for someone to think about it and say, *You know what, it's OK for you to ask, but I actually can't.*

Maybe you or your partner need to be able to talk about stuff that's going on in your relationship to your friends, and it includes disabled or MH stuff that is private. Maybe someone has shared about suicide and I'm not going to call the cops or post it on Twitter, but it's too big a secret for me to hold by myself. Or I have a need to get a reality check about a situation—because it is really easy for me to lose touch with what is OK or reasonable and blow past my limits, because of being autistic and taking things at face value, and growing up in a family where down is up and you're never allowed to say how it is. Growing up in a family with long-term lying, hustles, and intense fear around "telling anyone"—not even about the abuse, but about my dad's scams and deepfakes—it is really, really easy for me to fall into a thing where intimacy means secrecy and where the same place to be disabled is also the place where secrets live and go to rot. Things go sideways when that secrecy culture becomes control. It becomes everything I don't want as I keep breaking the cycle of violence I inherited.

And my parents are/were both disabled and ND. And a lot of their secrecy came from disabled passing to survive: my mom lying about being post-polio to keep her job, my parents both being Mad and ND and not having words for it or any sense they could assert that who they were was something that had dignity and common cause with others and deserved respect.

Sometimes those private small spaces of disabled secrecy are the best disabled spaces we've known or gotten to have. Sometimes things go bad in them and we're left feeling like our only choice is between the abled world that doesn't understand or this world that does but just got super toxic. Sometimes we are not wrong.

I think all of these dynamics and histories about secrecy, loyalty, control, and trust are common and important dynamics that pop up in disabled relationships and friend groups, that affect our community building and our attempts to build a fucking movement. We share a lot of secrets, and those are sacred. We trust each other with a hell of a lot.

That's not inherently bad: there's lots of ways we hold private disabled stuff that feels just fine and beautiful, and where there's lots of respect, consent, boundaries, and conversations about it. But I'm not kidding when I say I've been in one of those DJ cults, a group filled with abuse and abusive dynamics, where there was all the classic *To be good, you must be loyal, and to be loyal, you must never share what happens in Disabled Fight Club with anyone else, or you're a traitor* hallmarks of a small, controlling, and abusive group. A lot of those came out of scarcity: out of feeling we were the only four disabled BIPOC in the world, or who could be trusted in the world. When secrecy turns into control, the bad weird can grow fast like mold, and shit can get really awful really fast. As my friend Agustina said, "It's how I felt at times, like a robot that eats your secrets."

Sharing disabled secrets is a core part how we build relationships and groups. I want more choices for us, for us to keep growing more intricate ways of unpacking our disabled secret-holding and trust-building. More space to talk about our disabled skills and languages around secrets, about how our private sacred both holds and doesn't hold our movements. More possibilities around what we hold close and what we need to tell.

CHAPTER 14

What Really Happens in DJ Groups

I am going to tell you some secrets. Secrets you may already know. This is *Disability Justice: Behind the Music*. These are some of the things that happen when people try to start a DJ collective, told tongue-in-cheek and honestly. This is not ALL or INEVITABLY what happens in DJ organizing. But, boy, have I seen some of these patterns, and boy, did I feel like someone needed to write this down. I guess I am that guy.

The first, this is the classic: So you decide to start a DJ group. In the interests of not being exclusionary and because you know how badly people need this, you invite everyone you can think of who is disabled and BIPOC and/or queer and radical, and then they invite all their friends. And then, oh shit, people have major differences in political vision and/or personality conflicts, and because the thing has been kicked off in an ad-hoc way, there's no conflict-resolution plan.

We're all so isolated as disabled people that nobody wants to put limits on who can join. And nobody wants to be the bad guy who sets limits or kicks people out. But then there is that one crip who starts saying racist stuff, or transmisogynist stuff, or lecturing people about how they have the One Correct Political Line, or posts 37 million times on the group chat / Facebook thread / Discord that THEY are the only really disabled one and crazy people or anyone not on state benefits doesn't count and shouldn't be in the group. Maybe they are the most radical person who ever lived. Maybe they believe in respectability politics and admonish everyone, "We have to be on our best behavior for people to listen to us."

Or maybe they talk shit about people with some kind of disability other than the one they have. Physically disabled people putting down intellectually and developmentally people is always popular (sigh), but maybe they are Mad folks saying, "I'm not disabled like *those people*," or whatever. Usually they are white and often they are a dude and/or cis, but not always?

(Or maybe it's the older white crip lecturing everyone about what Real Activism is, or the older white-dude psych survivor who is sexually harassing all the young femmes. So many options. So many ways to have a horrifying community moment.)

Whoever is coordinating or co-running the thing really Mother Teresas it out—not infrequently when they have just found out they have cancer or some other really huge thing is going on—and attempt to be really patient and refer to the Values Statement and try to Be in a State of Curiosity and say, "It seems like you're feeling X, is that right?" But it doesn't work—the person keeps freaking out and repeating their point over and over, more and more dramatically.

At a certain point, people are really over it and someone wants to kick this person out of the group. Or if this is a racially mixed group and someone proposes having BIPOC-only space—because even though this is a DJ group and the leadership is all disabled BIPOC, white disabled people take over everything very fast because there are a lot of them, plus BIPOC are both shyer to identify as disabled and are more likely to leave quick when the first racist bullshit goes down—there is a huge protest. The group founder/moderator, inevitably a BIPOC disabled femme, at this point wants to take enough

Valium to sleep for a year or just quietly slink away and leave the group they founded because they are being worked to death trying to moderate the frothing sea of disabled emotional war.

What happens then? Sometimes the yelling person leaves. Sometimes BIPOC Craft Night happens anyway and the world doesn't end. Sometimes a lot of the BIPOC leave. Sometimes people get distracted. Sometimes the moderating/founding disabled BIPOC femme does indeed have a nervous breakdown or leave the group they founded. Sometimes there are attempts at getting a mediator that may or may not work and the group goes "on hiatus" right when it gets its first grant, and thus $890 sits in the bank account they just opened for a long time.

Other options:

- Somebody in the group freaks out and calls the cops on some-body else in the group or starts screaming at you when you are late or your computer breaks and you can't run the Zoom.

- A significant number of people are Highlander Crips, i.e., they have always been The Only Disabled One (or so they thought anyway) in their social group or social justice com-munity. They are used to being Right in the face of a bunch of trollups who don't know disabled anything. For them, being in a group of other crips is amazing at first and then confusing/distressing, because it turns out somebody knows something they don't know or makes a point that is valid, or people just disagree about strategy. They've never been in a group before and don't know how to be. No one has ever been able to call them on their shit before or meet them on their level or disagree. They don't know what to do. They leave in a huff, talk shit, storm off.

- Sustainability: great for everyone but them. They are lying on an ice pack in Level 9 pain facilitating being Captain SuperCrip Martyr. You can take a break, you should, but they're too Together for that.

- Doesn't want anyone to look at them or see them in public because of internalized ableism—gets angry when not recognized.

- Leader/Founderitis: so worried about being ripped off (is often being ripped off or not credited) that the group/project basically turns into Disability Justice: The Mafia.

- Some people have survived by being cute and pathetic and getting their needs met, some people have survived by having no needs. When those two things hit, it's a dangerous combination.

- A million ideas in the Google Doc, everyone enthusiastic: zero spoons.

- Structure: there isn't any, especially for decision-making, managing money, or kicking people out. What happens when someone says, *Oh, I can handle the bank account!* and then completely fucks it up?

- Money changes everything. There will probably be some money in an account and a huge fight and no one can resolve it so it sits there. It gets extra fun as funders Discover Disability.

- "Everyone can be a leader" is cool, but what happens if a person who assumes leadership is either a cop or acting like one?

- People identify as disabled, then have a miraculous recovery, but still want to run the organization despite no longer identifying as disabled.
- People say they will do something important (like come over and help) and don't, maybe because of flakiness but also out of general things like backs going out or having an access meltdown and not knowing how to talk about it because of shame. People needing the help then feel incredibly martyred and/or betrayed and/or enraged. Problems ensue.

In all seriousness, I need to also say: despite and alongside all this, there are a ton of groups doing magical, amazing things. I just wanted to be real about Some Things I Have Seen so you do not think DJ Is Supposed to Be Great, Why Does This Suck. These are all things a lot of new movements struggle with as they grow. Many of these are also dynamics we experience because we are making movements out of our own unique disabled bananagrams shit.

We are not failures. We are a bunch of disabled radical BIPOC/queer/trans people figuring out how to move together and where we want to go. Sometimes along the way, there are bumps and also completely absurd shit we also can maybe learn and build from.

FIN.

CHAPTER 15

Home Is a Holy Place: The Sacred Organizing Spaces of Disabled Homes

Home is a holy place: That was the title of one of the first social media posts the Disability Justice Culture Club made on their Instagram. Two months before COVID, when so many of us would be in our homes, they wrote:

> Disabled wisdom knows home is a holy place. Often times disabled homes are where it is safe to honor our sacredness and complexities. We hang our armor by the door. We center our own needs and the needs of our loves, wildly creative and inaccessible to abled gaze. Home is our sanctuary. Everyone deserves home. Houselessness is growing by 47% in Oakland. With the rent at $2500+, many are in living situations ripe for abuse. Elders are on the street. How is home your holy place? What can you do today to recognize the sacredness in each other? Of home?[87]

Good questions.

Every place a disabled person lives can arguably be called "disabled housing," but I draw a distinction between a place you live— which might be an institution or a hostile shared living space where

---

87 Disability Justice Culture Club (@disabilityjusticecultureclub), Instagram, November 21, 2019, https://www.instagram.com/p/B5Hv4L8g8Dd/.

you are abused or mocked—and the disabled homes we make for ourselves.

I've been in gorgeous crip homes made out of tiny precious apartments, bought for a friend by a million twenty-dollar contributions in grassroots community fundraising, or from an ally-friend with generational wealth they were passing on. I've fundraised for crip homes like Stacey Milbern Park's Disability Justice Culture Club and Aurora Levins Morales' Vehicle for Change, a chemically accessible mobile home, now parked at Finca La Lluvia, the land she stewards as a disabled Puerto Rican / Jewish elder in Indiera Alta, Puerto Rico. I've witnessed wild disabled experiments like Corbett O'Toole's Rolling Joy—a wheelchair-accessible rebuilt schoolbus with an accessible deep-soaking tub—37MLK, the empty lot in Oakland my friend Stefani Echevarria Finn and friends took over to build accessible, solar-powered tiny homes for houseless disabled Black elder women on her block, or the various iterations of accessible vans and RVs my friends have bought and lived in. I've listened to disabled Black and brown friends talk in hushed voices about the miracle of getting preapproved for a mortgage in our forties, celebrated when they got to the top of the co-op waiting list or won the lottery getting an accessible city unit, plotted about getting a double-wide not too far into Klan country.

I've had a lot of disabled, autistic, and Mad homes. From my various precious, shitty apartments in Toronto, to the Shark Pit, the queer femme collective house in South Berkeley I lived in for two years at the beginning of the 2010s, in a $175 environmental illness–safer shack-in-the-back with no lock and the only power coming from a heavy-duty extension cord from the house. Shark Pit was a house that practiced an easy working-class, majority BIPOC femme collective care that was accessible in so many ways: from the house money jar in the kitchen you could grab five bucks from when you were broke, to how I could walk across the yard to go be at a party, then walk back home forty feet away whenever I got tired or overstimmed. To my house in South Seattle, the nicest and most stable housing I've ever had as an adult, where I've lived in the Cheasty Greenspace woods for the past six years in fragrance-free, hot-tubbed living, where people leave you alone and you can be weird, but I'm still a three-minute drive to light rail and a ten-minute drive to the library and the local Black queer–owned coffee shop.

Disabled homes might be in broken-elevator Section 8 housing, a trailer, a tiny studio in public housing or a fucked-up house in the country or the exurbs that keeps getting citations, but if they are places we love and crip into our homes, they count. Our holy, sacred homes where we can unmask, let our hair down, hit a blunt, be naked, be weird, have all our access equipment out, be ourselves without shrinking.

The right to live alone is not on many access checklists or demands, but it is a key one for many disabled people, and especially many Mad or ND people. We need space where it is safe to be weird, or sick, without enforced "support" that is cruelty and control. Toronto-based Mad artist Agnieszka Forfa made a photo series I loved some years ago, where she photographed Mad people in Toronto in their beloved solo apartments, their sacred safe spaces. Home is where we get to be ourselves, on our own terms, without translation or negotiation. It's sometimes the only time we get to do this. Our one disabled autonomous zone, without staring, gawking, concern trolling, having to translate, and having to fight to get in the door or down the sidewalk.

Living with people has been beautiful and also tough for me. Sometimes I am too sick or tired or sad to clean up in ways that fit someone's chore wheel or sense of "responsibility." I've charmed my way through group-house interviews, but also there are times where every cell in my body has been screaming and I have had to force myself to be cheerful and normal and go clean, because if not, I will lose social points and get voted off the island.

In contrast, disabled sacred home is where my friends take their legs off, where there are five couches and we lay out on all of them. Where a roommate I loved and I had a joyful access happiness of being grumpy and word-free in the morning and not making each other chat or smile or do anything but grunt. Or when another room-mate once said, "We want to have the kind of house climate where no one will bug you if you've been in your room for three days, but we might leave a plate of food at your door"—a graceful understand-ing of Madness, that we understand that when you're in your room for days what you don't need is too-careful eyes and people saying, "Hey ... We're worried about your *mental wellness*," but a plate of food placed without hassle or comment is a gift. It's a hard thing to get on anyone's political agenda, the right to have a place of your own where you can be as messy and uncombed and sad and weird-bodied as you want. But it's a crucial one.

This is partly why so many of our disabled struggles have cen-tered on home: from fighting for the right to live in "community" rather than institutions, to our right to access sexuality and pleasure, to fighting for money to make our homes accessible, to creating accessible home spaces by and for houseless people, like 37MLK in Oakland and other encampments and tiny-house villages of houseless people, the majority of whom are disabled Black and brown women. Home is both a human right and the place we get to be our full disabled weird and messy selves. When we are able to organize from that place of our fullest, uncloseted disabled selves, whether we're connecting with other disabled people all over the world from a laptop in bed or in an in-person meeting as folks collapse on couches or gather around our hospital bed, our homes become spaces of organizing from our most potent, embodied disabled selves.

When I think of what disabled struggles for home have meant in a disability rights context, I think of pushing for Section 8, for public housing to be accessible, for elevators to work, and for funding to be approved. I support all of this. But in the long interregnum where often none of this seems to be happening—or it might take a good long time for Build Back Better to not just be approved but to actually build new housing—I think of the power that is in our hands, the disabled homes we are making right now.

It was October 2020, and I was hanging out with Leroy Moore after I was on his radio show. Leroy has famously written a lot about his battles with the public housing he lived in for years in Berkeley: the bedbugs and the years when the elevator was broken in a building that is supposed to be for disabled people. I knew he was getting ready to throw in the towel and figure out something else, especially after over twenty years living in and being a core participant of East Bay disability justice organizing. We were shooting the shit and I asked him, "What do you want next, Leroy?"

"I want the two-porch house for Krip Hop, for the archives. I've been keeping the whole archive in my apartment for twenty years. But no more Section 8—I'm done with this building. That's one thing Stacey Milbern taught me before she died, about disabled homes. The importance of them."

She sure did. Stacey bought the DJCC and joked she did it with everyone sending twenty bucks the first few days of the month. She lived in it for only a year before she died, but she burned rubber filling it with a home that became a community center. In the same weekend holding giant Korean dumpling–making parties for Chuseok and a big *Poor Magazine* collective meeting both in the same week, enough room in the living room for five or six powerchairs to dance, an accessible bathroom, a quiet spare bedroom with thick Korean blankets, a kitchen mural, a fridge filled with her friends' favorite drinks, orange trees in concrete outside. The last place I saw her alive and in person was there. The DJCC wasn't a Center for Independent Living, wasn't a 501(c)(3) disabled nonprofit lead by white people. It was and is a disabled BIPOC community center that was a disabled home.

The DJCC, in that same Instagram post, wrote: "A housemate has been describing the DJCC as a holy place where people come to do healing work. The house sometimes buzzes with liberation politics but most times it is slowpaced and quiet. It asks us to rest. We get blessed by community members who've made it routine to stop by a few times a week, many times sleeping the night. We sing, tell stories, practice medicine, and eat. This is the home dreamed of so long."[88]

It was.

88 Disability Justice Culture Club (@disabilityjusticecultureclub), Instagram, November 21, 2019, https://www.instagram.com/p/B5Hv4L8g8Dd/.

And I wonder: what if, as DJ grows, instead of thinking of our next steps in the typical ways typical movements think of them—nonprofits, buying a nonprofit building, funding, elected officials—we (both/also) think of them as creating more disabled homes? About continuing to organize out of our homes? Out of continuing a fight for disabled homes? Out of continuing to dream on and experiment with what disabled homes could be?

One of disability justice's strengths has always lain in how we defy traditional ideas of what a movement is—abled movement ideas and some disability rights movement ideas. Leaders, "smartness," meetings, sitting up, dressed, Contributing. In Sick and Disabled Queers once, there was a new member who asked us—in the midst of a then-buzzing online day of people problem-solving, asking for and sharing crip hacks and medical information and resources, and posting writing and actions, making each other laugh and sending hugs if wanted—to all list what kind of organizing we were doing, and chirped, *I don't see much organizing here!* We blinked and said, "We *are* organizing."

In their piece, "Collecting [a] Home for Disability Justice in the Library," Dustin Gibson and Dana Bishop-Root wrote,

> For many, the practice of Disability Justice is an attempt to find home. An access-centered[89] place that welcomes us to exist as we are, or create a home as Tupac described as, "a spot where we can kick it ... a spot where we belong."[90] The quest to do so is a continual building phase that provides foundation to the world

89 "Access Is Love," Disability Visibility Project, https://disabilityvisibilityproject.com/2019/02/01/access-is-love/.
90 Tupac, "Thugz Mansion."

that we have yet to imagine. Home is an inherent right that has purposefully been stripped away from Disabled and other marginalized communities for generations. Historically, home has been determined by people who create and uplift systems that torture,[91] abuse,[92] disappear,[93] and relegate Disabled people to confinement.[94] Most services promoted as residential living for Disabled people, such as "group homes" and "nursing facilities,"[95] provide an illusion of home with similar restrictions and uncare as traditional institutions have. Unlike prisons that disappear mostly Disabled people,[96] they're often not geographically dislocated from communities and still disappear people from the exact areas in which they're housed.[97]

I see those disability justice home dreams operating in many small, bold experiments now. Leroy Moore got into grad school and moved to UCLA with the goal of using its resources to secure a building and archive for Krip Hop International—that two-porch

91 "The Dallas Six Case: Some Background," *the dallas 6*, http://www.thedallas6.org/.
92 "Bearing Witness, Demanding Freedom: Judge Rotenberg Center Living Archive," *Lydia X. Z. Brown*, https://autistichoya.net/judge-rotenberg-center/.
93 Burton Blatt and Fred Kaplan, *Christmas in Purgatory: A Photographic Essay on Mental Retardation* (Syracuse, NY: Human Policy Press, 1974),https://www.canonsociaalwerk.eu/1966_Kerstmis/Xmas-Purgatory.pdf.
94 Mike Ludwig, "No Way to Call Home: Incarcerated Deaf People Are Locked in a Prison Inside a Prison," *Truthout*, August 22, 2016, https://truthout.org/articles/no-way-to-call-home-incarcerated-deaf-people-are-locked-in-a-prison-inside-a-prison/.
95 Occupational Therapy, "Our Homes Not Nursing Homes," October 10, 2018, YouTube video, 6:18, https://youtu.be/m0Oclpk1Us0.
96 Alice Wong, "Ep 41: Deaf in Prison," December 30, 2018, in *Disability Visibility Project*, produced by Cheryl Green and Alice Wong, podcast, 33:20, https://disabilityvisibilityproject.com/2018/12/30/ep-41-deaf-in-prison/.
97 Dana Bishop-Root and Dustin Gibson, "Collecting [a] Home for Disability Justice in the Library," *Disability Visibility Project*, February 24, 2019, https://disabilityvisibilityproject.com/2019/02/24/collecting-a-home-for-disability-justice-in-the-library/.

house he spoke of. My friend bought a house with her partner, both disabled and ND queers, and opened it to other disabled BIPOC who needed a home, as a space to live or to park their RV in the driveway. The Disability Justice Through Indigenous Ceremony project of Indigenous feminist project It Starts With Us / No More Silence is creating an accessible sweat lodge and figuring out where to site it, including potentially in Allen Gardens, a downtown Toronto park where many houseless Indigenous disabled people live. BLM Toronto bought an accessible building called Wildseed Centre with the goal of making a permanent, fully accessible Black cultural space in a city in hypergentrification. Friends dream of an accessible rural space where crips can be in the country, together and with personal space, but pooling resources, support, and community. Several friends have similar dreams of purchasing Black and brown community spaces in the city and committing to full access from the start. This may seem basic, but as someone who has witnessed years of the "let's buy a building/compound in the country" dreams of urban queers of color, almost all of which never thought about access except as an afterthought, who are guiltily apologetic when asked—"Um, well, there's a lot of stairs, but maybe it could be accessible eventually?"—or rural queer land projects with access statements that say, "Access Statement: This space is not accessible," this is a significant shift in people's ability to commit to access.

None of these dreams may work out perfectly or forever. People try living in a bus and realize they need a van instead; an encampment thrives for a time and then has leadership turnover; I move back East and closer to decade-olds friends, away from the greenbelt Seattle house I lived in for seven years and weathered the pandemic in. But them being imperfect and impermanent does not mean that they are worthless. They are examples of how we are building a home-rooted disability justice movement and communities right now.

We're also having a real-time experience of experimenting with this stuff because, well, it's COVID. There's a global housing crisis as corporations buy up all foreclosed housing they can. There are also massive rent strikes and eviction moratoriums allowing some folks to stay and live rent-free in their housing, for a time—until those moratoriums expire and there is a new peak of housing crisis. So many crips/immunocompromised people have had to move out of shared homes because living alone, or with one other highly COVID-cautious person, was crucial for our ability to survive. Nobody can find a roommate. Some people who have the means flee the cities to green space, and soon every place not completely trashed double triples in price. Anything two to three hours from a city is impossible, except for someone with an assload of white-people money.

It's me and my cat all year; nobody can come over except when we do porch and garden hangs.

Sometimes I feel desperately isolated, and I know I am not alone; I have friends with no immune system who have left the house only ten times during all the years of COVID. Some days I grow my tendrils, my skills at reaching to a small number of people regularly. We practice keeping each other alive. Then there's vaccinations and things shift again. Then the virus and the laws both mutate, and things shift again. God is change. God is a pain in the ass.

"Where are our places of power? Where are our sources of disabled strength, our liberated zones?"

Abled people and the ableist mainstream media talk about being "home bound" in hushed and terrible tones, just like they talk about the other disabled "bounds"—"wheelchair-bound," "bedbound"—they're prime numbers in the Fate Worse Than Death Olympics. Like it's awful to be bound to someone or something. Not even bringing consensual BDSM into it, I don't think being tied to something that goddamn awful. Why is it so bad to be linked to something gorgeous —a wheelchair, a home, a bed—that helps you fly?

"Bound" has connotations linguistically to nonconsensual bondage, to enslavement, to being tied to someone without consent, to being stuck, yes. But am I alone in finding something off about that phrase? Something that hates interdependence, the idea that one could, yes, be joyfully and consensually and reciprocally bound to an adaptive device, home, or bed? That one has a relationship and responsibilities to?

I was, am, more homebound during COVID than ever before. I didn't leave my house much for a full year between the beginning times and getting surprise early-vaccinated in late Jauary 2021 through a vaccine fridge breaking in the middle of the night and a nurse friend-of-a-friend tweeting that everyone who was a frontline worker, elder, or medically vulnerable should come get shots. Even post-vax, I barely left my neighborhood—going to North Seattle was a wild time. Me who used to be a crip road-warrior, the one who bucked expectations, hopped on a couple of planes with an almost dislocated knee every month, stood on stages and yelled into mics. My life has gotten beautifully rooted in my home, garden, and land. And it has been better for me.

There is safety and power in being hidden, and there is complexity in it for us. We've been hidden away in back rooms, staring out the windows of institutions. We have raged at being shut out from life, from being told *Oh, sorry, that party is up a flight of stairs* or *No, we won't turn off the smoke machine, we care about atmosphere*, by people who act like figuring out Zoom or CART is being asked to run a triathalon. So much of our movement is about visibility and the right to be in public, and that makes sense. We—the idea that there are disabled families, lovers, friends, communities, books, histories, skills, futures—have been so, so erased from consciousness, of course we want to take up space on front street.

But there is also power in retreat. In withdrawing from what does not serve or make room for us. In holding our fire. In choosing what our disabled priorities are, not responding to someone's ableist panic agenda or demands. Sometimes there is power in our invisibility. In the ways we get away with things, sneak into the headquarters of the corporation, because cripples couldn't possibly be doing anything. Organize quietly because no one could conceive we could. And there is power in the ways we claim our homes as liberated zones, and make them community centers in their spaces of retreat. We thrive in this place that is:

home life
home fly
home rooted
home joy
home decadence
home rich

Tina's house, a disabled community center. Leroy's apartment. My house. All the stops on the network of safe houses where there are ramps and fragrance-free soap and the permission to disabled fall apart. I am rooted. I am a homedweller. I have riches that happen in crip home space.

Adrienne maree brown defines fractals as "a never-ending pattern. Fractals are infinitely complex patterns that are self-similar across different scales. They are created by repeating a simple process over and over in an ongoing feedback loop ... what we practice at the small scale sets the pattern for the whole system."

Fractal. Instead of one big community center, a million different ones, connected in a crip mycelial network.

If there are a million different disabled homes in an ever-shifting network, how can we use this in ways that build out power, our resilience, our resources? Our joy?

LL COMES TO ME

It's the dark deep of 2021, the last month of this Gregorian calender. It got so cold last night, down to almost freezing. I snuggle down into my flannel sheets and sleep deep. I don't have nightmares. You come to me in a dream. It's two days after I mailed the last stack of your packages, things left in your house after you passed that no one wanted in our last frenzied giveaway, calling everyone we could think of and holding earrings and books and crystals up to the phone asking people if they wanted them. What was left was supposed to go to the queer thrift store, and I volunteered to drive it over, but when the time came I couldn't, and instead I took them home to what I called the LL Squared Thrift Store, where they sat in my house for months. Couldn't open the closet door for a while, all locked up with grief, but I slowly wrote the people I knew were some of your closest, made packages, pieces of you going to Borikén, Oakland, Chicago. Maybe this is why you're here, because I completed the work?

In the dream, I am at Hampshire College, the expensive liberal weirdo school in Western Massachusetts where you and a host of other beloveds went on scholarship, trying to write my PowerPoint at the last minute for a talk about what is disability justice, and my phone rings and it's you! I can see your face, so I guess you're FaceTiming me from the spirit world?!? And I was asking you, how the hell do I do this again, what do I say, how do I explain DJ to them? You're like, *Oh, when they ask you what is DJ don't let them get away with any bullshit, tell them about me! Tell them about this. Make sure they know about Patty, you can talk about the 10 Principles but also just talk about* WHAT IT IS. Halfway through I'm like, *Wait, you're dead, how are you FaceTiming me?* and was laughing and crying and you were like, *This is what* DJ *is, literally—we have connection to the disabled Black Latinx trans fat femme ancestors, you have connection to me. Stacey wasn't playing when she said that. I'm still here, even if they took me.*

You, with all your working-class Black Latinx fat trans femme loudass from Massachusetts self, you who said *oh I don't identify as disabled* when we spoke for the first time at the Sins show at NYU ten years ago, the really weird one where I was in a room that looked like a mirror-lined Jersey bar-mitzvah hall on a tiny platform six inches high, doing monologues in between videos because the college couldn't afford to bring the whole show. You who drove your Prius slowly from Atlanta to Seattle, stopping in the Bay on the way, went to the Sins show twice. Met me in Seattle when you moved here, where we were two loud Masshole QTBIPOC Tauruses in this grey and green cold white city, where Billie and me asked you to make a piece for our show about how our sick and disabled QTPOC ancestors survived fascism and you said yes and covered the whole stage in an altar, your Leo-rising asking us nonchalantly if we could buy you 100 bucks' worth of props. Another altar spread out back of your apartment that last year you were living and dying, the longass care collective Signal threads, the rebozo Satchél spread on your chest in the ICU. All altar.

When I woke up, the first thought that landed on my chest was: this time last year you were getting ready to live out your time on your terms. You had decided to quit your job—the one that had kept you on the whole year you were in the ICU and rehab—to write, heal. You were resting, buying delicious food, napping, writing down your dreams. I remember how I would get freaked-out texts from people who were like, *He didn't text me back, it's been 24 hours, do you think they're OK, should we go to their house?* How I'd text you first before I replied to them, being like, *hey, people are freaking out, I know you're OK because we talked yesterday but are you OK?* And how you'd roll your eyes on the phone and be like, *um, I'm just SITTING ON MY COUCH watching a Bourne movie after getting breakfast to go. I just don't feel like talking to them right now. I am resting.* You were both fighting to live, and in your last months on the planet, I felt how you had moved to a deep crip place of embracing a deeper kind of rest than many people know. I felt how you were between the worlds, in an intensely spiritual place from being close to death and your memory changing. You were close to the spirits, more than you had ever been.

When you died, some of your friends were like, *why didn't they call more, why didn't they tell us how bad it was? I just don't understand.* They clicked their tongues and shook their heads. *Sad.* I do understand. Maybe. I think you didn't want people fussing over you, taking your choices away, abled people panicking and scolding you. You were like, *I never mind texting with you because you don't trip when I don't get back to you right away, you know I'm just chilling. You understand.* I did understand. I was the friend who understood the deep crip sick need for autonomy and turning your phone off. For making choices even when they don't make sense to people. For going about your business without checking in with everyone's anxiety. For sleeping for days. Our right to remain silent.

On winter solstice 2019, right before all the everything, I hosted a gathering of people who were part of that small, imperfect disabled circle that survived those years together, to gather at the shores of

Lake Washington, Xacuabš. We met up at the disabled parking spaces in the south parking lot and threw fruit in the water to make wishes for the new year. Then we drove to my house, hung out, talked about Trump, organizing, getting ready for the election, the coup, the Three Percenters and militias gathering power, our food stashes and herbs and networks. None of us had any fucking idea what was coming in 2020 of course. But just getting together, praying, eating, and talking was actually preparation, even if we weren't prepping for what would actually come. All conversation, all talking out our fears, all connecting, all weaving is preparation.

We didn't know in March 2020 you would be in an early COVID ICU with a stroke, intubated, in a coma, no one allowed inside, you dreaming of glittery oceans of snow. Coming out, rehab, your short-term memory dreamy, testing positive for COVID after a million negative tests, us dropping arroz con pollo and soup in contact-free yogurt containers on your stoop, the altar for healing just outside. You and I cackling WHAT?!?!?! for hours on our couches COVID summer number one.

All of this is what DJ is.

CHAPTER 16

Loving Stacey: An Honor Song

Sometimes I feel impatient about how much ableism has forced us to emphasize accessibility to get people to pay even a modicum of attention to it. Collective access is revolutionary because disabled people of color (and disabled people in general) choosing each other is revolutionary. And, in many ways access should not be a revolutionary concept. It is the routine, every day part of the work. It is only the first step in movement building. People talk about access as the outcome, not the process, as if having spaces be accessible is enough to get us all free. Disabled people are so much more than our access needs; we can't have a movement without safety and access, and yet there is so much more still waiting for us collectively once we build this skillset of negotiating access needs with each other.

Tonight I am taking time to appreciate and enjoy access as a communication of our deepest desires. When my new friend makes their house wheelchair accessible so I can come over, a whole new level of safety and trust opens up. When a love takes initiative to reach out to event organizers to make sure my buds and I can fully participate, that's thoughtfulness, and also political commitment in practice. When I eat dinner with dear ones and they know which spoon or cup to grab, that's attunement. When I can ask a friend to move my body, it's because I know they want me to be comfortable out in the world. When I can do the impairment-related parts of my routine around someone, that's intimacy, a gift of letting each other into our most private worlds.

Feeling thankful for access—and interdependence—as an opportunity for us to show up for one another, and also for crip spaces that give us a taste of what can take place when we have each other. I am so hungry for us to be together. I am so ready for what is around the corner.

—STACEY PARK MILBERN[98]

She was one of the most brilliant organizers of her generation. I was an aging hater, a punk walkie with green hair and a cute cane who could fly in my thirties to all kinds of colleges with a half-assed PowerPoint and Recruit. She was the queer wheelchair tomboy femme with an MBA who was also a vanguard organizer, who could break down any concept, talk softly, and carry a big stick of brilliance, working to develop everyone she met as an activist, especially the disabled people who had been most written off as having nothing to contribute. She grew up a military kid, a Southern femme with one hell of a work ethic, a radical Christian, someone who believed she was going to die young. She was a young Republican who became a radical queer disabled feminist Asian blogger and poet. She took her accessible van and drove up from Fayetteville to the 2010 United States Social Forum in Detroit when she was twenty-three years old, and that thing was supposed to hold four people max, but there are so many photos of thirteen to fifteen of us crammed in, grins busting

98 Stacey Park Milbern, Facebook, December 22, 2017, https://www.facebook.com/smilbern/posts/780151464677.

off our faces, because we were so orgasmically happy. We had found each other in her crip clown car van, and we were never going to let go.

She and I wrote together for eleven years, even the years we couldn't figure out how to find our way to each other. Wrote intertwined pieces, showed each other pieces, wrote pieces that were responses to each other's pieces. She was always busy doing things like co-writing Bernie Sanders' disability platform during his 2020 presidential campaign or helping to lock down PG&E headquarters with a marvelously organized seventeen-group action. But a lot of the way she organized was writing: telling stories, writing her thoughts and observations down, in essays and in Facebook notes so epic they counted as essays, in language that was beautiful and solid and that everyone could understand.

She knew that if we had a project we could work on together we'd hang out because we were both Tauruses for whom work is love, so she figured out ways we could get jobs together. One of us was always making the slides for the training two hours before it started, after the other was like, "Shit, femme I was puking / had a terrible doctor visit / didn't sleep / took too many edibles, could you do it?" We were there at the beginning of DJ, and for eleven wild years I was blessedly lucky enough to be part of co-creating a movement with many other disabled BIPOC, in relationship with her. She was the Magician in the tarot deck, alchemizing brilliance out of many tiny threads, one who was deeply committed to being ordinary and not seeking fame or ego. We were a double-Taurus crip dream team, and together we felt unstoppable. Stacey had a ton of power-duo friends. I was lucky to be one of them. She was twelve years younger than me and dealt with a lot of people infantilizing her because of her soft face, Southern manners, Asianness, and wheelchair use. Me, though, I sat at her feet. She taught me everything I knew.

Stacey Park Milbern was a working-class, Southern, deeply spiritual, Korean and white, femme disability justice organizer who started organizing and writing DJ into being in her late teens. All of those identities are crucial to understanding who she was and is as an organizer, thinker, writer, and dream-maker into being of DJ.

She was born on May 19, 1988, the same birthday as Malcolm X and Yuri Kochiyama. Like both of them, she was a deeply revolutionary person with an ambitious vision of liberation. However, when I think of the people who remind me of her the most, I think of the great Southern Black freedom organizer Ella Baker,[99] a movement worker whose organizing helped develop the heart and bones of the 1950s and '60s Black Freedom Movement. Ella Baker is famous for saying "Strong people don't need strong leaders," and is credited with birthing what is called facilitative leadership. Working against the model of charismatic, often male, individual leadership—someone fancy up on a podium giving a speech—Baker believed her organizing work lay in supporting and amplifying the genius of everyday Black poor people in the South, and that her work as an organizer was to support them in knowing they had the ability and brilliance to make change happen—that they were the ones they'd been waiting for.

Similarly, Stacey never wanted to be seen as a leader of DJ, and a cornerstone of her organizing was her belief that every single disabled person had crucial things to contribute and leadership skills to be nurtured. She especially supported disabled people who had

---

99 For more information about Ella Baker, see Barbara Ramsey's *Ella Baker and the Black Freedom Movement: A Radical Democratic Vision* (UNC Press, 2003).

been marginalized from communities and movements, who didn't go to the Ivy League or aren't the one disabled person all the abled activists know: developmentally/intellectually disabled, poor, young, "uncool," Black and brown, small-town, institutionalized disabled people, who had been told all our lives we are not capable of contributing, that we can only be "clients." She knew that it was the disabled people who had been written off the most who had the most crucial, valuable skills that are needed if we are going to win. That they/we just need to be witnessed, presumed competent, and given support and a place to shine. DJ is insistently a horizontal movement of "nobodies" because of this vision.

Stacey was involved in more kinds of DJ organizing projects than I can count, from her early work with the Disabled Young People's Collective of Fayetteville, NC, to her work with the Azolla Story, Creating Collective Access, Sins Invalid, BAD CRIPP (Bay Area Disabled Community Rising in Protest and Power), the Disability Justice Culture Club, the #PowerToLive campaign, and many more. She used the Neflix film *Crip Camp*'s platform to launch radical programs centering disabled BIPOC, like the Ki'tay D. Davidson Fellowship. But just as, if not more, crucial were the million ways she built relationships with and brought disabled multiply oppressed people together. The hashtag #StaceyTaughtUs, created by the radical young Black and brown Girl Scout–alternative group Radical Monarchs after she visited them, is one that many people who loved her used after her death to encourage people to share the organizing strategies and crip knowledge we learned from her. (It was also used by Alice Wong and I when we created the "StaceyTaughtUs Syllabus," collecting her available online writing, poetry, speeches, and trainings immediately after her death.) A friend also pointed out that what she likely would've said was that she didn't teach people anything, but that we learned it together.

In writing this piece, I am loving my friend and comrade who loved me and many of us, and used her love to love disability justice community into being. I am loving my friend by sitting with her legacy, the great work of what she created, thought, and dreamt. I offer these meditations on her work and thinking as a way of not just helping to keep that work present, but to do work she asked as to do—to crip ideas of ancestorhood and to love, learn with, and engage with our disabled ancestors as a source of strength and wisdom.

ON THE ANCESTRAL PLANE

I think about crip ancestorship often. It is tied to crip eldership for me, a related but different topic. So many disabled people live short lives, largely because of social determinants of health like lack of healthcare, housing, clean air and water, or having basic needs met ... I do not know a lot about spirituality or what happens when we die, but my crip queer Korean life makes me believe that our earthly bodyminds is but a fraction, and not considering our ancestors is electing only to see a glimpse of who we are. People sometimes assume ancestorship is reserved for those of biological relation, but a queered or cripped understanding of ancestorship holds that, such as in flesh, our deepest relationships are with people we choose to be connected to and honor day after day.

Ancestorship, like love, is expansive and breaks manmade boundaries cast upon it, like the nuclear family model or artificial nation state borders ... I believe that our ancestors laugh, cry, hurt, rage, celebrate with us. Most importantly, I believe they learn as we are learning, just as we learn from them. We grow knowledge and movements with them. We crip futurism with them. We demand and entice the world to change the way things have always been done, with them. We change ourselves with them. They learn through us. When we become ancestors, we will also continue to learn.

—STACEY PARK MILBERN, "ON THE ANCESTRAL PLANE"[100]

It's a trip, writing about your friend and comrade's thoughts about crip ancestorhood that she wrote before she became an ancestor—when she is now an ancestor.

What is Stacey learning from us? What am I learning from her as an ancestor?

How do I demand and entice the world to change with her?

I will be answering these questions all my life, asking them and answering and answering again. It's a lifelong grief stewardship practice, one that is not quite ancestral reverence, more an ongoing ancestral conversation.

Right now, if you asked me those questions, I would say personal things. That I hear her telling me, in the middle of COVID and war, to not forget about my joy. To not just work hard and do serious things and all that lifesaving crap. To tease, to play, to flirt. To move across the country, away from the city that was beautiful but never fully felt like home and often felt like exile, to a city where I have always felt

---

100 Stacey Park Milbern, "On the Ancestral Plane: Crip Hand Me Downs and the Legacies of Our Movements," *Disability Visibility Project*, March 10, 2019, https://disabilityvisibilityproject.com/2019/03/10/on-the-ancestral-plane-crip-hand-me-downs-and-the-legacy-of-our-movements/.

inexplicably happy. To not forget good food, sweet community, sex, love, fresh water and warm salt water, mangos and sitting on a stoop with my coffee.

I hear her telling me to have patience, always and especially in a community writhing from seventy-eight kinds of grief and loss every day, where no one is acting with their best self—to extend grace where I can, to not burn bridges where I can. To allow for the unfolding of trust. To pump the brakes when it doesn't feel right. To be present with the ever-changing chaos, and to have faith in what we don't know yet. We never could have predicted any of this.

I am also dreaming of creating disability justice archives. About preserving our legacies for each other. I dream of creating an oral history series of DJ activists and artists. I dream of interviewing different disabled BIPOC artist about our life paths, the ways we create, what fruit we love best.

Creating disabled archives, of our friends' and comrades' work, dreams, and lives, before and after we die, is a form of DJ resistance in a world that wants to kill us and then erase us. It is a way we love each other and protect each other, to paraphrase Assata Shakur.

White queer disabled activist Corbett O'Toole once said, "Crips who die are libraries." All of us living disabled people hold so much crip knowledge, history, and survival skills—some of which may be written down, and some of which may live within us. When our disabled kin die or are murdered, one of the pieces of grief we often feel is how quickly their lives and work can be erased. People die without wills all the time, leaving their birth families to claim their property, including their intellectual/creative property and their online presence. It may be lost, taken offline, or hidden by family members who are overwhelmed, confused, homophobic or transphobic, or just don't understand their family member's work and life. Facebook and other online platforms may lock the content of disabled creators if a legacy holder is not designated—and the internet is where so many disabled people do our creating and sharing. I spent some of the hours after Stacey died with some of her other grieving friends, frantically copying and pasting her FB texts into a Google doc in case Facebook took her work offline.

COVID has made people talk about wills more than ever. But disabled estate planning is complex. Some of us are deemed legally incompetent to make our own decisions, and that specter hangs over so many of us. I have had a will since I was in my early twenties to protect myself from my abusive family; I did not want them to have the right to claim my body, my belongings, and creative work after my death. At the same time, I've spent the last two years of the pandemic waffling over my will and power of attorney. Some of the questions on the standard checklist are complicated for disabled people: The phrase "low quality of life," standard in living wills, as a "please do not revive me or use heroic measures if ..." is weaponized by ableist MIC people to deem nonspeaking people and people in comas "vegetables," said pejoratively to mean "not human," "not thinking," and to presume that they'd rather be dead. How do I write a power of attorney that understands that the medical system may be more likely to neglect me into death than fighting to use lifesaving technologies on me, and that fighting for my life is something I need my POA to do?

I don't have all the answers, but as we move into disabled death work—connecting with our many, many ancestors, and facing down our deaths to work to protect our legacies, I have faith we will keep asking and anwering the questions. I have faith we will keep cripping death, as we do everything else.

DISABLED UNCONDITIONAL LOVE IS LIFE FORCE

Stacey Park Milbern taught me a lot about unconditional disabled love. I hadn't had a ton of it. I had a mom who bragged casually throughout my childhood about how I had it lucky because "I don't have to hit you, I just stop loving you for a couple of days and you fall right in line." As an autistic kid, a lot of people's love or liking of me was really conditional on me being able to mask or pass as normal, be speedy and speaking. That love got pulled away as soon as I freaked out or went nonspeaking or had a meltdown. This followed me into adulthood, where I would default to being a wisecracking storyteller, a bedrock bottom liner, an automatic helper to the people I called friends, to try and make up for all the "weirdness" that was being autistic before I had words for it. I hid my private, "weird," neurodiverse parts I was ashamed of.

The second act of my and Stacey's friendship came after a period where both of us had gone through some struggles within disability justice community. She left DJ work for a time; I left the Bay Area and moved back to Toronto, saying it would be just for six months while it ended up being much longer. Some of my core relationships had ended or imploded, some of them because, even though I wasn't out about being autistic yet, some people couldn't deal with the me that was neurodivergent, and neither could I. At the time I was terrified that I was losing all my community and would be alone for the rest of my life. I did lose some people, but I was also surprised by the kinds of new friendships that emerged, the kinds of older friendships that grew deeper because they were, whether we said it out loud or not, places where it was OK for us to at least risk being ND without hiding it.

My friendship with Stacey was one of the friendships that surprised me during this period. As my friend and comrade Max Airborne said, "Stacey gave that (kind of disabled love and cherishing) to so many people, in fun ways and in areas they'd been hurt or considered disposable."[101] She loved my neurodiversity; I didn't have to closet things or apologize for them. That didn't mean she didn't tell me when something bothered her or that we didn't work out conflict, but it did mean that she had a fundamental love for disabled me as the bedrock that held us up during those times. She showed me this love in such everyday ways, without making a big deal out of it. And this feels like such a disabled way of showing love to people who have been shunned for their disabled parts, so we cringe when people try and overtly beam love at us because it's never been safe for us to be seen.

I think of the GIF she sent me unprompted one night that talked about how the core traits of autism was an inability to bullshit and a passion for justice. Or how, the time I had a full-scale meltdown when I missed my train to Portland, where we were co-facilitating an all-day training the next day and I was the only one of us who was going to be there in person, and after problem-solving with me about how I was going to get there, when I was still freaking out about *What if I lose it during the workshop and everyone thinks I'm crazy? What if they fire us?*

---

101 Max Airborne, Facebook, May 20, 2020, https://www.facebook.com/maxairborne/posts/1015 9845079308135.

It's bad enough I'm sick, I can't also be nuts, she said, *Hey, have you ever thought that your panic and meltdowns are also access needs? What if, if you start panicking, you just tell the room you have an access need to take care of and will be right back?* Even after coming of age in the psychiatric survivor movement at a young age, I had never, ever conceived of mental health access needs as being something I had a right to. This changed my life. I've told that story so many times, passing it on to others who worry about having a panic attack or another Big Crazy in Public moment at work.

If, as bell hooks said, "love is an action, never simply a feeling,"[102] these are two examples of disabled love in action. Unconditional disabled love that loved my shamed parts, that still could be real, say when something bothered her or have hard conversations or move away from abuse.

In thinking about ways I can work out of her lineage, bend the future, and build the movement out of what I learned from and with her, I think about: what are the ways we can be in a practice of unconditional disabled love, as a way we organize and live our lives?

When I talk about unconditional disabled love, I don't mean having relationships without boundaries, cosigning abuse, or letting anyone do anything. I've seen that play out in community, where people fuck up and say, "DJ means you have to love and accept everything I do!" No. Being able to be loved by Stacey equally for my goofy, nerdy, nonspeaking self as much as for the shiny, verbal, talkative, entertaining self—for years, the only one I thought could be shown to the world—didn't mean she didn't tell me when something bothered her or that we didn't have to work out conflict. It did mean that

---

102 bell hooks, *All About Love: New Visions.*

she had, that we practiced, a fundamental love for our disabled, ND selves, as a bedrock that was the core of our organizing, disability justice dreaming, our relationship.

I am thinking of unconditional disabled love as a rigorous commitment to reaching to each other with love. Many of us already practice this. As Stacey wrote, "I learned how to love hard from disabled QTPOC and our communities. We create places of refuge and imagine revolutionary care and belonging for one another. We try to be present in each other's joys and pains. The Disability Justice Movement's biggest political projects have been our relationships, the sites where we do the generative work of supporting each other to be the people we have fought and dreamed ourselves to be."[103] A rigorous, critical, learning commitment to reaching with love to each other. In a disabled way.

A disabled love politic could mean so many things. It could mean being committed to an ongoing practice of learning our own and each other's languages of disability, access, and care. I often think of cross-disability solidarity—the practice of being in solidarity with people with other kinds of disabilities than the ones we currently have—as being a process of learning a new language. Just like several different languages can share roots and have similar words (like Dravidian languages or Romance languages), many disabilities also share core experiences (for example, the ways some Deaf and Autistic people often feel like cousins because of our cultures' directness; the ways people with facial differences and amputations and dwarfism have a shared experience of being stared at). But there are

---

103 Stacey Park Milbern, Facebook, May 11, 2018, https://www.facebook.com/smilbern/posts/797 884841847.

still so many things we don't automatically know about each other, some languages we have to learn from scratch: Mad to physically disabled, sick to Deaf. (Of course there are people who are all or both.) We stumble when we assume that because we are oppressed by the same people, we don't have to do this work as part of our struggle to get everyone free.

A disabled love politics could be about doing deep listening, to take in the things a person may be shamed about or may not know they can do—like leadership and organization, like living on their own, going back to school, moving out of their family's house or across the country—and to believe in them. It could mean starting with ourselves, to be curious in our practices of learning to love the places in ourselves that have been most hated, and to be creative in how we invite ourself, Spirit, and others in to love those places.

Disabled love like this is not something we automatically know how to do. It makes me think of the words of Audre Lorde in her essay "Eye to Eye: Black Women, Hatred, and Anger": "We have to consciously study how to be tender with each other, until it becomes a habit ... because what was native has been stolen from us, the love of Black women for each other." This first part of the quote is often what is cited—what gets left out is that Lorde was specifically writing about internalized racism and misogynoir among Black women, and how the theft of that "native tongue" of Black women's love directly affected Black feminist organizing.

I think of Lorde's thinking as I think about the work of overcoming internalized hatred of ourselves and each other as disabled BIPOC, as a crucial part of the work of building disability justice. She continued, "But we can practice being gentle with ourselves by being gentle with each other. We can practice being gentle with each other by being gentle with that piece of ourselves that is hardest to hold, by giving more to the brave bruised girlchild within each of us."[104] I think of the ways I have witnessed disabled BIPOC give each other tenderness. I think about the work I witness us doing, little spoken of, of giving love to the brave bruised disabled young Black or brown self within each of us.

"Unconditional disabled love" or "disability justice love practices" are some of those crip-made phrases, like "crip doulaing," that we invented, that are not present in the dictionary or everyday mainstream discourse—so their very existence is hidden from many people who might need them. As disabled people, we often live in isolation with few or no disabled peers or mentors who can bring us into disabled community and mentor us in disabled language, skills, ways of loving. We may learn to love on our own, but loving in community is also a precious gift. Many of us have been taught not to listen to or trust our bodily sensations—at times very overtly, as with autistic people who are taught to mask and ignore our bodily symptoms of distress in "compliance training" within ABA programs. Part of our process of learning to love ourselves and each other means doing the incredibly risky work of tapping back into the disabled body/mind we have been taught to supress and abandon, to learn what our boundaries are, what we want, need, and desire.

Whether we have a disabled community or not, this kind of disabled love work does not come automatically. In attempting to love ourselves and each other, we often make shit up out of thin air as we

---

104 Audre Lorde, "Eye to Eye: Black Women, Hatred, and Anger," *Sister Outsider* (Berkeley, CA: Crossing Press, 2007).

invent these practices, trying stuff out, having no idea if it'll work. Sometimes, our attempts to love each other are messy and imperfect and fail, and it's easy to throw up our hands and say "that was garbage" and walk away from the community. Yet, I don't believe this means that our attempts at disabled love work and community-building aren't valuable. I think our messy imperfectness is disabled genius in action, even if it truly doesn't always feel that way. Admitting we don't know what we're doing, improvising things the way crips always do, and being honest when we fail, can be a disabled organizational strength. How many times have I seen organizers, abled and sometimes disabled, insist that they are the experts and refuse to be honest when mistakes or harm happen in organizing, keeping face and continuing the damage?

And how many times have I seen disabled relationships stumble when mistakes are made or harm is caused, and the ways that can feel like betrayal—of the idea that "You must automatically know how to love me just right, and fill all the holes left gaping, because we're both disabled"—leading to long-lasting fissures in the community, people who haven't been able to talk with one another or work together for years? There's no heartbreak like crip heartbreak.

But I believe when we practice disabled love with curiosity about each other, we can build relationships that are more likely to withstand the bumps. There is room for crip bitterness and complexity, for coming back together after not speaking for years, for moving in and out of contact with the seasons of our lives. Maybe even for forgiveness, for a communion of coming back together after time passes, accountability happening and change occurring—or, if not, just being able to be in the same meeting together.

One of my earliest and most often cited disability justice essays is "Making Space Accessible Is an Act of Love for Our Communities," a piece I wrote as an act of service in the lead-up to the 2010 Creating Collective Access disability justice space at the Allied Media Conference and US Social Forum in Detroit. In it, I argue that radical spaces needed to move towards a politic and practice of making space deeply accessible, collectively/together, from a deep place of loving and valuing disabled people, rather than as a reluctant, resentful act of complying with the bare minimum of the ADA in order to avoid a lawsuit, or feeling like "I guess we have to accommodate THEM." I believe that people who responded to that essay did so because it lifts up a radical disability justice love politic of truly loving and valuing disabled people as we are, building relationships with each other, and as disabled people, being in an ongoing practice of learning to love each other and ourselves that we have not been taught, that is an act of undoing internalized ableism. Love in the bell hooks sense of "being an action, not a feeling."

Yet, I also received some backlash, anger, and critique from other disabled people. One commenter on my blog was furious about an early version of the piece, insisting that disabled people should not have to be loved to receive the access that are our legal rights. I understand: so many of us have been told we must be loved and liked to get our basic access needs met, that we do not have a right to exist and get what we need on our own. Their critique made me understand I needed to make it clear that I differentiate between love and desirability, that what I was advocating for was a deep and unconditional love of all disabled people—"pretty" and "ugly," both "good cripples" and those of us who are the most hated and deemed undesirable by ableist society—as a politic and a practice. The critique also made me feel the tension between the aims of a rights-based framework—used by disability rights advocates to fight for legal protections and rights for disabled people—and the interventions of disability justice to name the "cliffhangers" found in a rights-based framework: namely the ways so many of us, in particular Black and brown, poor, criminalized, and non-citizen people are left out. If you can't sue because you don't have papers or money, you're shit out of luck if the law is the only way to get what you want. Multiply marginalized disabled people are often saved more by the relationships and networks of support we build outside the system.

This essay is a continuation of "Making Space Accessible Is an Act of Love for Our Communities." In loving and learning from my friend, in her life and as she resides on the ancestral plane after death, as she continues on in studying her life's work and organizing and sitting with my grief at her death—as so many of us are sitting with our disabled beloveds who are gone—I am asking: What does it mean to center a practice of unconditional and critical disabled love in how we organize to save our lives, and build communities of resilient and beautiful disabled love?

Maybe some examples of disabled love-in-action practices that Stacey thought of. Like:

We are in a climate crisis. There is no way to know the specifics of what happens next. It makes sense that we all will be called into the unknown, needing to do things we have not done before. Please step out into it with us.

Socioemotional skills to sharpen so the women & femme organizers in your life don't have to do everything:

- approach people for money
- have a sense of how much you have and how much you need
- make decisions about resources
- write grants & do gigs
- make sure there are contracts, leases, insurance etc
- host dinners to get to know people or bring people deliberately together
- keep a mental log of people who are looking for work and people who are hiring
- keep a mental log of people who are looking for friends or dates, introduce them
- vouch for people, take your referrals super seriously
- provide emotional & mental health support
- build relationships with partner orgs
- befriend the people in your org
- remember people's surgeries, cat's birthdays, first days at a new job
- ask people to slow down
- provide care work or find care workers
- fundraise and collect resources for people
- pump the brakes if something isn't right
- be the heavy/messenger/boundary keeper
- bring up hard topics
- encourage people to approach each other if they have a conflict

- mediate conflict
- give a pep talk or cheerlead
- observe emotional temp of room & adjust group
- be a consistent, sometimes public, presence so people know who to go to
- write about the work
- create the social media content
- represent your group at events
- speak on panels
- respond to emails in the group inbox
- respond to the DMs
- figure out who in group can do a task, ask them, brief them on details
- problem solve
- hear people's negative experiences and apologize on behalf of group
- create the event promo
- create the meeting agenda and facilitate
- check or create access
- encourage groups to take care of each other
- demonstrate what having fun looks like
- take photos and document moments
- A million more ... What would you add?

—STACEY PARK MILBERN[105]

105 Stacey Park Milbern, Facebook, March 20, 2020, https://www.facebook.com/smilbern/posts/882436888867.

Black queer feminist maestra poet, essayist, teacher, and thinker June Jordan said, "Love is lifeforce."[106] I believe in the radical power of disability justice love as lifeforce. It found me, the disabled Divine, when I was sick and alone on a futon with no spoons and community, and it has stayed with me, something I am continuously learning together with Stacey and many other disabled kin, a rippling crip ribbon that weaves through all the moments of my crip life.

I am going to continue to shape my life around it because it has been what has brought me home. More than ever, even and especially as times get harder, I think this rigorous, messy learning and devoted disabled love will be what keeps us and leads us.

I know like any kind of love it will surprise me, shake me up, turn me inside out, scare me, and set me free. I believe it can be a piece of the disabled Divine on earth.

I invite you to join me and us in this practice, and to witness the ways you are already doing it, as real.

---

106 June Jordan, "The Creative Spirit and Children's Literature," originally written and not published in 1977, published in *Revolutionary Mothering: Love on the Front Lines*, edited by Alexis Pauline Gumbs, China Martens, and Ma'ia Williams (San Francisco: PM Press, 2016).

ADAPTIVE TRIKE

Disabled people aren't supposed to be exist in the public world, let alone the woods, or just about anywhere having a great time. As evinced by the tiny blonde girl screaming in confused rage as I speed by in my racing recumbent trike, "But WHY is she riding that, Mommy? WHY IS SHE RIDING THAT THING?"

"BECAUSE IT FEELS AMAZING!" I scream at her over my shoulder. I have upset the entire orientation of her universe just by being me, in public, completely shredding the hell out of the Magnusen Park trail network in this adaptive trike that weighs maybe 18 pounds. It doesn't work; she's still bellowing "WHY?" and being shushed by her no-doubt embarassed parents. But I'm already half a mile away.

Michel Foucault said, "Visibility is a trap," a concept echoed by Black trans disabled scholars like Tournaline: trans visibility doesn't equal less trans murder or more trans justice. I agree. Cute disabled Paralympian ads don't counter right-to-die legislation or help raise SSDI / SSI / state disability rates from below the sub-sub-poverty line. But it's also true that our vibrant, weird, improbable crip bodyminds enjoying ourselves in ways the abled and normal may not have ever considered has the power to shock and upend both their ableism and their idea of the way things—bodies, movement, life—are supposed to be.

I didn't come here to be a teachable moment for this tiny white kid, though. I'm here because my current town of Seattle is the home of Outdoors for All: a truly incredible adaptive sports center that has a WAREHOUSE of handcycles and trikes and quadcycles that anyone disabled can just show up and borrow for free. I was a disabled, autistic kid whose dad raged at them because bikes aren't accessible to my body and my lack of ability to ride one was a huge shame to him. Then I was a disabled autistic twenty-three-year-old who figured out how to buy a used Pashley trike from a bike place called Parts Unknown, down an alley in Kensington Market, and started speeding all over the city, riding my trike standing up to go up hills and looking like the Road Warrior, and just having massive crip body-joy all the time.

It's been a minute though. I've mostly been hanging out in my crip homespace for a year and change, and it's been a terrible year. My friend Stacey died, my friend LL died, my dad died, more people than I can count who I knew a little bit or were friends or relatives of loved ones died. And like every disabled person I know, I spent the year terrified that everyone I loved—because my whole beloved community is disabled—were going to be murdered by a virus plus care rationing. I wore a hole in my couch crying out my grief, and my life mostly didn't get that far from my house and the Cheasty Greenspace, the urban forest where my house is located. I went for slow cane walks by the blackberry vines, western red cedars, bigleaf oak, and trickling urban streams of my neighborhood. When I was the most terrified, I visited the ring of cedars by the mailboxes to pray.

A month after Stacey died, bereft and looking for a place to hold me, I went to an online grief workshop held by BIPOC Grief Circle,[107] a Toronto collective that started doing grief workshops at the beginning of COVID. They asked us to pay attention to the land we were on as we began to write and meditate on grief—both what Indigenous

107 Instagram: @BIPOCgriefcircle

land it is and what our treaty rights and responsibilities were to it, and to just spend some time breathing and connecting with the land we were on, including the land that as bed-living people we saw out our windows. I was grateful, because as a bed-dwelling person I do often connect the most with the land I can see through my window when I'm sick or sad. Grief is held by and with land, not separable, the facilitators said.

Grief lives in the body, crip grief lives in the crip body. And I am working out my crip grief by moving in a crip way on this land, on this trike. I am luxuriating in sinking into this inches-from-the-ground chair. I am whipping by everyone, and easing off the gears and moving slow. I am leaning back, pedaling through all the ecosystems this 350 acre park has: the lake, the wetlands, the grasslands, the many sportsfields with kicking children and picnicking adults, all of us looking to this land to hold our hearts. I have a map, but it's not the world's greatest and it's not the point. The point is to enjoy going whichever way my body wants to go, to get lost and figure my way back, with my brain and my muscles, my felt sense of what direction I want to stretch into.

At one point I'm reclining and pedaling through a long wetland boardwalk path, the boards quietly clanking under my wheels. The blackberries are at eye and hand level, and I get to cruise slowly, pick them, and throw them in my mouth as I ride in a luxurious slow. I get to see all the wheel-high things walkies miss because they're five or six feet up, not two.

Three or four miles later, I pull up by the pebbly Lake Washington beach. My trike is my chair. I lean back and watch the lake's waves, her giant inland ocean. I think of all the stories she holds.

I bring my grief to her, and my leaning-back adaptive joy, and she takes everything I have to give her with wide open hands.

CHAPTER 17

Wild Disabled Joy: Disabled Pleasure Activism

HANGING OUT WITH OTHER DISABLED QUEER/TRANS BIPOC PEOPLE IS MY PLEASURE ACTIVISM

My Twitter account's pinned post just says WILD DISABLED JOY. All caps.

We're not supposed to be happy. We're not even supposed to exist, or be alive. Happy? What the fuck? Who do you think you are?

And our lives as disabled people often contain a fair amount of bullshit, pain, and struggle. And yet.

I'm staring at a photo taken during the *I wanna be with you everywhere* study day at the Whitney. The image description would read, *Four sick and disabled queer Black and Asian femmes—some wheelchair-using, some with facial differences, some chronically ill, all neurodivergent, sit in a room laughing and talking and listening to each other intently.* Looking at it, I think, hanging out—just hanging out—with other disabled BIPOC is one of my deepest joys. The fabric of our days, how we enjoy, laugh, listen, notice, and show up, makes me rich.

"Pleasure activism," the term coined by writer and activist adrienne maree brown to mean a politic that uplifts joy and pleasure in activism and radical life, is both a beloved and controversial concept amongst people I know. I have a piece about the pleasures of giving and receiving care in brown's book *Pleasure Activism.*

I appreciate a focus on joy and sensuality in activism and the lives we make, as a form of healing, prefiguratively making the lives and communities we want in the Good Future to happen now, and also just helping us withstand the struggle. I also have had friends make reasonable critiques of how they see some people using the term "pleasure activism" to lift up individual self-care and hedonism as the world burns, without a class analysis of who gets to afford certain pleasures and how we define pleasure with regards to what things cost. *Not everything is fun! Someone has to take out the garbage, and who does that if some people who have more class-stability are off enjoying themselves?* This is a fair question.

However, I am a big fan of the working-class and poor disabled Black and brown femme pleasure activism I see as a crucial part and not-always-discussed part of disability justice. I think of listening to Patty Berne talk about her insistence that Sins Invalid have a high aesthetic standard, beautiful photography on the posters, and a sensuality about the theatrical experience. I think of the Black disabled femme maximalist aesthetic of my friend Naima Niambi Lowe's gorgeous, cunty, huge cashmere scarves with FUCK THE POLICE silk-screened on them. I think of the joy of my best friend's house, where she gave me a key so I can always come home, and we sit on the couch, let it all hang out, order iddly, curd rice, and dosas, smoke a little tiny joint and listen with great care and knowledge and laughter and kindness to each other.

I find lacking some sites that call for rest as radical without talking about class or race or disability; I understand some spaces that say that all these pro-rest people are privileged and don't name their privileges enough. I resonated with Ijeoma Oluo's recent article "Capitalism Sucks, but Don't Be Shamed for Your Hustle,"[108] where she advocated for both a critique of burnout always-working culture, and an understanding that a lot of poor and working-class Black and brown people are not choosing to work all the time because we love capitalism, but because our hustle pays for both the rent and pleasures we want for ourselves and our kids.

I find that both sides of the coin frequently don't talk about the original resters I know: disabled people, including a shit ton of poor disabled people, especially disabled people whose bodies leave us no choice but to rest a lot, and who often do so when we are poor. Disabled people know about resting because when your body literally has an hour of spoons a day and you have no choice but to rest, you might as well learn how to organize from a space of resting a lot. How we learn what one-spoon organizing looks like, and also, how to have fun on a serious fourteen-dollars-for-extras-a-month budget while we do it.

As disabled people, particularly disabled BIPOC, wild disabled joy and disabled forms of pleasure—including kinds that are not legible to abled and neurotypical people, or that they are repelled by—are a core part of our resistance. A few years ago everything was shit and I texted my friend, a genderful queer amputee artist, asking if they wanted to get out of town. *Oh yeah*, they text back. They pick me up in their sexy black Jeep with hand controls, we get coffees and we google *best accessible swimming hole within 45 minutes*. We drive, and talk, and go through the drive-through at TacoTime so we don't have

---

108 Ijeoma Oluo, "Capitalism Sucks, but Don't Be Shamed for Your Hustle," *Behind the Book* (Substack), January 6, 2022, https://ijeomaoluo.substack.com/p/capitalism-sucks-but-dont-be-shamed/.

to get out and walk, and spontaneously stop by for five-dollar joints at this suburban-country strip-mall weed place. When we get to the unmarked pull-off, walk carefully down a hill that is way slopier than we thought, slowly and crip-careful. They say, *We can stop whenever we want and go as slow as we need*. They share with me the tips they share with their clients, about how walking with your feet angled gives you more control. We talk and sweat and finally get to the prize: a tiny swimming hole with waterfalls next to cliffs wreathed with vines, with three naked people lounging who cheerfully wave then ignore us. My friend walks with their brand new cheetah feet prothesis into the river I navigate with my cane.

Disabled people are the best people I know at prioritizing pleasure in our lives. Whether it's my friend who tops me into getting a goddamn massage already, to my friends who are champions of rest and of innovating ways to make bedlife feel fun even when you want to poke your eyes out you're so sick of it, to my disabled friends who love Disneyland (because it's accessible for fat and disabled people and filled with working-class families, and lots of ND folks and folks with inner younger parts love the whimsy and alternate world), or hot springs, accessible casinos or all-in resorts with a patio, my disabled friends who have crip game night, including visiting when someone is in a nursing home for a spell, to the crip dance night at *I wanna be with you everywhere* with protheses, chairs, canes, and ear defenders aplenty. I think of the hours I've witnessed other disabled people spend curating our makeup and clothes and the crip ravers I've known who just loooove drugs, and budget weeks of low-spoon bed/rest time to go dancing. We are disabled creative in both how we pursue pleasure, and how we crip pleasure-making and -enjoying.

Crip sex looks different than abled sex. I think of C.K. Kaufman's recent writing on what disabled sex and sensuality in the pandemic has looked like:

> It has looked like separating my sensuality from my sexuality, and deepening my understanding of the erotic.
>
> it looks like developing and nurturing kinky dynamics through long texts, voice memos, and tons of nudes.
>
> it looked like breaking up with a lover in spring 2021 when he chose going to the club over my safety/boundaries.
>
> it looks like struggling to write the sex toy reviews, because of not being in the mood to try the toys.
>
> it looks like not knowing when I'll be able to cuddle and kiss a precious sweetie.
>
> it looks like reading erotica to my friends over the phone.
>
> it looks like taking deeper care of myself and upgrading my skin-care routine.
>
> it has looked like having the space to excavate and feel the depths and effects of sexual violence and trauma in my body and figuring out what's needed for the pain of it all.
>
> it has looked like undefining and redefining my own sexuality.
>
> it looks like moving in a wavy line so that the leaves of my tallest house plant touch and tickle my face when I roll by.[109]

Consciously choosing to create disabled pleasure is a radical act when ableism tells disabled people that all we deserve is an abusive and nasty bare-bones nursing home life, and then dying in a corner. A

---

[109] C.K. Kaufman (@rosesarespread), Instagram, January 7, 2022, https://www.instagram.com/p/CYczKPZhpFJ/.

central way ableism punishes us is saying that all we deserve is functional utility, that we should be desperately grateful for the basics and not ask for more.

Dig deeper, and there's a million examples of ableism saying that because our bodyminds are monstrous we are less than "human," and deserve punishment, not pleasure. Think of the disabled kids at the Willowbrook State School, fed a ground-up slop in a trough for their meals, three minutes maximum a day. Think of almost every psych inpatient unit you've ever known. Think of the deep eugenic fear of disabled sexualities, of "out of control" developmentally/intellectually disabled people who "don't know what they're doing," and the work to forcibly sterilize disabled people or use "the Ashley X treatment" to stop disabled young people from going through puberty, in order to control our sexualities and prevent us from reproducing. Think of the ugliness of much adaptive equipment or medical equipment—how, until recently, many protesthetics and adaptive devices came only in DOA Caucasian skin tones, or were functional, never beautiful. So much of ableism comes from a core belief that a can of Ensure in a nursing home is all we are entitled to, and we are incredibly uppity if we insist on "frills" like beauty, pleasure, and choice.

I've seen rage launched at anyone—but in a particular way at disabled femmes, particularly BIPOC femmes—when we ask to live not just on bread and water and a cot. This mostly comes from abled people, but I've also witnessed it coming laterally from other disabled people. I've seen rage launched at a disabled femme of color elder because she wanted to make her accessible mobile home beautiful. Friends of mine, all masculine, grumped, *Why does it have to have wall paneling of that particular kind of nice wood? Why does it have to have tiles she likes?* I understood some of their trepidation, because when people are asking for food, shelter, electricity, a wheelchair, back-rent, or milk for their babies, there are complicated things about asking for money for pleasure. Yet there is also a rage that is abled sexism/femmephobia mixed with a certain rage at daring to have a disabled erotic—like, *How dare you ask for more than the bare minimum?* And a lack of certain understandings of disabled life. When I see disabled BIPOC femmes asking for something considered a femme luxury, I see both a demand to live with full vibrancy and an acknowledgment that we may not live forever or for long and we want to maximize our time here. When people got pissed at my friend, I often thought, *After years of inaccessible homes, she wants to raise the money to have something beautiful. She has every right to insist on beauty.*

There's something about being told you're a sad-sack medical tragedy with violins ready to be cured all the time that makes you just go, *fuck it, I'm going to live.*

And there's something about claiming a body you've been taught to despise, told it's a broken toy that should be hidden from public space, that makes it a courageous and radical act to have a good goddamn time unapologetically taking up as much space as possible. It is a particular disabled Black and brown femme politic (often fat too) of loudness, excess, and maximalism that I adore. It is an insistence of our right to joy and to take up space. It is resistance. It is a cripping of pleasure. It is freedom work, insisting that we deserve our roses, lilies, peonies, jasmine, orgasms, fresh water when we are still here—and that joy and pleasure are key parts of what both helps us make the disabled world-to-come we are dreaming of now, in this moment, and what helps us keep going when the work is hard and heartbreaking.

Disabled people pursuing pleasure also bring crip doulaing to the work—creating and sharing spaces of disabled pleasure are one of the ways we model for other disabled people. When she was alive, Stacey Park Milbern was the most brilliant practitioner of disabled pleasure that I've known. We were both Taurus crips, we both worked all the damn time, but I have never had spreads of food like we had at her house. The last time I ate with her before she died, it was Wednesday, for fuck's sake, but "Oh we have fried chicken ... this grilled lavender salmon ... mac and cheese ... sweet and purple potatoes ... greens ... oh and I think there's a cheesecake?" she said, innocently, her eyes twinkling. Stacey had a lot of different circles of friends, but central to the crew were her "vacation buddies" who she went on big crip weekends off with. She went to Yosemite, she went to Harbin Hot Springs once they got accessible cabins, she was the master of the hotel vacation with drinks on the patio. She is far from the only crip I've known who has deliberately practiced making space for pleasure.

When I wrote "Cripping the Apocalypse," some of my points felt simple. Get abled people, especially BIPOC, to get their heads out of their asses about disability. Build multigenerational disabled communities. Build disabled work for climate justice. Save Ourselves. Sure. And this book is a lot of that too.

But I don't want to leave out: it's never just Hard, Activist Work. It's disabled pleasure. It's wild disabled joy. It's us on the dance floor, throwing our heads back laughing. It's the permission, the utter permission to be as we are. It's the ways we create pleasure to both make the work sweeter and more accessible—pleasure as a form of access.

It's a lot easier to get people to sign up for the long struggle of changing the world if we have fun and disabled joy while we do it.

I also think about the power and the ways our pleasures are often illegible to abled minds. I think about the way I budgeted for and bought really great sheets this year (they're not a million dollars or anything, but they're also no longer IKEA Basics) and the great joy I get from stimming as I slide into them at night. When we slide under the radar of abled vision, there are many things we can get away with, many sneak-attack possibilities where we can strike where they're not looking.

I know a lot of people who, throughout the pandemic, found it necessary to fight hard for joy. I knew a lot of people who, when Trump hit, did the same. Immediately after the 2016 election, queer Arab writer Randa Jarrar wrote, "When Trump won in 2017, I decided I wanted to live more and work less; to walk my dog, to smoke my weed, to eat Ethiopian food with a lover, to swim in warm water, to breathe deeply, to cry, to drive to mountains, to drink tea copiously, to sleep next to my pets. To live."[110]

I felt similarly in the pandemic. Everyone was dead and there were so many explosions in my heart every month, and somehow, joy in the horror was something I found. I made new routines. Farmers market on Wednesdays, ice cream once a week in the park at night on the secret picnic bench, Friday-night takeout with Neve and Tony on the pink velvet couch with all the TV, my big autistic *Star Trek Discovery* weekly watch party, going to the lake and putting my body

---

110 Randa Jarrar, "Ask Auntie Randa: On Writing, Coffee Grounds, and the Flavors of Oral Sex," *Bitch Media*, January 17, 2018, https://www.bitchmedia.org/article/ask-auntie-randa/writing-coffee-grounds-and-flavors-oral-sex.

in it at least once a week with a cane and water shoes. I worried it looked on IG like I was just blithely having a wonderful time, but I mostly didn't care. And it wasn't that. It was me finding the autistic awe, the disabled joy, in the middle of so many things burned down, ripped out of my heart with no warning and no sorry, the crushing weight of how casually the system murdered people I loved who were treasures.

It wasn't just surviving as a burnt-out husk. It was insisting on claiming my right to live after murderous loss, with joy.

BEDAZZLED FOR GOD AND INSISTING ON VELVET: BIPOC DISABLED FEMME MAGICAL PROTECTION RITUALS

"The visibility which makes us most vulnerable is that which also is the source of our greatest strength."
—AUDRE LORDE

When I was working on this essay, I received criticism from one comrade, who said that insisting on pleasure was not the most radical DJ act—that going to Disneyland with a posse of crips could never be a radical disability justice act because Disneyland was a corporation. I was taken aback by his feedback, but it made me think more deeply about the argument I am making.

Beauty, ugliness, and the place of pleasure are ongoing conversations within disability justice. The tagline of disability justice performance collective Sins Invalid—whose works have often centered explorations of disabled BIPOC and/or queer and trans beauty, sexuality, and embodiment—reads, "An unashamed claim to beauty in the face of invisibility." Disabled Asian queer writer Mia Mingus in her

2010 essay, "Moving Towards Ugly: Beyond a Politics of Desirability,"[111] wrote about her experiences of feeling excluded from nondisabled femme communities and genders, and argued that disability justice advocates should move away from a politic of celebrating disabled beauty and towards embracing what she called "magnificance"—a term encompassing bodyminds categorized as ugly and undesirable.

Sins Invalid's work and Mingus's writing opened doors for a lot of disabled femmes of color and disabled BIPOC to talk about beauty and ugliness in our lives and to begin to unpack the ways racist ableism had affected our relationships to our sense of our own desires and desirability. Some of Mingus's writing, to me and other disabled femmes I know, strayed into statements that felt femmephobic and critical of all femme aesthetics and genders as necessarily ableist, uncritically loving of consumerism, and depoliticized—something I disagree with.

A decade after Mingus wrote "Moving Towards Ugly," Reclaim Ugly, an organization founded by Black disabled fat femme writer and organizer Vanessa Rochelle Lewis (and lead by a team of disabled BIPOC and/or queer trans organizers who have experienced uglification) is a community organization that invites people to "rewrite and decolonize (their) understanding of beauty from white supremacy, the patriarchy, and other social hierarchies." Reclaim Ugly names "uglification ... as a system of personal and cultural beliefs, behaviors, practices and laws that dehumanize people as ugly, undesirable,

---

111 Mia Mingus, "Moving Toward Ugly: A Politic Beyond Desirability," *Leaving Evidence* (blog), August 22, 2011, https://leavingevidence.wordpress.com/2011/08/22/moving-toward-the-ugly -a-politic-beyond-desirability/.

immoral and unworthy."[112] Reclaim Ugly is doing crucial work to center the knowledge and experience of people who have been deemed ugly, to talk about the ways we've been called ugly, to name ugliness as something that was invented—not a "natural" concept that has always meant the same thing—and uglification as a system that can be resisted and destroyed.

When I was getting down to the wire on working on this piece, my disabled Jewitch friend Dori Midnight and I had a spirited conversation on traded voice-memos about disabled aesthetics and beauty as a specifically disabled femme protection practice that really helped me figure out why I believe that crip beauty and pleasure practices are radical and important. Dori shared with me her Jewish culture's concept of *hiddur mitzvah* (which she teaches about in her workshops and writing on Jewish protection magic), a tradition of putting extra time, style, sparkle, flair, resources into a practice or thing to make it as beautiful as possible.

"It's about bedazzling for God, that beauty itself is the way—a way to connect, protect, heal, deepen, and express devotion and love. It's the lineage of centuries of femme armor, of dressing ourselves as the altars," she said. "It's like, yeah, you can do this thing but why do you put pomegranates on it, why do we put gold on it, why do we make it velvet? Why do we create ornamentation? To me that is femme adornment, which is a form of protection magic and healing that's thousands of years old. Things don't have to be ascetic. We live in capitalism, and capitalism co-opts those things and tries to sell it back to us, but creating beauty is a life-affirming practice and

112 "5 Things We Should All Know about Uglification," *Reclaim Ugly*, February 12, 2021, https://reclaimugly.org/2021/02/12/5-things-we-should-all-know-about-uglification/.

something that has been going on for millennia—not just as part of capitalism."[113]

Ah ha. Of course. How could I have forgotten? How could I have forgotten that the heart of disabled pleasure practices, for me, are my own brown disabled femme adornment, armor, and pleasure practices—inspired and in conversation with many other BIPOC queer disabled friends and comrades? I thought about Rebirth Garments' disabled, trans, Southeast Asian garments, binders, packers, breast forms, masks and hijabs, filled with bright metallics, prints, hot pinks and purples—and their founder Sky Cubacub's "Radical Visibility Manifesto,"[114] where they point out, "Cultural norms don't encourage trans and disabled people to dress stylishly or loudly. Society wants us to 'blend in' and not draw attention to ourselves. But what if we were to resist society's desire to render us invisible? What if, through a dress reform, we collectively refuse to assimilate?" Where adaptive devices are never made to be gaudy or beautiful, the clothing and access tools Rebirth Garments creates are a counter to this. I thought about disabled superfat Indigeous femme artist Shilo George's Fat Femme Warrior Regalia art series, an art installation which includes a war club made of broken glass shards and an artillery of lipsticks. My friend Naima Niambi Lowe, a Black disabled fat femme visual and multimedia artist who makes gorgeous, huge paintings, silk and cashmere scarves in bright colors with FUCK THE POLICE and ABORTION IS HEALTHCARE screenprinted onto them, tweets, "Naima lives in Oklahoma where she makes luxury abolitionist accessories

113 Dori Midnight, personal conversation with the author, January 2022.
114 Sky Cubacub, "Radical Visibility: A Queercrip Dress Reform Movement Manifesto," *Rebirth Garments*, abridged and updated October 2019, http://rebirthgarments.com/radical-visibility-zine.

that she markets using IPhone thirst traps in her back yard." All of us are rejecting a world that would shame us into hiding.

We are navigating unsafe worlds—the bus, the internet, the world where we may be doxed—by taking up space with our bright colors and gorgeousness. This is femme of color crip magic—the ways we decorate our canes and wheelchairs and CPAPs, the way Frida Kahlo painted on her casts and back corsets. They are ways we insist on our right to be here and create vibrant lives. And they are also forms of protection magic. There are times we survive by hiding and making ourselves small, and those are valid. And so many BIPOC femmes also know that getting bigger, louder, and shinier is also a way we protect ourselves. When we go out with our sharpest fade, our eyebrows done right, our shiniest jewelry and most well-ironed button-down or best dress, we don our femme armor, blades so sharp anyone wanting to fuck with us gets cut.

In creating spaces and an aesthetic of disabled brown femme maximalist pleasure in my life, I'm being a gaudy, loud, working-class-raised Sri Lankan / Galician / Irish disabled femme who finds resilience and joy in big gold, bright colors, tight clothes, button-ups, all-fuchsia everything, black mesh, sensory friendliness, big earrings and amethyst studs, the memories of my grandmother's wedding set of bigass Sri Lankan amethyst rock jewelry set in dark Southie gold. I am possibility modeling and recruiting for other crips in shame who see me limping down the street being cute and joyful with it, and I'm also creating a disabled brown queer life of pleasure. This is just the way I love and live when I wake up, put on some earrings and gold glitter sneakers and pick up the cane my chosen brother bought off the internet and drew roses on with nail polish for my fortieth birthday, saying we made it, we lived. It is also a process of de-assimilation from whiteness, Christian hegemony, and ableism, and finding and creating power.

When I had to do some protective magic after a scary roommate moved out, my friend told me to put on my tightest dress and my shiniest jewelry and walk around the house scattering the salt. The salt was important, but so was the shine. In these times where we both desperately need the power of the imaginary to create liberated disabled futures and presents, and which are times where we are under attack, we need both kinds of magic: the kind that invokes beautiful, hot disabled BIPOC lives and futures into being, and the kind that are protection amulets against those who want to kill us.

Luckily, disabled BIPOC pleasure and beauty practices are often both.

THE EROTICS OF UNMASKING

A lot changed for me when I hit forty-six and started tracing how my pleasure history had been so deeply woven with my autism. It's easy to look at much of my life as being one big wreckage of car crash after car crash of trauma. CSA, sexual assault in junior high suicidal best femme rape almost murdered #1 almost murdered #2.

All of this is true. But it's also true that my life has contained green gardens, saved-up-for lipstick in hot orchid (MAC Epic, if you want to know, circa 2001, now it's Too Faced Melted Matte Unicorn, except it's discontinued, so I bought Fenty Unlocked and a tube of MAC's Heroine for when my last tube runs out), living alone, ferality, short skirts, tight jeans, that tiny lavender mylar bra top I wore riding a trike home at three a.m. when I was twenty-five, femme clothing swap hordes, lovers, Value Village heels, and later, really good sneakers and boots, the whole autistic disabled femme sexual life I have that lives in dreams, porn, fantasies, various lovers at various times. The erotics of my autistic feral femme solitude, the erotics of my erotic decade friendship romances.

When my relationship ended and my dad died and my friend died, not in that order. And my ex moved out and I was going to, but then my other friend died and there was a huge North American rental and moving crisis and moving while disabled is never ever easy, so I decided to stay a little longer in the miracle rental that I couldn't really afford but I couldn't afford to move either. COVID divorcée paying the whole-ass rent, got another job and a Patreon to pay the difference. And in that sacred space of no eyes, I found myself, my sex and my pleasure. Found my sex dreams and the compression garments and button-ups I'd been afraid to try. I found my nonbinary, autistic gendered and sexual self, and its pleasures.

So many autistics unmasked during COVID. So many trans/NB folks were able to soften and harden, lean into our genders in our own four walls if we had them. This was true of me, and the two were related. Living alone, in a COVID-divorcée solo house, I leaned into both.

I figured out I was autistic in 2016. The four years before the pandemic were a long slow process of reading everything I could get my hands on, following hashtags, reviewing my whole entire life as a silent movie with my mouth slightly open, slowly coming out to friends, losing some who had shit reactions (like the secret trust-fund white kid who said, "I'm not surprised, you've always been rude!"—bye), slowly leaning into wanting to build more with other autistic friends and making new ones. I wasn't out all the time. I felt like I had a lot to learn and I wasn't ready. I was also really really scared of losing jobs, social connections, the grease that kept me fed.

But leaning into being autistic felt so good. The first time I saw a pile of ear defenders at IWBWE and slipped them on, or orally stimmed with my roommate (*boop boop boop boop boop!*), or had such joy being silent and grumpy and happy with my other roommate in the morning, all of those things healed me to myself and just felt good. The unconditional love and acceptance of some of my autistic friends, and also, I just liked hanging out with them.

It was also permission to stop hermetically sealing the bilateral halves of my brain—the autistic/ND stuff I had always loved but kept private, and my public world, including my sexual and romantic relationships, they could never meet. The first was delicious but gross, weird, annoying. No one would ever like or enjoy that. No one could see it. Instead, I could be all of me, more.

My neurodivergent femme therapist listening to me talk about this, nodded and said, *It makes me think of the phrase, "the erotics of unmasking,"* and all the doors of my heart opened up. I wanted to send her all the edible arrangements and flowers in thanks, but didn't because she has good boundaries and would probably say no to them.

What is an erotic, pleasure-centered disabled world like where the pleasure is centered on our unmasked selves? What do our unmasked selves leaning deeply into our ND joy look like, what are they able to create? What theories and practices and tools and hangouts and sex or sensuality can we make out of that autistic and ND unmasked erotic?

You can't have good sex and/or pleasure—sex and pleasure not about functionality but about intimacy, connection, embodiment, joy—while lying about essential, core things about your self. This might include splitting them off and burying them, and essentially moving from a place of deep shame and masking.

Audre Lorde famously defined the erotic, in her work "Uses of the Erotic: The Erotic as Power," as

> a resource within each of us that lies ... firmly rooted in the power of our unexpressed or unrecognized feeling ... When released from its intense and constrained pellet, it flows through and colours my life with a kind of energy that heightens and sensitizes and strengthens all my experience. We have been raised to fear the yes within ourselves, our deepest cravings ... But when I become in touch with the erotic, I become less willing to accept powerlessness, or those other supplied states of being which are not native to me, such as resignation, despair, self-effacement, depression, self-denial.[115]

Reading Lorde's words decades after she first wrote them, through my lens as a brown autistic nonbinary femme, I resonate strongly with them, finding my erotic as power in my experience of the erotics of unmasking. Following what brings me joy, doing what feels good, living in my comfort zone, practicing loving my autistic facets unconditionally, loving into sensory joy and autonomy, all are an autistic erotic that builds my power.

---

115 Audre Lorde, "Uses of the Erotic: The Erotic as Power," *Sister Outsider* (Berkeley, CA: Crossing Press, 2007).

What is this disabled future we are creating if it is not rooted in all the everyday, daily moments of a joyful disabled present, in the middle of the crap? The everyday, yet not-taken-for-granted, things—the *it's always OK for your access needs to change* text, the honesty where we discuss the risks we are taking and needing not to take, the re-jigging of a small Christmas *Matrix* and dim sum crip gathering to mean me driving dim sum and slices of my molasses ginger pear upside-down cake (GF, not vegan) to friends as the snow comes down, love through the windows, and then watching it from home.

What future would you create if you leaned into the wild crip imaginings you maybe have not let yourself imagine?

What futures come from autistics and other NDs unmasking and creating the conditions where we can unmask and not be murdered (by cops or our communities)—from our being our truest and wildest selves?

When we crip pleasure, when we lean into the erotics of unmasking and autistic and NB pleasure, when we make crip pleasure in our couch hangs, our delivery, our slow couch sits, our cat pics, our backyard porn shoots, our buying a grabber and using it to get our vibrator, our putting an accessible deep-soaking tub in the schoolbus we remake into a house, our raucous wheelchair and caney crowd blocking traffic at the farmers market, our drooling laughter, we make a new world in the craters of this present one. We make amazing lives, and they are possibility models for other crips who see us for a moment, a glimpse, in-person or in the pages of the internet.

Our crip pleasure activism is a fist in the face of those who say we only deserve utility—Ensure in an institution, basic clothes but not gender euphoria, survival but not pleasure. We create movements and imagine futures from our deepest disabled and ND erotics—ones full of not just survival, but particular disabled and ND pleasure and joy.

The work of imagining a radical disabled future must be guided by the wild disabled joy we are figuring out how to fight for in the present. And it is.

Our disabled erotic is powerful.

CHAPTER 18

Wild Disabled Futures:
The Future Is Now

MAYBE WE WILL ALL BE SICK AND SAD

The future is disabled, unknown, and unwritten. I don't know what the world will be like when this book comes out, or the year or decade after that. Yet, there are a few clues about how it might go.

Two years into the mass disabling event of COVID, there are massive numbers of newly disabled people—from long COVID, from getting COVID twice or three times, from CPTSD, anxiety, and overwhelming grief from mass death. This means a lot of things.

On the one hand, the pandemic has meant that there's a huge wellspring of disabled culture, collective care, communities, love, grief work, joy. A cripping of the world, more than ever before. And on the other hand, especially as 2022 bears on, there's an oh-well acceptance of eugenics and survival-of-the-fittest, in the "learn to live with COVID" and "most of the people who died from Omicron are disabled, that's encouraging," statements and policies, in the ways it feels like we're being gaslit and ghosted by a state acting like a bad boyfriend, as we go into the sixth and seventh waves and the powers that be tell us that COVID is over, to go back to normal and forget everything we've done to keep each other alive. It's like living in a tilt-a-whirl. I feel nauseous. Some days, I think that the cripping of the world will make the crip world to come that I want. Some days,

I think we will all be sick and sad forever and be crushed under the weight of fascist ableism, as trans ban after trans ban passes, mask mandates get torn up, and everyone is forced back to work and school in-person, accomodations fluttering in the breeze.

Jewish autistic anti-fascist organizer Eric Warwick notes, "Everyone keeps talking about how after the 1919 pandemic there was a huge surge in eugenics laws and discourses in the US and Europe. No one seems to be mentioning that after the massive polio outbreaks of the 1950s we got the disability rights and independent living movements of the 1960s and '70s. I think we're becoming too invested in fatalistic narratives to fight for a better world."[116]

I think both things can be true. I think our fears are real because we see the unrelenting ways Amazon, governments, and masses of everyday people don't give a shit if people die of COVID, particularly if we are broke Black and brown disabled people. But if the majority of the world really is or will be disabled because of COVID, massive numbers of disabled people could be *huge potential resources for the revolution we need*.

If we really are the majority, if masses of people—parents, teachers, low-wage/high-vulnerability workers—are already lying down, quitting, organizing Amazon's first union, and gathering to primal scream at night out of utter exhaustion, could there be so many of us we are impossible to ignore? Will the masses of us have the collective power to fuck the world into justice? Even if we don't make the revolution the way I continue to long for, the world will be permanently fundamentally changed—and full of disabled possibilities.

---

116 Eric Warwick, Facebook, January 4, 2022, https://www.facebook.com/eric.warwick7/posts/4729497680459474/.

SCALING UP CRIP DOULAING

This potential revolution isn't just going to happen. There will be (already is) a need for crip doulaing on a massive scale, linking newly disabled people living with long COVID with people who have been sick and disabled longer, sharing our skills in living with chronic illness and fighting the medical industrial complex. In particular there are people in chronic illness community, like folks living with CFIDS and MCS and late-stage Lyme, who have done community research on post-viral syndrome that millions of people living with long COVID desperately need. Our disabled histories of activism and survival skills are crucially needed—and most people outside disabled / chronically ill community don't know they exist.

When I read a January 2022 *Guardian* article[117] about Heidi Ferrer, a British screenwriter committed to social justice who killed herself because she felt despair at the huge changes long COVID had made to her energy level and life and the lack of support she got from the medical establishment, I feel such rage at the medical establishment and compassion for her, her husband, and loved ones, as well as for everyone struggling in isolation with long COVID. I very much believe in the importance of newly long COVID disabled people who are struggling and suicidal being able to access crip doulaing and supportive community with people navigating similar disabilities, like CFIDS and ME, that lead to vast changes in their amounts of energy and mobility. Disabled community and crip doulaing save lives, altering experiences of "fates worse than death" to lives that

117 Nick Güthe, "My Wife Had Long COVID and Killed Herself. We Must Help Others Who Are Suffering," *Guardian*, January 12, 2022, https://www.theguardian.com/commentisfree/2022/jan/12/long-COVID-wife-suicide-give-others-hope.

are precious and contain pleasure. But because our very existence as disabled communities and people with disabled skills is incomprehensible to the abled world, I don't anticipate a mass crip doulaing funding rollout by the state or a local HMO any time soon. I *do* see individual disabled-controlled community organizations, like Senior and Disability Action of Berkeley, California, who are starting a group partnering new long COVID patients with more seasoned disabled people as mentors.

We have to keep sharing crip community–sourced info about what helps long COVID: the drugs, acupuncture, herbs, and cognitive tools. We also have to demand that the existing medical and social systems support long COVID disabled people, including listening to the community-sourced treatment wisdom ME/CFS disabled people have created over the last decades of ME and CFS not being taken seriously. We already see some of this work, as with the recent call for Long COVID Justice.[118] But right now I hear so many stories from folks with long COVID being dismissed or brushed off by long COVID clinics and their regular PCPs, telling them that they're just fine. Just as welfare systems are designed to deny money to as many people as possible, the insurance and health care systems are invested in denying people the MRIs and accommodations they need so they can save money and pretend everything is just fine. We need a complete overall of the MIC as we know it, full funding of community and home-based care, guaranteed annual income way above the poverty level, and a care revolution. Nothing more or less. Even if the chances of

---

118 "Pandemics Are Chronic: A Statement of Commitment to Long COVID Justice," *Long COVID Justice*, https://docs.google.com/document/d/1062ERIbI1A-VMaNRysYPPxSVsavQU1oGyfmRlW Lv3JQ/edit.

winning it feel fucking futile, I have to remember other communities where we have fought and won socialized medicine and community care.

Because we still need a revolution. It's real that our mutual aid staved off the worst of the apocalypse, and it's also shown how deeply we need to keep scaling things up. As Mask Oakland, the disabled and neurodivergent mutual-aid group that has distributed hundreds of thousands of free masks in North California during wildfires and COVID surges, wrote in their 2021 end-of-year email:

> We have a lot of accomplishments. We could list them—thousands of masks, hundreds of air purifiers that got donated in-kind … But the reality is they aren't enough. You could donate, which would be great, get us a head start on financing our fire season 2022 response (because this is only going to get worse every year for the rest of our lives). But … small hopeful donations to a nonprofit aren't going to be enough to turn this thing around. We really need a revolt. An uprising … Mutual aid isn't enough, but the lessons of mutual aid can inform the kind of deep revolutionary work that will need to happen.[119]

In a Twitter post written slightly earlier in 2021, Mask Oakland wrote, "Every Inspiring Mutual Aid project we know of is pretty burned out right now. Like … we don't got this … Volunteers [are] too exhausted. Public Health is like water and sewage infrastructure: [it] should not be left to unpaid mutual aid.[120]

119 Mask Oakland, "Obligatory year-end email," January 1, 2022.
120 Mask Oakland (@MaskOakland), Twitter, December 24, 2021, https://twitter.com/Mask Oakland/status/1474248471385313282.

I agree. I also believe that the next step does not have to be a resigned "Well, I guess we have to stick with the failing system we have," but a disabled and trauma-infused re-imagining—again—of how we can support movements that are exhausted and are still doing more than state systems are to keep each other alive. Alongside all the devastating losses, the pandemic has also given us a window into how everything can be different.

The projects investing in community care, alternatives to the cops, the Mad and psych-survivor-lead alternatives to emergency service organizations, the fact that Sikh gurdwaras provided some of the most effective emergency response to the fall 2021 flooding in British Columbia: Our work may not have taken over the government yet, but we need to remember it is still more effective than the government is. The disability justice solution is not to abandon those projects when people are exhausted, but to continue to figure out how to resource the work. Our crip skills and working, living, and organizing with low spoons are going to be crucial. They already are. I know all of us long-term disabled people are already tired, and the work shouldn't just land on us. Yet, we have knowledge the world needs, and I'm not holding out hope the abled or the state will get it together to do that work, as much as we need to make demands of both.

EVERYTHING WAS DIFFERENT. EVERYTHING IS DIFFERENT. EVERYTHING CAN BE DIFFERENT.

In January 2022, in the midst of the first Omicron wave, trying to figure out how to keep safe, I realized that none of the local grocery stores had elder/immunocompromised hours anymore. Elder/

immunocompromised hours were a practice initiated by stores early in the pandemic—usually right after opening, the idea was that all us vulnerable people could be in the store early, while the air was still un-breathed in, and that we might be safer surrounded by all us other careful ones. As an immunocompromised person, those hours made me feel seen in a way I'd never felt before—the public acknowledgement that there was this thing called the immunocompromised, and maybe there could be special early hours for all us careful ones, was a rare moment of disability being normalized.

But a year later, even during a COVID infection wave much more virulent than the initial one, those hours disappeared, along with the outdoor dining area outside of the diner in my neighborhood where I would take myself out and eat pancakes feeling fairly safe. The diner couldn't get its permits renewed, said the server at the counter, and after all, people were vaccinated now, right? I took my cooling pancakes home with me in a to-go container, watching through the window at the happy non-disabled people eating and sipping coffee.

This could just be sad, and it is—the corporate ableist refusal to let access stay. But it's also a remembrance: nothing has to be the way it is. Access is created, it gets taken away/destroyed, but it can be created again.

In her essay "Choosing the Margin as a Space of Radical Openness," Black feminist writer and theorist bell hooks cites a statement constantly repeated in *Freedom Charter*, writing from the South African anti-apartheid movement: "Our struggle is also a struggle of memory against forgetting." This is our disabled futurist struggle now too.

We can choose to remember: our dead, our losses, and what they taught us, but also the vibrant spaces of disabled creativity and imagination we have made during the pandemic, that we have been building all our lives. And we can insist that the world continue to be cripped with our wild imaginings, as we continue to make this future, the only one we have. The wild disabled future is for disabled people and for everyone, led by lifetimes of DJ practice.

As my friend and editor Lisa Factora-Borchers said in the last days of sitting with this manuscript, "More and more people going to find that they need DJ—DJ writers, DJ thought, DJ intellectualism, theory-making, praxis, writing, poetry, lyricism *because of* the pandemic. Because of COVID and because of Trump, people are realizing more and more we need to do things in a different way, and these are things that disabled folks have known for lifetimes and lifetimes, but mainstream folks are coming into an awareness that there is actually a spot in the world where disability justice writers and thinkers exist."[121]

I may be a portal, but I can't predict the future. All I know is to have faith in the complete unpredictability of what comes next. That there will be suffering and death, eugenic glee as mask mandates are canceled by Trumpian judges and the abled and oblivious rip off their face masks in mid-flight and laugh at our fear. And we will also keep doing all the lifesaving disabled shit we have been doing. We will keep disabled innovating, building, grieving, surviving, inventing. There will be ableist backlash and predictable nightmare violence. And our wild disability justice dreams and imaginings cannot be murdered.

All I know is that disability justice dreaming is audacious and bold and will take us to the future of the world. Whatever it is. Whatever we make it be.

121 Lisa Factora–Borchers, personal conversation with the author, January 2022.

The *Certain Days* calendar hanging on my kitchen wall asks: *What can we grow out of crisis?*

I answer: The wild disabled futures we are making with the rest of our lives.

Leah Lakshmi Piepzna-Samarasinha (she/they) is a queer nonbinary femme disabled writer, performance artist, and disability and transformative justice movement worker of Burgher and Tamil Sri Lankan, Irish, and Galician/ Roma ascent. They are the author or co-editor of ten books, including (with Ejeris Dixon) *Beyond Survival: Strategies and Stories from the Transformative Justice Movement*, *Tonguebreaker*, *Bridge of Flowers*, *Care Work: Dreaming Disability Justice*, and *Bodymap*. A Lambda Award winner who has been shortlisted for the Publishing Triangle five times, she is winner of Lambda's 2020 Jean Cordova Award "honoring a lifetime of work documenting the complexities of queer of color, disabled, and femme experience," and is a 2020–2021 Disability Futures Fellow. Since 2009, they have been a lead performer with disability justice performance collective Sins Invalid; since 2020 they have been on the programming team of the Disability & Intersectionality Summit. Raised in rust belt central Massachusetts and shaped by T'karonto and Oakland, they are currently at work building Living Altars, an organization creating space for disabled QTBIPOC writers, including the Stacey Park Milbern Liberation Arts Center, an accessible writing retreat for disabled BIPOC creators. They are a hot, haggard porch and couch witch and a very unprofessional adaptive trike rider.

brownstargirl.org